N	O	P	Q	R	S	T	U	V	W	X	Y	Z		
21	—	22	24	24	25	28	29	29	30	—	30	30	a	ACTIVE CAT
45	45	46	47	48	50	52	53	53	54	54	55	55	e	HEALTHY ELEPHANT
81	81	82	83	84	87	90	91	91	92	—	—	93	i	BIG PIGLET
105	106	108	109	110	111	113	113	114	114	—	115	115	o	WATCHFUL DOG
127	127	128	128	129	130	133	134	136	136	—	136	—	u oo	DUCK AND WOODPECKER

N	O	P	Q	R	S	T	U	V	W	X	Y	Z		
146	147	147	148	148	149	151	151	151	152	—	152	—	ae	BABY SNAIL
165	165	166	167	167	169	172	—	173	174	—	175	175	ee	BREEDING EAGLE
187	187	188	189	189	190	192	—	193	193	194	—	194	ie	LIVELY LION
202	203	204	206	206	207	208	—	208	209	—	209	209	oe	LONELY GOAT
218	218	219	219	220	221	222	223	223	223	—	224	224	ue oo	SMOOTH NEWT

N	O	P	Q	R	S	T	U	V	W	X	Y	Z		
232	—	233	233	233	234	235	—	235	—	—	235	235	ar	BASKING SHARK
—	—	239	—	240	240	241	—	241	241	—	—	—	air	RARE BEAR
249	249	250	251	251	252	253	254	254	255	—	255	—	er	EARLY BIRD WITH WORM
263	264	265	266	266	267	268	—	268	269	—	269	—	or	WARLIKE HORSE
273	273	274	274	274	275	275	—	275	—	—	—	—	oi	JOYFUL OYSTER
281	281	282	—	282	283	283	—	284	284	—	284	—	ou	AN OWL SOUND

Acknowledgements

The author would like to thank all those who took part in the original field trials in England, Northern Ireland, Scotland and Wales. Special thanks are due to Bess Moseley for the animal drawings, to Gwyn Singleton for editorial and proofreading assistance and to George Macbride for help in meeting the pronunciation requirements of Scottish users. I am also grateful for many suggestions for improvement made by users of the *ACE Spelling Dictionary* since its first publication in 1985.

ACE Spelling Dictionary
102521
ISBN-13: 978 1 85503 478 5

First published 2009
Reprinted 2010

Printed in the UK for LDA
Pintail Close, Victoria Business Park, Nottingham, NG4 2SG, UK

ACE

Aurally Coded English

SPELLING DICTIONARY

THIRD EDITION

David Moseley

LDA

ACE INDEX

Index

Contents

Introduction

How can you look up a word in a dictionary if you do not know how to spell it?

The *ACE Spelling Dictionary* is designed for writers of all ages who need to check spellings, and it is intended for use in educational settings and at home. The unique index always directs you to the page you need, taking away the frustration of hunting around in a conventional dictionary. After a little practice you will be able to find any word in just a few seconds, many times faster than in other dictionaries.

Another great advantage of using the ACE dictionary is that it actually improves your spelling. This is because the words are listed by vowel sound in alphabetical columns. This makes common spelling patterns stand out and draws attention to unusual features. Using the Index and choosing the correct syllable column on a page is itself a learning process, as you have to think about how a word sounds when spoken. This distinguishes the ACE dictionary from an electronic spelling checker, which forces the writer to attempt a spelling and then provides a long list of words from which little can be learned. Using the ACE dictionary is largely error free and many safety-nets are provided to take account of regional differences in pronunciation, indistinct speech and phonetically based guesswork.

The main concern of any writer, whatever their age, is communication. All too often difficulty with spelling gets in the way of expression and many people become frustrated to the point of giving up.

English spelling often appears illogical and does not obey simple rules. How to represent the vowel sounds ('singing-like' sounds like *aaaah* made with the mouth open) can be a real headache as you have to choose between two hundred ways of representing the eighteen vowel sounds of spoken English. This may lead to confusion and delay when looking up words in a standard dictionary.

The *ACE Spelling Dictionary* is aurally coded – it confronts the multitude of spelling patterns by grouping words according to the vowel sounds heard at or near the beginning of each word. In the *ACE Spelling Dictionary* the eighteen vowel sounds are reduced to sixteen by grouping together two related pairs.

To use the dictionary successfully you need to **LISTEN** for the first clear vowel sound and the initial letter, **LOOK UP** the word on the page shown on the index table and **LEARN** something about how the word is spelled. The process of choosing the correct column of words according to the number of spoken syllables is an important built-in aid to learning.

After reading this introduction you can practise finding words on your own, or with a teacher or helper. Learning to use the *ACE Spelling Dictionary* with a teacher or helper (see p. xi) includes four lessons that are suitable for use by individuals or in groups.

The Index is the key to the sixteen different sections of the dictionary. Once you have understood how it works, you should never again have to ask someone else how to spell a word that is in the ACE dictionary. Eventually you will be able to save time by going straight to the right vowel-sound section without using the Index at all.

The 20,000-word vocabulary contained in the *ACE Spelling Dictionary* is extensive, up to date and suitable for.both formal and informal types of writing. While beginning writers will recognise most of the shorter words in the one- and two-syllable columns, older learners will find that specialised vocabulary for academic subjects is also included.

The *ACE Spelling Dictionary* consists of three main parts, each including five or six sections. All the words in a section have the same or nearly the same vowel sound.

The first five sections of words with 'short' vowel sounds are printed on pale blue paper. These vowel sounds are usually introduced at an early stage of phonic instruction:

Part 1

/a/ as in c**a**t
/e/ as in **e**lephant
/i/ as in p**i**g
/o/ as in d**o**g
/u/ as in d**u**ck and /oo/ as in w**oo**dpecker

Words containing vowel sounds that sound like or rhyme with letter names are printed on darker blue paper. These are 'long' vowel sounds:

Part 2

/ae/ as in sn**ai**l
/ee/ as in **ea**gle
/ie/ as in l**i**on
/oe/ as in g**oa**t
/ue/ as in n**ew**t and /oo/ as in sm**oo**th

The last six sections are also printed on pale blue paper and include spellings with the letter 'r' and two double sounds. These sounds are often spoken in English as 'long' vowels (but not when the 'r' is rolled):

Part 3

/ar/ as in sh**ar**k
/air/ as in b**ear**
/er/ as in w**or**m
/or/ as in h**or**se
/oi/ as in **oy**ster
/ou/ as in **ow**l

The *ACE Spelling Dictionary* provides word meanings when two or more words sound the same or nearly the same. This allows you to choose the meaning you want. The options are usually nearby in the same column. The ACE dictionary is in fact the best resource there is for the study of such easily confused words, which are called *homonyms* (meaning 'same name').

Using the *ACE Spelling Dictionary* to look up spellings will make it easier to use other dictionaries for looking up meanings. The words within each section are arranged alphabetically, with subsections beginning with the same two letters (e.g. sc- sh- si- sk- sl- sm- sn- sp- sq- st- sw-) separated visually. Finding a word within a column makes use of exactly the same dictionary skills as finding a word in a dictionary that gives full definitions.

At the back of the book there is a section on improving spelling. The main focus is on much-needed words, especially those that are often misspelled. Personalised learning strategies for learning and correcting spellings are provided, as well as suggestions for studying spelling patterns. It is a good idea to write down unusual spellings in a personal spelling book, noting the 'tricky' part or parts and learning them by well-proven methods such as simultaneous oral spelling (naming the letters as you write them in chunks), 'look–say–cover–write–check' or visualisation with eyes closed. These and many more learning activities for use with the *ACE Spelling Dictionary* are also available in a separate publication, *ACE Spelling Activities* (Moseley and Singleton, 1993).

How to use the *ACE Spelling Dictionary* (self-help guide)

You need to understand the sixteen vowel sections of the Index and the clear vowel sounds they cover. To do this, open the dictionary at each of the sixteen sections in turn. You will see that each section has a different vowel sound symbol at the top right of each page. Read aloud a number of the shorter words in each section until you can recognise that they contain similar clear vowel sounds.

Make sure that you can say aloud the vowel sound symbols as listed on page viii and printed in blue at the top right-hand corner of each dictionary page. Outside the dictionary itself, slashes (e.g. /or/) are used to indicate sounds rather than letters.

To use the Index you have to do two things:

- Say the first clear vowel sound (the one that 'stands out').
- Name what you think is the first letter.

Reading across from the vowel sound and down from the first letter will take you to the page you need. Then you choose the correct column, according to the number of syllables in the word. Each column has one or more stars at the top showing the number of syllables. To begin with, say the word slowly and tap out the syllables at the same time. Try this rhyme if you need help:

* One tap for 'fun'
** And two for 'begun';
*** Three taps for 'stadium'
**** And four for 'gymnasium'.

If you want to find the word 'skyscraper' on page 190, for example, look in the column of three-syllable words. Words containing four or more syllables are on the right-hand side of each page. You will notice that every syllable contains a vowel sound.

The basic routine

To look up 'rhinoceros':

First	Say 'rhi' (say the first syllable really slowly)	Say /ie/ (say the vowel sound on its own)	Use the ACE Index (it's on pages ii and iii)
Second	Find /ie/ (as in lion) (the vowel sound /ie/ is next to the lion picture)	Find 'R' (from the alphabet across the top)	Go along from /ie/ and down from 'R' (you'll get to page 189)
Third	Find page 189 (in Part 2)	Open book in Part 2 (the darker blue pages)	Turn to page 189
Fourth	Tap out rhi-no-ce-ros (**** 4 syllables)	Go to the 4th column (**** 4 or more syllables)	YOU'VE GOT IT!

Neutral vowel sounds in the first syllable (what the white boxes are for)

When using the ACE Index, go for a strong, clear vowel sound in the first or second syllable, one that really stands out. Neutral vowel sounds are not clear sounds and require very little effort to pronounce. They are not given a separate section in the ACE Index. So if you think that there is a neutral vowel in the first syllable of the word you want (e.g. annoy, prepare, observe, success), go for the vowel sound in the second syllable – in these words the sounds /oi/ /air/ /er/ and /e/.

The Scottish pronunciation of vowel sounds is much clearer than is usual in England, making virtually no use of neutral vowels. It is therefore important that Scottish users look up words according to the vowel sound in the syllable with the first strong beat.

Say you want to look up 'suspicious'. The vowel sound that stands out when you say the word is the /i/ sound in the second syllable, and you will find 'suspicious' in the /i/ section on page 88. However, if you were to go for the weaker sound in the first syllable, you would still find the word, on page 132, in the white 'neutral vowel' box. So, if you cannot see a word where you think it should be, see if it is in a white box. You will soon notice that the weak neutral vowels sound much the same as each other, rather like a quiet grunt or squeak.

Listen to the way you pronounce 'balloon', for example:

Say 'buh' (start to say the word)	Say 'uh' (this sound is weak and unclear)	It's a neutral sound (it's not like the /a/ sound in 'cat')

To find 'balloon' in the dictionary, listen for the clear vowel sound (in the second syllable):

Say 'balloo'	Say /oo/	Then use the Index

In all the following words the strong beat (stress) is on the second syllable. You will probably succeed in finding the words if you try to identify the letters used for the first (neutral) vowel sound. However, it is easier to go by the first strong, clear vowel sound.

above	SHORT /u/	laboratory	SHORT /o/
advertisement	SOUND /er/	magician	SHORT /i/
appearance	LONG /ee/	manoeuvre	LONG /oo/
approach	LONG /oe/	observer	SOUND /er/
because	SHORT /o/	particular	SHORT /i/
before	SOUND /or/	performer	SOUND /or/
circumference	SHORT /u/	potatoes	LONG /ae/
collision	SHORT /i/	production	SHORT /u/
conductor	SHORT /u/	remain	LONG /ae/
confetti	SHORT /e/	remarkable	SOUND /ar/
despair	SOUND /air/	request	SHORT /e/
destroy	SOUND /oi/	reverse	SOUND /er/
discuss	SHORT /u/	surrender	SHORT /e/
emotional	LONG /oe/	surroundings	SOUND /ou/
enough	SHORT /u/	survivor	LONG /ie/
exhaust	SOUND /or/	towards	SOUND /or/
guitar	SOUND /ar/	trapeze	LONG /ee/
infectious	SHORT /e/	vocabulary	SHORT /a/

Learning to use the *ACE Spelling Dictionary* with a teacher or helper

Lesson 1 (counting syllables)

Aim: You need to be able to say how many syllables there are in any spoken word (up to four syllables). Counting syllables is a skill which is easier than counting phonemes and which can be built up from the age of 5. The 'Clap and Count' activity in *Letters and Sounds* (DES, 2007) is intended as an aid to both word recognition and spelling.

In one-to-one work a parent or friend should read out the words and say whether your responses are correct. A teacher can work with a group or whole class, asking for individual or group responses. The three stages below should be followed.

1 The teacher/helper (T/H) says a word slowly and taps out the syllables at the same time. You repeat the word and tap out the syllables. The T/H asks, 'How many taps?' This should be done with the following words, or with people's names.

play-ground	win-dow	ba-na-na	mud	un-for-tu-nate
Tap - Tap	Tap - Tap	Tap - Tap - Tap	Tap	Tap - Tap - Tap - Tap

Repeat more slowly if necessary, with the words in a different order.

2 The T/H says a word without tapping and asks you to repeat the word and tap it out. Each time the T/H asks, 'How many taps?' This is done with words from the following list until you tap out ten words correctly.

* * *	newspaper	* *	picture	*	paint	* * * *	television
* *	spider	*	mice	* *	monster	* * *	dinosaur
* *	postman	* *	burglar	* * *	acrobat	* * * *	politician
* *	pancake	* * *	margarine	* * * *	supermarket	* *	kitchen
*	crash	* * * *	helicopter	* *	rocket	* * *	motorbike

3 The T/H says a word and simply asks, 'How many syllables?' You carry on, taking words at random from the list below, until you achieve a success rate of 19/20.

* *	money	*	shop	* *	birthday	* *	present
* *	bedroom	*	door	* * *	wallpaper	*	stairs
* * *	holidays	*	weeks	* * *	underground	* * * *	underwater
* * *	crocodile	* * * *	alligator	*	shark	* *	danger
* * * *	caterpillar	*	moth	* * *	butterfly	*	eggs
* *	rabbit	* * * *	invisible	*	hat	* *	magic
*	win	* * *	manager	* *	football	* * * *	competition
* * * *	everybody	* *	children	* *	mother	* * *	grandfather
*	clock	* *	morning	* * *	afternoon	* * *	yesterday
* * * *	mysterious	* * *	horrible	* * *	beautiful	* * *	exciting

Lesson 2 (vowel sounds in Part 2)

Aims: You will correctly

a) identify long vowel sounds in words of one and two syllables

b) use the long vowel sounds part of the Index to find the page numbers for various words

c) look up words in the darker blue part of the dictionary.

1 Begin with listening and speaking activities only, starting with the long vowel animal names: **snail**, **eagle**, **lion**, **goat** and **newt**.

The T/H asks about a vowel sound in each of the five long vowel animal names. The expected answers are either 'yes' or 'no'; for example, 'Can you hear /ae/ in **snail**?' 'Can you hear /ee/ in **snail**? The vowel sounds can be made longer and louder if necessary. If you need further practice, your T/H may also ask you to identify these vowel sounds, giving a choice of three (e.g. 'What is the vowel sound in **snail**: /ae/, /ee/ or /ie/?)'. You will need to continue until you can correctly identify the sounds.

When you are confident and accurate with the animal names, you may move on to listening for long vowel sounds in other words, answering questions like 'Can you hear /ee/ in **fine**?' 'Can you hear /ae/ in **baby**?' Carry on until you can do this correctly with most words of one or two syllables.

It may also be helpful to play Odd Vowel Out with groups of four words. For example, your T/H asks which is the odd one out in:

- pail, sail, tail, tile
- cheap, choose, cheat, beach
- mice, dive, save, smile
- heap, slope, coach, slow
- stew, queue, duke, spoke.

You may then be asked to explain the difference between the two vowel sounds; for example, '**Tile** has an /ie/ sound, but the others have an /ae/ sound'.

2 Practise using the darker blue part of the Index to find page numbers. If working in a group each person should have an ACE dictionary to use (at least one between two) or else a copy of the Index from pages ii and iii. The T/H may like to make an OHT from *ACE Spelling Activities* (Moseley and Singleton, 1993) or display the Index on a whiteboard for class instruction.

Referring to the animal picture words, your T/H asks you to point first to the snail picture next to the letters 'ae' that stand for the sound /ae/. They then ask which letter 'snail' begins with and ask you to find the letter in the alphabet across the top of the page. You are then shown how to move one finger along the line of page numbers and another finger down, until they meet at a page number. **Snail** is on page 149. The same exercise is repeated with **eagle** (p. 157), **lion** (p. 185), **goat** (p. 199) and **newt** (p. 218). There is no reason why you should not look in the dictionary to find these words. In the case of **eagle** you will have to look in the second column.

You can then practise finding page numbers with some more animal words: **ape**, **beaver**, **bison**, **mule**, **poodle**, **reindeer**, **sheep**, **snake**, **tiger**, **whale**. This time you will need to listen for the vowel sound, find the correct sound symbol and confirm your choice with the animal picture. For example, what is the first vowel sound in **tiger**? It is /ie/, which you can also hear in **lion**.

Here are some more long vowel topic lists that you may use until you have mastered using the Index to find page numbers.

bacon, cake, cereal, cheese, doughnut, mousse, pie, steak, trifle, tuna
beans, beetroot, coleslaw, cucumber, leeks, maize, peanuts, peas, seaweed, swede
apricot, coconut, dates, grapefruit, lime, peach, pineapple, prunes, raisins, rhubarb
basin, bowl, knife, ladle, microwave, plate, scales, soap, teapot, toast

3 Now you are ready to look up words from the above lists or elsewhere in the darker blue part of the dictionary itself. After turning to the right page, say the word, tap out and count the syllables and then search down the appropriate column. If there is a homonym (e.g. leaks/leeks, stake/steak), check the meaning. Where the word is not given in plural form (e.g. prune), an 's' should be added. Note that in one case (swede) the target word is in a column that extends to three pages.

Lesson 3 (vowel sounds in Parts 1 and 2)

Aims: You will correctly

a) identify short vowel sounds in words of one and two syllables
b) use the short vowel sounds part of the Index to find the page numbers for various words
c) look up words in the first two parts of the dictionary.

1 Begin with listening and speaking activities only, starting with the short vowel animal names: **cat**, **elephant**, **pig**, **dog**, **duck** and **woodpecker**.

Your T/H asks about a vowel sound in each of the six short vowel animal names. The expected answers are either 'yes' or 'no'; for example, 'Can you hear /a/ in **cat**?' 'Can you hear /e/ in **pig**?' If you need further practice, your T/H may also ask you to identify these vowel sounds, giving a choice of three (e.g. 'What is the vowel sound in cat: /ae/, /a/ or /e/?') You will need to continue until you can correctly identify the sounds.

When you are confident and accurate with the animal names, you can move on to listening for short vowel sounds in other words, answering questions like 'Can you hear /a/ in **active**?' 'Can you hear /i/ in **big**?' Carry on until you can do this correctly with most words of one or two syllables.

It may also be helpful to play Odd Vowel Out with groups of four words. For example, your T/H asks which is the odd one out in:

- pat, fat, mat, pet
- nest, fist, chest, best
- giggle, wiggle, waggle, jiggle
- slope, stop, clock, stock
- shut, dust, shock, must
- look, book, cooker, cooler.

You may then be asked to explain the difference between the two vowel sounds; for example, '**Pet** has an /e/ sound, but the others have an /a/ sound.'

2 Practise using the first two parts of the Index to find page numbers, first for short and then for both short and long vowel words. If working in a group, each person should have an ACE dictionary to use (at least one between two) or else a copy of the Index from pages ii and iii. Teachers may like to make an OHT from *ACE Spelling Activities* or display the Index on a whiteboard for class instruction.

Referring to the animal picture words, your T/H asks you to point first to the cat picture next to the letter 'a' that stands for the sound /a/. They then ask which letter 'cat' begins with and ask you to find the letter in the alphabet across the top of the page. You will remember how to move one finger along the line of page numbers and another finger down, until they meet at the page number you want. **Cat** is on page 7. The same exercise is then repeated with **elephant** (p. 36), **pig** (p. 82), **dog** (p. 99), **duck** (p. 120) and **woodpecker** (p. 136). There is no reason why you should not look in the dictionary to find these words. In the cases of **elephant** and **woodpecker** you will have to look in the third column.

You can then practise finding page numbers with some more animal words: **camel**, **donkey**, **frog**, **hedgehog**, **kangaroo**, **leopard**, **monkey**, **pigeon**, **rabbit**, **rook**. This time you will need to listen for the vowel sound, find the correct sound symbol and confirm your choice with the animal picture. For example, what is the first vowel sound in **rabbit**? It is /a/, which you can also hear in **cat**.

Here are some more short vowel topic lists that you may use until you have mastered using the Index to find page numbers.

biscuit, bread, butter, chicken, chocolate, crisps, haddock, jam, popcorn, pudding
broccoli, cabbage, cauliflower, celery, lettuce, mushroom, onion, pepper, pumpkin, spinach
apple, blackberry, cherry, damson, fig, lemon, melon, orange, plum, tangerine
bottle, brush, clock, fridge, matches, mirror, rack, scissors, sieve, whisk

After working with the short vowel part of the Index, you can practise finding the page numbers for both short and long vowel words from the following lists. If there is any confusion between short and long vowels, ask, for example, 'Is it short /a/ as in **cat**, or long /ae/ as in **snail**?' as appropriate.

black, blue, buff, crimson, gold, green, indigo, red, ruby, white
apron, boots, collar, dress, jeans, nightdress, shoes, sweater, tie, vest
bicycle, boat, glider, helicopter, motorcycle, scooter, submarine, train, van, yacht
bus, coach, cycle, ferry, hovercraft, liner, lorry, rocket, tricycle, truck
chewing, cooking, drinking, eating, helping, listening, nodding, sleeping, watching, writing
baker, bricklayer, cook, miner, optician, sailor, scientist, secretary, soldier, teacher

3 Now you are ready to look up words from the above lists or elsewhere in the first two parts of the dictionary. After turning to the right page, say the word, tap out and count the syllables and then search down the appropriate column. If there is a homonym (e.g. blue/blew, red/read), check the meaning. Where the word is not given in plural form (e.g. boot), an 's' should be added. Note that in some cases (apple, biscuit, bus, butter, crimson, drinking, fridge, indigo, matches, optician, orange, spinach, sweater) the target word is in a column that extends to two or more pages.

Lesson 4 (vowel sounds in Part 3)

Aims: You will correctly

a) identify vowel sounds in the third part of the dictionary, in words of one or two syllables

b) use the Index to find the page numbers for various words

c) look up words in all three parts of the dictionary.

1 Begin with listening and speaking activities only, starting with the animal names from the third part of the dictionary: **shark, bear, bird, horse, oyster** and **owl**.

Your T/H asks about a vowel sound in each of the six animal names. The expected answers are either 'yes' or 'no'; for example, 'Can you hear /ar/ in **shark**?' 'Can you hear /or/ in **owl**?' If you need further practice, your T/H may also ask you to identify these vowel sounds, giving a choice of three (e.g. 'What is the vowel sound in **shark**: /ar/, /ae/ or /or/?') You will need to continue until you can correctly identify the sounds.

When you are confident and accurate with the animal names, you can move on to listening for ACE part 3 vowel sounds in other words, answering questions like 'Can you hear /ar/ in **harmless**?' 'Can you hear /oi/ in **early**?' Carry on until you can do this correctly with most words of one or two syllables.

It may also be helpful to play Odd Vowel Out with groups of four words. For example, your T/H asks which is the odd one out in:

- car, fir, jar, tar
- stair, store, fair, chair
- farmer, nervous, person, service
- horse, north, south, score
- point, noise, choice, nice
- ground, grand, mountain, fountain.

You may then be asked to explain the difference between the two vowel sounds, for example, '**Fir** has an /er/ sound, but the others have an /ar/ sound.'

2 Practise using the third part of the Index to find page numbers, and then move on to all three parts. If working in a group, each person should have an ACE dictionary to use (at least one between two) or else a copy of the of the Index on pages ii and iii. The T/H may like to make an OHT from *ACE Spelling Activities* or display the Index on a whiteboard for class instruction.

Referring to the animal picture words, your T/H asks you to point first to the shark picture next to the letters 'ar', which stand for the sound /ar/. They then ask which letter 'shark' begins with and ask you to find the letter in the alphabet across the top of the page. You will remember how to move one finger along the line of page numbers and another finger down, until they meet at the page number you want. **Shark** is on page 234. The same exercise is then repeated with **rare** (p. 240), **worm** (p. 255), **warlike** (p. 269), **noisy** (p. 273) and **sound** (p. 283). There is no reason why you should not look in the dictionary to find these words. In the cases of **warlike** and **noisy** you will have to look in the second column.

You can then practise finding page numbers with some more animal words: **armadillo, cow, earthworm, hound, mouse, partridge, sardine, starfish, tortoise**. This time you will need to listen for the vowel sound, find the correct sound symbol and confirm your choice with the animal picture. For example, what is the first vowel sound in **partridge**? It is /ar/, which you can also hear in **shark**.

Here are some more topic lists that you may use until you have mastered using the Index to find page numbers.

---

burger, cornflakes, flour, lard, marmalade, oil, pork, prawn, sardine, trout
garlic, herbs, parsley, parsnips, pear, soya, sprouts, strawberry, turnip, walnut
boiler, carton, door, fork, jar, larder, margarine, starch, torch, towel

---

After working with the third part of the Index, you can practise finding the page numbers for words from any of the three parts, using the following lists. If there is any confusion between any pair of patterns, ask, for example, 'Is it /a/ or /ow/?' 'Is it /o/ or /ar/?' as appropriate.

---

aquamarine, brown, cream, ginger, grey, lilac, orange, pink, purple, rose, scarlet, silver, turquoise, violet, yellow

blouse, braces, coat, jacket, overalls, sandals, scarf, shorts, skirt, slippers, socks, sweater, tights, trainers, trousers

brushing, counting, cutting, ironing, learning, marking, painting, reading, serving, sewing, shaving, shopping, sweeping, swimming, working

actor, artist, dentist, diver, doctor, fisherman, hairdresser, joiner, journalist, musician, nurse, plumber, priest, tailor, warden

---

3 Now you are ready to look up words from the above lists or elsewhere in all three parts of the dictionary. Note that in some cases (aquamarine, cutting, slippers, sweeping, swimming) the target word is in a column which extends to two or more pages.

What you can achieve with ACE

As a learner:

- extend your vocabulary
- come to think well of yourself as a writer
- enjoy the processes of planning, writing, redrafting and proofreading
- never again have to ask how to spell a word
- spell correctly all the words you know, including homonyms ('sound-alikes')
- avoid confusing yourself by repeatedly misspelling certain words
- confidently use words that are hard to spell
- never limit the quantity and quality of what you write
- give priority to purpose, audience, communication and impact
- automatically improve rapid word recognition and spelling skills
- become familiar with common linguistic patterns and identify unusual spellings easily
- use the dictionary to search for words with rule-based features
- develop an interest in word derivations, patterns and families
- develop effective strategies for learning really hard spellings painlessly
- voluntarily study the words you want and need to learn
- improve alphabetical dictionary skills so you are more likely to use other dictionaries.

As a teacher/helper:

- use the ACE dictionary as a rich resource for phonic and linguistic instruction
- make spelling a positive experience as learners increasingly take responsibility for it
- develop personalised, paired and group learning approaches to word study
- meet and comfortably exceed all Key Stage spelling objectives
- have learners of all abilities proofread and correct their work from initial outline onwards
- see the quantity and quality of writing improve dramatically when the ACE dictionary is used daily
- ensure that learners can spell all specialist subject vocabulary up to A-level correctly.

A

SHORT VOWEL a

*

act
*acts more than one act

add
*adds does add
*adze tool

-aft

-alms
Alps

am
amp

an
and
*ant insect

apt

as
ash es
-ask ed
ass es

at

*-aunt relative

*axe d chopping tool

for H . . .
see page 16

* *

aback
abbess es
abbey
abbot
abscess es
abseil
absence
absent
abstract

accent
access es
accessed
acid
acne
acted
acting
action
active
actor
actress es
actual ly

adapt
added
addend
adder
addict
adding
adept
adult
-advance d
advent
adverb
adverse
advert

affix es
Afghan
-after

aggro
-aghast
agile

alas
album
alcove
algae
Allah
alley
alloy ed
ally -ies
allied
☛

* * *

abacus es
abandon ed
abattoir
abdomen
abnormal ly
absentee
absolute
abstraction

accident ally
accurate
acetate
acquiesce d
acrobat
acronym
activate
actively
activist
actual ly
actuate

adamant
adapter / adaptor
additive
addressee
adenoids
adequate
adjective
admirable
admiral
adulthood
-advancement
-advancing
-advantage
-advantaged
adversary -ies
advertise d
advocate

affluence
affluent
Africa
African
-aftermath
-afternoon
-afterwards

aggravate
aggregate
agitate
agonise d
ze
agony -ies

albatross es
*albumen white of egg
*albumin protein
☛

* * * * * *

abnormally
abolition
aboriginal
aborigine
absolutely

academic ally
academy -ies
accentuate
accentuating
accessory -ies
accidental ly
accuracy
accurately
accusation
acquiescence
acquisition
acrobatic ally
activity -ies
actuality -ies
actually
acupuncture

-adagio
adaptable
adaptation
adequacy
adjectival ly
admirable
admiration
adolescence
adolescent
advantageous
-advantaging
adverbial ly
adversary -ies
advertising
advocating
advocacy

affirmation
Afghanistan

aggravation
agitation
agoraphobia
agoraphobic
agricultural ly
agriculture

alacrity
Albania
☛

for Scots: a -r
is on page 225

A

SHORT VOWEL **a**

* *

-**almond**
alpha
Alpine / alpine
alto

amass es
amassed
amber
amble d
ambling
ambush es
ambushed
ampere
ample
amply

anchor
anger ed
angle d
***angler** person who fishes with hook and line
angling
angry -ier, -iest
anguish ed
ankle
annexe d
annual ly
annum
anode
-**answer** ed
anthem
anthill
anthrax
***antics** strange behaviour
antique
***antiques** very old objects
antlers
anvil
anxious

aphid / aphis
apple
aptly

Arab
arid
arrow ed
☛

* * *

alchemy
alcohol
algebra
alibi
alkali
alkaline
allegory -ies
allergy -ies
allocate d
alphabet
Alsatian
altitude
Alzheimer's

amalgam
amateur
ambition
ambitious
ambulance
amethyst
ammeter
amnesty -ies
ampersand
amplify -ies
amplified
amplitude
amputate
amylase

anagram
analyst
analogue
analyse d
ze
anarchy
ancestor
ancestral
ancestry -ies
anchorage
andante
Anglican
angora
angrier
angriest
angrily
***angular** sharp-cornered
animal
animate
aniseed
annual ly
anodise d
ze
anorak
-**answering**
antarctic
anteater
antelope
☛

* * * * * * *

alcoholic
alcoholism
algebraic ally
Algeria
algorithm
alimentary
allegation
allegorical ly
allegory -ies
allegretto
alligator
allocating
allocation
alphabetical ly
alphanumeric
altimeter
aluminium

amalgamate
amalgamating
amalgamation
ambassador
ambidextrous
ambiguity -ies
ambiguous
ambivalent
ammunition
amphibian
amphibious
amphitheatre
amplification
amplifier

anachronism
anaerobic
anaesthesia / anesthesia
anaesthetic / anesthetic
analogous
analogy -ies
analysing
zing
analysis [analyses]
analytic ally
anatomical ly
anatomy -ies
angiosperm
Anglo-Saxon
animation
anniversary -ies
annually
anonymity
antagonise d
ze
antagonism
antagonistic ally
☛

for H . . . see page 16

for Scots: a -r is on page 225

In these words you can hear the vowel sound a as in cat

A

SHORT VOWEL a

* *

ashtray
-**asking**
aspect
asphalt
aspirin
asset
aster
asthma

athlete
atlas es
atoll
atom
attach es
attached
attack ed
attic
attract

-**Auntie / Aunty**

average d

*__axes__ more than one axe or axis
axing
*__axis__ fixed or imaginary line
axle

azure

impasse

* * *

antenna [antennae]
anthracite
anthropoid
antidote
antifreeze
antonym
anxiously

apathy
aperture
apparent
appetite
applicant
appliqué
apprehend
aptitude

aquatic
aqueduct
aqueous

Arabic
arable
arrogance
arrogant
arrowhead

asbestos
aspirin
assassin
assonance
asterisk
asteroid
astronaut
asymptote

athletic ally
athletics
Atlantic
atmosphere
attaché
attachment
attacker
attitude
attracted
attraction
attractive
attribute

avalanche
avant-garde
avarice
avenue
average d
averaging

axial ly
axiom

* * * * * * *

Antarctica
antecedent
anthology -ies
anthropologist
anthropology
antibiotic
antibody -ies
anticipate
anticipating
anticipation
anticyclone
antimony
antipathy -ies
antiquated
antiquity -ies
antiseptic ally
antisocial
antitoxin
anxiety -ies

apostolic ally
apparatus
apparently
apparition
appetising
applicable
application
apposition
apprehension

aquamarine

aristocracy -ies
aristocrat
aristocratic ally
arithmetically

asparagus
aspiration
assassinate
assassinating
assassination
astronomical ally
astrophysics

athletically
atmospheric ally

avaricious
averaging
avocado

axiomatic ally

for H . . . see page 16

for Scots: a -r is on page 225

In these words you can hear the vowel sound a as in cat

A

In these words the first letter 'a' is a neutral vowel.

AMAZING WORDS

abate
abating
abbreviation
abeyance
abide
abiding
ability -ies
ablaze
aboard
abode
abolish es
abolished
abominable
abominate
abominating
abortion
abound
about
above
abrasive
abreast
abroad
abrupt ly
abscond
absorb ed
absorber
absorption
abstain ed
absurd
abundance
abundant
abuse d
abusing
abysmal ly
abyss es
accelerate
accelerating
acceleration
accelerator
accept able
acceptance
accepting
accessibility
accessible
accession
accessory -ies
acclaim ed
accommodate
accommodating
accommodation
accompaniment
accompany -ies
accompanied
accomplice
accomplish es
accomplished
accomplishment
accord
accordance
according ly
accordion
account
accountability
accountable
accountancy
accountant
accrue d
accruing
accumulate
accumulating
accumulation
accumulator
accusative
accuse d
accusing
accustom ed
acetylene
achieve d
achievement
achieving
acidic
acidity
acknowledge d
acknowledgement /
acknowledgment
acknowledging
acoustic ally
acquaint ance
acquire d
acquiring
acquit ted
acquittal
acquitting
acropolis
[acropoles]
across
acrylic
acute
addicted
addiction
addictive
addition al ly
address es
addressed
adhere d
adhering
adhesive
adieu
adjacent
adjoining
adjourn ed
adjudicate
adjudicating
adjudication
adjudicator
adjust er
adjustment
administer ed
administrate
administrating
administration
administrator
admire d
admiring
admission
admit ted
admittance
admitting
ado
adopt ion
adorable
adore d
adoring
adorn ed
adrenalin
adrift
adsorption
adultery
adventure
adventurous
adverbial ly
adversity -ies
advertisement
advice
advisable
advise d
adviser
advising
advisory
Aegean
aesthetic ally
afar
affair
affect ed
affection
affectionate ly
affiliate
affiliating
affiliation
affirm ed
affirmative ly
affix es
affixed
afflict
affliction
afford
affront
afloat
afoot
afraid
afresh
again
against
agenda
aggression
aggressive
aggressor
agility
ago
agog
agree d
agreeable
agreement
ahead
ahoy!
ajar
alarm ed
alert
alight
align ed
alignment
alike
alive
allege d
allegedly
allegiance
alleging
allegro
allergic
alliance
alliteration
alliterative
allot ted
allotment
allotting
allow ed
allowable
allowance
allude
allusion
alluvial
alluvium
aloft
alone
along side
aloof
aloud
amaze d
amazing
amenable
amend
amendment
amenity -ies
America n
amid st
amino
amiss
ammonia
ammonium
amoeba
among st
amount
amuse d
amusement
amusing
anaemia / anemia
anaemic / anemic
anaesthetist /
anesthetist
anemone
anew
anneal ed
annihilate
annihilating
annihilation
announce d
announcement
announcer
announcing
annoy ed
annoyance
annoying
anoint
anon
anonymous
another
apart
apartheid
apartment
apologetic ally
apologise d
apologising
apology -ies
apostle
apostrophe
appal led
appalling
appeal ed
appear ed
appearance
append
appendicitis
appendix
[appendices]
applaud
applause
appliance
applicable
apply -ies
applied
applying
appoint
appointment
appreciate
appreciating
appreciative
apprentice d
apprenticeship
apprenticing
approach es
approached
approaching
appropriate ly
approval
approve d
approximate ly
approximating
approximation
aquarium
Arabia
arena
arise
[arose]
[arisen]
arising
arithmetic
aroma
arose
around
arouse d
arousing
arrange d
arrangement
arranging
array ed
arrest
arrival
arrive d
arriving
ascend ing
ascension
ascent
ascribe d
ascribing
ashamed
ashore
aside
asleep
aspire d
aspiring
assail ed
assailant
assault
assemble d
assembling
assembly -ies
assent
assert
assertion
assertive
assess es
assessed
assessment
assign ed
assignment
assimilate
assimilating
assimilation
assist
assistance
assistant s
associate d
associating
association
associative
assorted
assortment
assume d
assuming
assumption
assurance
assure d
assuring
astern
astigmatism
astonish es
astonished
astonishment
astound ed
astounding
astray
astrology
astronomer
astronomy
asylum
atomic
atone d
atonement
atoning
atrocious
atrocity -ies
attain ed
attainment
attempt ed
attend ed
attendance
attendant s
attention
attentive
attorney
attribute d
attributing
aurora
Australia
avail ed
availability
available
availing
avenge d
avenging
avert
avoid ed
await
awake d
[awoke]
awaken ed
awaking
award
aware
awareness
away
awhile
awoke n
awry

B

SHORT VOWEL a

*

backed
***bad** not good
***bade** did bid
badge
bagged
-**balm**
banned
***band** strip of material / stripe / group
***bands** more than one band
banged
banked
***banned** forbidden
***banns** announcement in church of plan to marry
bashes
bashed
*-**bask**ed enjoy
***Basque** person living near the Pyrenees
batted
batches
-**bath**ed

blacked
blagged
bland
blanked
-**blast**

-**bra**
brad
bragged
bran
-**branch**es
-branched
brand
brash
-**brass**es
brat

* *

babbled
babbling
backbone
backcloth
background
backhand
backing
backlashes
backlog
backpacked
backstage
backstroke
backup
backward
backwards
backyard
badgered
badly
baffled
baffling
baggage
bagging
baggy -ier, -iest
bagpipes
balanced
ballad
ballast
***ballet** dance
***ballot**ed voting
-**balmy**
bamboo
-**banal**
bandaged
bandit
bandy -ies
bandied
banger
banging
bangle
banishes
banished
banjo es / s
banker
banking
bankrupt
banner
banning
banquet
baptised
ze
Baptist
***baron** lord
barracked
barracks
barraged
barrelled
***barren** not fertile
barrowed

- * * *

bachelor
backbencher
backstory -ies
badminton
-**Bahamas**
balancing
balcony -ies
balloted
bamboozled
bamboozling
-**banana**
bandaging
bandwagon
Bangladesh
banishment
banister
bankruptcy -ies
baptising
zing
baptism
baritone
barraging
barrelling
barricade
barrier
barrister
-**basketball**
bathysphere
battalion
battery -ies
battlefield
battleship

blackberry -ies
blanketed

bombastically
bonanza
-**Botswana**

*-**brassier** more showy
***brassière** bra
-**bravado**

* * * * *

bacteria
bacterial
ballerina
barracuda
barricading

beatitude

bombastically
botanical

brutality

for Scots: a -r is on page 226

In these words you can hear the vowel sound a as in cat

* *

basalt
-**basket**
-**basking**
-**bastard**
-**bathroom**
batik
***baton** short stick
batsman [batsmen]
***batted** did bat
***batten** board
batter
***battered** did batter
battery -ies
batting
battle d
battling

began
-**behalf**

bhangra

blackbird
blackboard
blacken ed
blackhead
blackmail ed
blackness
blackout
blacksmith
bladder
blagging
blanket ed
-**blast-off**

bracken
bracket
bradawl
braggart
bragging
bramble
-**branches**
brandish es
brandished
brandy -ies
brassière
-**brassy** -ier, -iest

for Scots: a -r is on page 226

In these words the first letter 'a' is a neutral vowel. It sounds like the 'a' in 'astonish'.

baboon
balloon ed
barometer
bazaar
bazooka
blancmange
Brazil

C

SHORT VOWEL a

*

cab
*__cache__ storage space
cadge d
-**calf**
-**calm** ed
-**calve** d
cam
camp ed
can ned
*__cant__ insincere talk / sloping edge / tilt
*-**can't** cannot
cap ped
*__cash__ money
cashes
cashed
*-**cask** barrel
*__casque__ helmet
*-**cast** throw / mould / decide parts in a play / squint
-[cast]
*-**caste** social class
cat
catch es
[caught]

champ ed
*-**chance** lucky event / risk
-**chanced**
-**chant**
*-**chants** does chant / more than one chant
chap
chapped
chat ted
chav

clad
clam med
clamp ed
clan
clang ed
clank ed
clap ped
clash es
clashed
-**clasp** ed
-**class** es
-classed
☛

for Qu . . . see page 24

* *

cabbage
cabin
*__caching__ storing away
cackle d
cackling
cactus es / -i
*__caddie__ person paid to carry golf clubs
*__caddy__ -ies caddie / box to hold tea
caddied
cadging
cafe / café
caffeine
*__callous__ hard
*__callus__ es hard growth
-**calmly**
camber ed
camel
camera
campaign ed
camper
*__campers__ people in a camp
campfire
camphor
camping
*__campus__ es college or university grounds
camshaft
canal
cancel led
cancer
*__candid__ frank
*__candied__ sugar-coated
candle
candy
canning
*__cannon__ gun / stroke in billiards
cannoned
cannot
canny -ier, -iest
*__canon__ musical round / rank in church / laws / list of works
canteen
*__canter__ ed gentle gallop
*__cantor__ leader of the singing
*__canvas__ cloth
*__canvass__ ed seek opinions and/or support
*__canyon__ deep and narrow valley
☛

* * *

cabaret
cabinet
cadmium
calcium
calculate
calendar
calibrate
calibre
calico
callipers
calorie
camcorder
camembert
camera
cameraman [cameramen]
camouflage
campaigner
Canada
*__canapé__ party nibble
cancelling
candidate
candlelight
candlestick
canister
cannabis
cannibal
*__canopy__ -ies protective covering
capital
capturing
caramel
caravan
caribou
carolling
carriageway
carrier
carrion
carrycot
carrying
cascading
casserole d
castanets
-**castaway**
casually
casualty -ies
catalogue d
catalyst
catapult
cataract
category -ies
*__catholic__ wide-ranging
*__Catholic__ belonging to the Roman Catholic church
cavalier
cavalry
cavity -ies
☛

* * * * * * *

cafeteria
calamity -ies
calculation
calculating
calculator
calibrating
Cambodia
cameraman [cameramen]
camouflaging
cantankerous
cantilever ed
capacitor
capacity -ies
capitalise d
ze
capitalising
zing
capitalism
capitalist
cappuccino
captivity
Caribbean
caricature d
caricaturing
casually
casualty -ies
cataloguing
catalytic ally
catamaran
catastrophe
catastrophic ally
category -ies
caterpillar

championship
chandelier
characterisation
zation
characterise d
ze
characteristic ally
charioteer
charismatic ally
charitable
chrysanthemum

clarification
classically
classification
☛

for Scots: a -r is on page 227

In these words you can hear the vowel sound a as in cat

C

*

crab
cracked
-craft
crag
crammed
cramped
cranked
crashes
crashed

for Qu . . .
see page 24

* *

capping
capstan
capsule
captained
caption
captive
captor
captured
carafe
*carat measure of purity of gold
*caret insertion mark
carolled
carriage
*carrot vegetable
carry -ies
carried
cascade
cashew
cashiered
*cashing turning into cash
*-caster / castor powdered sugar / swivelling wheel
-casting
-castle
-castling
*-castor castor oil
casually
catching
catchment
cathode
*catholic wide-ranging
*Catholic belonging to the Roman Catholic church
catkin
cattle
catty -ier, -iest
cavern

chaffinches
chalet
challenged
champagne
-chancing
-chandler
channelled
chapel
chaplain
chapter
-charade
chasm
chassis

* * *

ceramic

challenger
championed
-chancellor
chandelier
channelling
-chapati
character
chariot
charity -ies
chatterboxes

clarify -ies
clarified
clarinet
clarity
classically
classify -ies
classified

collapsing
combatted
combatting
-commander
-commandment
companion
compassion
contraction
contractor
contractually
contraltos
contraption

-craftier
-craftiest

kangaroo
-karate
Kazakhstan

-koala

* * * * *

collaborate
collaborating
collaboration
collapsible
companionship
comparative
comparatively
comparison
compassionate
compatible
congratulate
congratulating
congratulations
constabulary -ies
contaminate
contaminating
contamination
contractually

Karaoke

for Scots: a -r
is on page 227

* *

chatroom
***chatted** had a chat
chatter
***chattered** talked quickly and too much / rattled
chatting
chatty -ier, -iest
*-**chorale** hymn tune

cladding
clamber ed
clamming
clammy -ier, -iest
clamour ed
clanger
clanking
clapper
clapping
claret
classic ally
-**classmate**
-**classroom**
clatter ed

collapse d
combat ted
-**command**
compact
contract
-**contrast**
*-**corral** enclosure for cattle and horses

crackdown
cracker
crackle d
crackling
-**craftsman** [craftsmen]
-**crafty** -ier, -iest
craggy -ier, -iest
cramming
crankshaft
cranny -ies
crevasse

kebab

-khaki

-Koran / Qur'an

In these words the first letter 'a' is a neutral vowel. It sounds like the 'a' in 'astonish'.

cacao	capillary -ies	catarrh
cadet	capricious	cathedral
Canadian	career ed	chameleon
canary -ies	caress es	charisma
canoe d	caressed	
canoeing	casino s	

for Qu . . . see page 24

for Scots: a -r is on page 227

D

*

dab bed
dad
-**daft**
-**dal / dhal**
***dam** water-barrier / mother of animal
***dammed** held back by a water-barrier
***damn** swear word / condemn
***damned** cursed
damp ed
-**dance** d
dank
dash es
dashed

drab
*-**draft** rough plan / selected group
drag ged
drank
*-**draught** current of air / depth of ship in water / piece in game
-**draughts**

* *

dabbing
dabble d
dabbling
dachsund
daddy -ies
dagger
dally -ies
dallied
damage d
dampness
damsel
damson
-**dancer**
-**dancing**
dandruff
dandy -ies
dangle d
dangling
dapple d
dashboard
-**data**
dazzle d
dazzling

decamp ed
-**demand**
***despatch** es send off
despatched
detach es
detached
detract

***dispatch** es despatch / message
dispatched
distract
divan

dragging
dragon
-**drama**
drastic ally
-**draughty** -ier, -iest

* * *

daffodil
dalmatian
damages
damaging
damnation

-**demanded**
-**demanding**
detachment

didactic
-**disaster**
-**disastrous**
dismantled
dismantling
distraction
distractor

dogmatic ally

dragonfly -ies
dramatic ally
dramatise d
ze
drastically

* * * * *

daddy-longlegs
dandelion

decapitate
declarative
defamatory

diagonal ly
dilapidated
dissatisfy -ies
dissatisfied
distractible

dogmatically

dramatically
dramatising
zing
drastically

for Scots: a -r is on page 228

In these words you can hear the vowel sound a as in cat

*

for H . . . see page 16

for I . . . see page 17

* *

elapse d

enact
encamp ed
-enchant
-enhance d
-entrance d

exact
exam
expand
expanse
extract

* * *

ecstatic ally

elaborate
elastic ally

embankment
embarrass es
embarrassed
emphatic ally

enamel led
enamour ed
-enchanting
-enhancing
entangle d
entangling
-entrancing

erratic ally

establish es
established

exactly
examine d
-example
expanded
expanding
expansion
expansive
extraction
extractor

* * * * *

ecstatically

elaborate
elaborating
elaboration
elastically
elasticity

emancipate d
emancipating
emancipation
embarrassing
embarrassment
emphatically

enamelling

erratically

establishment

evacuate
evacuating
evacuation
evacuee
evaluate
evaluating
evaluation
evangelism
evangelist
evaporate
evaporating
evaporation

exacerbate
exaggerate
exaggerating
exaggeration
examination
examiner
examining
exasperate
exasperation
expandable
explanatory
extrapolate
extrapolating
extravagance
extravagant
extravaganza

for Scots: a -r is on page 228

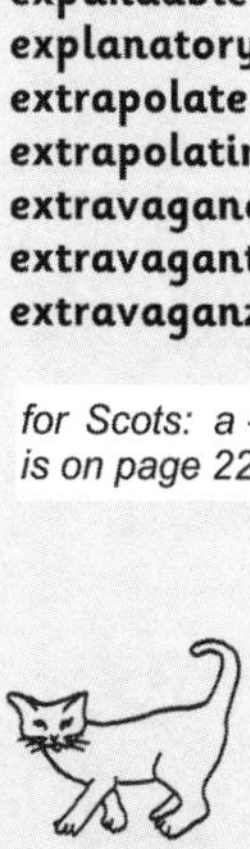

F

SHORT VOWEL a

*

fact
***facts** more than one fact
fad
fag ged
fan ned
fangs
-**fast**
***fat** ter, test plump
***fax** es machine for sending copies faxed

flag ged
flan
flange d
flank ed
flap ped
flash es
flashed
-**flask**
flat ted
flax

***franc** French coin
-**France**
***frank** plain and honest
franked

*phat excellent

for th . . . see page 28

* *

fabric
-**facade / façade**
facet
facile
faction
factor
factory -ies
factual ly
faddy
fagging
faggots
fallow
family
famine
famish es
famished
fanbelt
fancy -ies
fancied
fanning
fascist
fashion ed
-**fasten** ed
-**faster**
-**fastest**
-**father**
-**fathered**
fathom ed
fatten ed
fattening
fatter
fattest
fatty -ier, -iest

finance d

flabby -ier, -iest
flagging
flagpole
flagship
flannel led
flapjack
flapper
flapping
flappy
flashback
flasher
flashing
flatmate
***flatted** made flat
flatten ed
flatter
***flattered** did flatter
flattest
flatting

forbade / forbad

* * *

fabricate
fabulous
factorise d
ze
factory -ies
factual ly
faculty -ies
Fahrenheit
fallacy -ies
fallible
family -ies
fanatic ally
fanciful
fantasise d
ze
fantastic ally
fantasy -ies
fascinate
fascism
-**fastener**
fattening
fatuous

fiasco s
-**finale**
financial ly
financing

flamboyant
flannelling
flashforward
flattery -ies

fractional ly
fracturing
fragmented
franchising
frantically

* * * * *

fabricated
fabricating
fabrication
facsimile
factorising
zing
factually
fanatically
fantasising
zing
fantastically
fascinating
fascination
fashionable
fastidious
-**father-in-law**

financially

flabbergasted

fractionally
fragmentation
frantically

philatelist

for Scots: a -r is on page 229

In these words you can hear the vowel sound a as in cat

for th . . .
see page 28

for Scots: a -r
is on page 229

* *

fraction
fracture d
fragile
fragment
franchise d
frankly
frantic ally

phantom

In these words the first letter 'a' is a neutral vowel. It sounds like the 'a' in 'astonish'.

facetious	familiar
facilitate	familiarity
facilitating	fatigue d
facility -ies	flamingo es / s
fallacious	

G

*

***gaff** hook / pole to support sail
***gaffe** embarrassing act
gag ged
gang
gap ped
gas es
gassed
gash es
gashed
-**gasp** ed

glad der, dest
-**glance** d
gland
-**glass** es

gnash es
gnashed
gnat

-**gouache**

grab bed
*-**graft** cause to grow together / hard work
gram / gramme
gran
grand
-**grant**
graph ed
***graphed** made a graph
-**grasp** ed
-**grass** es
-grassed

* *

gabble d
gabbling
gadget
gagging
gaggle
-**gala**
gallant
***galleon** ship
galley
***gallon** measure
gallop ed
gallows
gambit
***gamble** d risk
gambler
***gambling** taking risks
***gambol** led frisk
gamma
gammon
gander
gangling
gangplank
***gangsta** member of youth gang / type of rap
***gangster** member of violent criminal gang
gangway
gannet
gantry -ies
gapping
garage d
garret
gasket
gassing
gastric
gasworks
gâteau
gather ed

-**Ghana**
-**ghastly** -ier, -iest

-**giraffe**

gladden ed
gladder
gladdest
gladly
glamour
-**glancing**
-**glasses**
-**glassy** -ier, -iest

-**gouache**

* * *

galaxy -ies
gallantry
gallery -ies
galvanise d
ze
***gambolling** frisking
garrison
gathering

-**Ghanaian**

glacier
glamorous
glandular

gradual ly
graduate
gramophone
grandchildren
granddaughter
grandfather
grandiose
grandmother
grandparent
granular
graphical ly
-**grasshopper**
gratify -ies
gratified
gratitude
gravelling
gravitate
gravity -ies

guarantee d

-**gymkhana**
gymnastics

* * * * *

galvanising
zing
gasometer
gastronomic

gelatinous

gladiator
gladiolus [gladioli]

gradually
graduation
grammatical ly
graphically
gravitation
gravitational

-**Guatemala**

for Scots: a -r is on page 229

* *

grabber
grabbing
gradual ly
grammar
grandad / granddad
grandchild
grandeur
grandma
grandpa
grandson
grandstand
granite
granny -ies
-granted
granule
graphic ally
graphite
grapple d
grappling
-grasping
-grassland
-grassy -ier, -iest
-gratis
gravel led

for Scots: a -r is on page 229

In these words the first letter 'a' is a neutral vowel. It sounds like the 'a' in 'astonish'.

galena
galore
galoshes
gazelle
gazump ed
gradation
graffiti
gratuitous

H

SHORT VOWEL a

*

hack ed
had
-half [halves]
-halve d
ham med
hand
hang
[hung]
hanged
has
hash es
hashed
hat
hatch es
hatched
hath
have
[had]

* *

habit
hacker
haddock
hadn't
haggard
haggis
haggle d
haggling
-half-time
-halfway
hallo
-halving
hamlet
hammer ed
hamming
hammock
hamper ed
hamster
hamstring
[hamstrung]
handbag
handbook
handbrake
handcuff ed
handed
handful
handgun
handle d
handler
handling
*hand-made made by hand
*handmaid servant
handout / hand-out
handshake
*handsome fine-looking
handspring
handy -ier, -iest
*hangar shed for planes
*hanger coat hanger
hanging
hanky -ies
*hansom cab
happen ed
happy -ier, -iest
harass ed
harrow ed
hasn't
hassle d
hassling
hatchback
hatchet
hatching
hatter
haven't
having
havoc
hazard

* * *

habitat
Halloween /
Hallowe'en
hamburger
handicap ped
handicraft
handiwork
handkerchief s
handlebar
handwriting
handwritten
handyman
hangover
haphazard
happening
happier
happiest
happily
happiness
harassment
haricot
haversack
-Hawaii
-Hawaiian
hazardous

heptathlon

* * * *

habitation
handicapping

Here the first 'a' is spoken as a neutral sound.

habitual ly
hallucination

for Scots: a -r is on page 230

In these words you can hear the vowel sound a as in cat

I

SHORT VOWEL a

*	**	***	**** **
	impasse	imagine d	imaginary
		imbalance	imagination
	intact	impasto	imaginative
			imagining
	-Iran	inhabit ed	immaculate
	-Iraq		-impassable
		-Iraqi	implacable
	Islam		impractical
		Islamic	
			inaccuracy -ies
		Italian	inaccurate
		italic	inadequate ly
			infallibility
			infallible
			infatuate d
			infatuation
			inflammable
			inflammatory
			inhabitant
			inhabited
			inhabiting
			insanitary
			insanity
			intractable
			intransitive
			invaluable
			irrational ly
			italicise d
			ze
			italicising
			zing

for E . . .
see page 11

J

*

jabbed
jacked
***jam** fruit boiled with sugar / crush / block
jammed
***jamb** side post of door or window
jazzes
jazzed

* *

-giraffe

gymnast

jabbered
jabbing
jackal
jackdaw
jacket
jack-knifed
jackpot
jagged
jamjar
jamming
jampot
jangled
jangling
Japan
jasper

* * *

-gymkhana
gymnastics

jaguar
jamboree
Japanese
javelin

* * * *

gelatinous

January

for dr . . .
see page 10

for Scots: a -r
is on page 230

In these words the first letter 'a' is a neutral vowel. It sounds like the 'a' in 'astonish'.

Jacuzzis Jamaica Jamaican

K

*

knack
***knap** chip off

*nap short sleep / take a snooze

* *

kebab

-khaki

knapsack

-Koran / Qur'an

* * *

kangaroo
-karate
Kazakhstan

-koala

* * * *

Karaoke

Here the 'a' is neutral.
kaleidoscope

for C . . .
see page 7

for Qu . . .
see page 24

In these words you can hear the vowel sound a as in cat

L

*

lab
lacked
***lacks** does lack
lad
lagged
lambed
lamp
-**lance**d
land
***lap** thighs of seated person / once round a track / splash gently / drink by using tongue / be placed together or overlapping
***Lapp** native of Lapland
***Lapps** more than one Lapp
***laps** more than one lap
***lapse**d slip / end through disuse
lashes
lashed
lasses
-**last**
latches
latched
-**laugh**ed
***lax** slack

* *

lacking
lacquered
laddered
lagging
lambing
lamp-post
lampshade
-**lancing**
landed
landfill
landing
landlord
landmark
landscape
landslide
language
languid
languishes
languished
languor
lanky-ier, -iest
lantern
Lapland
lapping
lapsing
laptop
lapwing
larynx
lassos / es
-**lasted**
-**lather**ed
Latin
latte
latter
latticed
-**laughter**
-**lava**
lavishes
lavished

-**llama**

* * *

Labrador
labyrinth
lacerate
laminate
Lancashire
landlady-ies
landowner
landscaping
lariat
-**lasagne**
laterally
latitude
Latvia
lavatory-ies
lavender
lavishing
laxative

-**legato**

* * * *

labradoodle
lamentable
laminated
laminating
laryngitis
laterally
lavatory-ies

legality-ies

for Scots: a -r is on page 231

In these words the first letter 'a' is a neutral vowel. It sounds like the 'a' in 'astonish'.

laboratory-ies
laborious ly
laconic ally
lagoon
lament
lapel

M

*

-ma
ma'am
mac
mad der, dest
mall
man [men]
man ned
manse
Manx
map ped
mash es
mashed
-mask ed
mass es
*massed crowded
*-mast pole
*mat small rug
match es
matched
maths
*matt not shiny

* *

macho
mackerel
*madam English form of address
*madame French form of address
madden ed
maddening
madder
maddest
madness
maggot
magic ally
magma
*magnate wealthy businessman
*magnet iron which attracts iron
magpie
malice
mallard
mallet
malware
-mama
mammal
mammoth
manage d
mandate
*mandrel spindle
*mandrill baboon
mangle d
mangling
mango es / s
manhood
manic ally
mankind
*manna food
*manner way
mannered
manning
*manor landed estate
mansion
*mantel frame round fire
*mantle cloak
manual ly
mapping
marriage
married
marrow
marry -ies
married
mascot
massage d
masseur
masseuse
*massif highlands
*massive huge

* * *

-macabre
mackerel
mackintosh
maddening
mademoiselle
madrigal
mafia
magazine
magical ly
magistrate
magnetic ally
magnetise d
ze
magnify -ies
magnified
magnitude
majesty -ies
-Malawi
malleable
management
manager
managing
mandolin
manganese
manically
manicure d
manifest
manifold
*mannequin model
*mannikin dwarf
manpower
manslaughter
mantelpiece
manual ly
manuscript
marathon
marigold
mariner
marital
maritime
mascara
masculine
masochist
masquerade
massacre d
massacring
massaging
-masterpiece
-mastery
mastodon
masturbate
matador
matinée
maximise d
maximum

* * * * **

macaroni
Madagascar
magically
magnanimous
magnesium
magnetically
magnetising
zing
magnetism
magnification
magnificent
magnolia
maladjusted
malleable
malnutrition
mammalian
manageable
manageress es
managerial
mandatory
manically
manicuring
manicurist
manifestation
manifesto
mannerism
manometer
manually
manufacture d
manufacturer
manufacturing
marijuana
marionette
masculinity
masochism
masochistic ally
massacring
masturbating
masturbation
mathematical ly
mathematician
mathematics
matrimonial
matrimony
maturation

mechanical ly
menagerie
metabolism

miraculous ly

morality

for Scots: a -r is on page 232

M

**

-**master** ed
mastiff
matches
matching
*__matted__ twisted in a thick mass
matter
*__mattered__ did matter
matting
mattress es
maxim

meringue

-**mirage**

-**morale**
-**moustache** d

***

meander ed
mechanic ally
medallion

Mohammed
molasses

In these words the first letter 'a' is a neutral vowel. It sounds like the 'a' in 'astonish'.

machine d
machinery
machining
machinist
Madeira
magician
mahogany
majestic ally
Majorca
majority -ies
malaria
Malaya
Malaysia
malevolent
malicious
malignant
manipulate
manipulation
manoeuvre d
manure d
marauder
marauding
marina
maroon ed
material ly
materialism
materialist ic
mature d
maturity

for Scots: a -r is on page 232

N

*

gnash es
gnashed
gnat

knack
*knap chip off

naff
nag ged
nan
*__nap__ ped take a snooze

**

knapsack

nagging
nana
nanny -ies
napkin
napping
nappy -ies
narrow ed
-**nasty** -ier, -iest
natural
-**Nazi**

***

narrative
narrowly
-**nastier**
-**nastiest**
national ist
nationalise d
ze
nationally
natural ly
naturalise d
ze
naturalist
navigate
-**Nazism**

nomadic
nostalgia
nostalgic ally

**** **

nationalise d
ze
nationalising
zing
nationalism
nationalistic
nationality -ies
nationally
naturalisation
zation
naturalise d
ze
naturalising
zing
naturalist
naturally
navigable
navigating
navigation
navigator

normality
nostalgically

In these words the first letter 'a' is a neutral vowel. It sounds like the 'a' in 'astonish'.

narrate
narrating
narrator
nasturtium
nativity -ies

for Scots: a -r is on page 232

P

SHORT VOWEL **a**

*

*fat plump

pack
***packed** tightly filled
***pact** agreement
padded
pal
-**palm**ed
panned
pang
pant
pants
-**pass**es
*-**passed** went by
*-**past** time that has passed / beyond
patted
patches
patched
-**path**

***phat** excellent

plaid
plait
planned
planked
-**plant**
plaque

pram
-**prance**d
prank

-**psalm**

* *

packaged
packer
packet
packing
padded
padding
paddled
paddling
paddock
paddy-ies
padlocked
pageant
palace
***palate** taste
***palette** board for mixing colours
***pallet** mattress / tool
pally-ier, -iest
pampas
pampered
pamphlet
panache
pancake
***panda** animal
***pander**ed encourage by bad example or taste
panelled
panic
panicked
panning
pansy-ies
panther
panties
pantry-ies
-**papa**
para
parish-es
parrot
parry-ies
parried
passage
-**passing**
passion
passive
-**passport**
-**password**
pasta
***pastel** crayon / soft colour
***pastille** sweet
-**pastime**
-**pasture**d
pasty-ies

* * *

pacifist
packaging
-**Pakistan**
Palestine
pancreas
panelling
panicking
pantograph
pantomime
paprika
parable
parachute
paradigm
paradise
paradoxes
paraffin
paragraphed
parakeet
paralleled
paralysed
ze
paramount
paranoid
parapet
paraphrase
parasite
parasol
paratroop
parity
parody-ies
passageway
passenger
-**passers-by**
passionate
passively
-**Passover**
-**pasteurise**d
ze
-**pastoral**ly
-**pasturing**
patio
patriot
patronage
patronised
ze

pentathlon

pianist
pianos
-**piranha**

* * * * **

-**Pakistani**
palaeontologist / paleontologist
palaeontology / paleontology
Palestinian
panacea
panorama
paparazzo [paparazzi]
papier-mâché
parabola
paracetamol
paradoxically
paraglider
paragliding
parallelogram
Paralympic
paralysing
zing
paralysis [paralyses]
paralytic
paramecium
parameter
paranoia
paraphernalia
parasitically
paratrooper
passionately
-**pasteurising**
zing
-**pastorally**
pathologically
patriotically
patriotism
patronising
zing

philanthropist
philanthropy
philatelist
philately

pianoforte
-**pistachio**s

planetary

polarity-ies
potassium

for Scots: a -r is on page 233

In these words you can hear the vowel sound a as in cat

* *

patchwork
patchy -ier, -iest
patent
-**pathway**
***patted** did pat
patter
***pattered** did patter
pattern ed
patting
patty -ies

perhaps

phantom

pince-nez
pianist
piano s

placard
placid
planet
plankton
planner
planning
-**planted**
-**planter**
-**planting**
plasma
-**plaster** ed
plastic
plateau
platen
platform
platter

***practice** action
***practise** d do or act / repeat for improvement
-**prancing**

* * *

planetary
-**plantation**
-**plasterboard**
plasticine
platinum
platitude
platypus es

practical ly
practising
pragmatic ally
protractor

-**pyjamas**

* * * * *

practicable
practically
practitioner
pragmatically
pragmatism
preparatory

for Scots: a -r is on page 233

In these words the first letter 'a' is a neutral vowel. It sounds like the 'a' in 'astonish'.

pagoda	pathetic ally
papyrus	pathology
parade	patrol led
parading	patrolling
parental	pavilion
parenthesis -es	placebo s
parishioner	platoon

Q

*

quack ed

* *

quagmire
quango s
-Qur'an / Koran

* * *

quackery

* * * *

R

*

*rack ed stretch to the limits / framework with bars / cogged bar
-raft
rag ged
ram med
ramp
ran
-ranch es
rang
rank ed
*rap knock / speech music
*rapped knocked / performed rap
*rapt entranced
rash es
-rasp ed
rat ted

*wrack seaweed
*wrap cover by winding or folding
*wrapped covered

* *

rabbi
*rabbit animal
*racket racquet / din / dishonest way of making money
*racquet bat with strings
radish es
raffle d
-rafter
ragged
ragging
rally -ies
rallied
ramble d
rambler
rambling
ramming
rampant
rampart
rancid
random
ranking
ransack ed
ransom ed
rapid
*rapper rap artist
*rapping knocking / performing rap
rapport
rapture
*rarebit cheese on toast
-rascal ly
rasher
-raspberry -ies
ratchet
-rather
ration ed
ratted
ratting
rattle d
rattling
ratty -ier, -iest
ravage d
☛

* * *

rabbitted
rabbitting
radical ly
raffia
Ramadan
ramshackle
randomise d
ze
randomly
rapidly
-rascally
-raspberry -ies
ratify -ied
rational ly
rationale
rattlesnake
ravaging
ravenous

reaction
reactor
refraction
refractive
regatta

rhapsody -ies

romancing
romantic ally

* * * * * * *

radicalism
radically
randomising
zing
Rastafarian
ratification
rationalisation
zation
rationalise d
ze
rationalising
zing
rationality
rationally
ravioli

reactionary -ies
reality -ies
retaliate
retaliating
retaliation

romantically

for Scots: a -r is on page 233

In these words you can hear the vowel sound a as in cat

R

for Scots: a -r is on page 233

* *

react
refract
relax es
relaxed

romance d

wrangle d
wrangling
*wrapper protective covering
*wrapping covering

In these words the first letter 'a' is neutral.

raccoon / racoon
rapidity
ravine

S

*

-psalm

***sac** pouch
***sack** large bag / plunder / dismiss from a job
sacked
***sacks** more than one sack / does sack
***sacs** pouches
sad der, dest
sag ged
sand
sang
sank
sap ped
sash es
sat
***sax** saxophone

scab
scalp ed
scam
scamp
scan
***scanned** did scan
***scant** hardly enough
scrap ped
scratch es
scratched

shack
-**shaft**
shag
shall
sham med
shank
shrank

* *

chalet
champagne
-charade
chassis

sabbath
***sachet** small soft bag
sadden ed
sadder
saddest
saddle d
saddling
sadly
sadness
-**saga**
sagging
salad
salmon
salon
salsa
salvage d
samba
-**sample** d
-**sampler**
-**sampling**
sanction
sandal led
sandbag
sandbank
sander
sandstone
sandwich es
sandwiched
sandy -ier, -iest
Santa
sapling
sapphire
sapping
sapwood

* * *

ceramic

chandelier

sabotage d
saboteur
saccharin / saccharine
sacrament
sacrifice d
-**safari**
-**Sahara**
-**salami**
salaried
salary -ies
salutary
salvaging
salvation
sanctify -ies
sanctified
sanctity
sanctuary -ies
sandpaper
sandpiper
sanitary
sanity
Santa Claus
satanic
satellite
satisfy -ies
satisfied
saturate
Saturday
savaging
savanna
saveloy
saxophone

* * * * * *

chandelier

sabotaging
sacrificial ly
sacrificing
salivary
salmonella
salutary
salutation
sanatorium
sanctuary -ies
sanitary
sanitation
satisfaction
satisfactorily
satisfactory
satisfying
saturated
saturating
saturation

Scandinavia
-**scenario** s

semantically

-**Somalia**

spasmodically
spectacular ly
sporadically

for Scots: a -r is on page 234

S

*

slab bed
slack ed
slam med
slang
-slant
slap ped
slash es
slashed

smack ed
smash es
smashed

snack
snag ged
snap ped
snatch es
snatched

spam med
span ned
spank ed
spat
splash es
splashed
sprang
sprat

stab bed
stack ed
-staff ed
stag
stamp ed
-stance
stand
[stood]
stank
strand
strap ped

-suave

swag
swam
swank ed

* *

***sashay** glide forward at an angle
satchel
satin
satire
sat-nav
Saturn
savage d
Saxon

scabbard
scabby -ier, -iest
scaffold
scallop ed
scalpel
scamper ed
scandal
scanner
scanning
scanty -ier, -iest
scatter ed
scavenge d
scrabble
scrabbling
scraggy -ier, -iest
scramble d
scrambling
scrapbook
scrapping
scrappy -ier, -iest
scrapyard
scratchy -ier, -iest

shabby -ier, -iest
shadow ed
shaggy -ier, -iest
shallow
shambles
shamming
shampoo ed
shamrock
shandy -ies
shanty -ies
shatter ed
shrapnel

-slalom
slamming
slapping

smasher
smashing

snagging
snapping
snappy -ier, -iest
snapshot

* * *

scaffolding
scandalous
scantiest
scavenging

semantic ally
semantics

-soprano s

sparrowhawk
spasmodic ally
spatula
sporadic ally

-staccato
staggering
stalactite
stalagmite
stamina
stampeding
standardise d
ze
statically
statuesque
stratagem
strategy -ies
stratify -ied
stratosphere

substantial ly
subtracting
subtraction
-sultana
-surpassing

syllabic ally

* * * * * *

standardisation
zation
standardising
zing
statically
statistician
statutory
strangulation
stratification

substantially

syllabically
syllabification
syllabify -ies
syllabified

for Scots: a -r is on page 234

In these words you can hear the vowel sound a as in cat

* *

spammer
spamming
Spaniard
spaniel
Spanish
spanner
spanning
sparrow
spasm
spastic
splashdown

stabbing
stagger ed
stagnant
stallion
stammer ed
stampede
standard
stand-by
standing
standpoint
standstill
stanza
static ally
statue
stature
statute
straggle d
straggling
stranded
strangle d
strangling
strapping
-**stratum** [strata]

subtract
-**surpass** es
-surpassed

swagger ed

for Scots: a -r is on page 234

In these words the first letter 'a' is a neutral vowel. It sounds like the 'a' in 'astonish'.

sadistic ally	saluting	stabiliity
salinity	samosa	statistic al ly
saliva	satirical ly	statistics
saloon	Savoy	strategic ally
salute	spaghetti	

T

SHORT VOWEL a

*

tab
tack
***tacked** did tack
***tacks** more than one tack
***tact** skill in putting things to people
tag ged
tan ned
tank
tap ped
-**task**
***tax** es money taken by government
taxed

than
thank ed
thanks
that
thatch es
thatched
that's
***thrash** es beat
thrashed
***thresh** es beat corn
threshed

track
***tracked** did track
***tract** pamphlet
tram
tramp ed
-**trance**
trap ped
trash es
trashed

twang ed

* *

tabby -ies
tableau
tablet
tabloid
tacit
tackle d
tackling
tacky -ier, -iest
tactful ly
tactic s
tactile
tactless
tadpole
tagging
talcum
talent
tally -ies
tallied
talon
tamper ed
tampon
tandem
tangent
tangle d
tangling
tango s
tangoed
tankard
tanker
tanner
tanning
tantrum
tappet
tapping
tariff
tassel led
tattered
tavern
taxi s

thankful ly
thank-you
that'd
that'll

timbre

tracksuit
traction
tractor
traffic
trafficked
tragic ally
trample d
trampling
tramway

* * *

tabulate
tactfully
tactical ly
taffeta
talented
tambourine
tangerine
tangible
tantalise d
ze
tapestry -ies
taxable
taxation
taxpayer

thankfully
thematic ally

-**tiara**

tobacco s
-**tomato** es

trafficker
trafficking
tragedy -ies
tragically
trampoline d
tranquilly
transaction
transcendent
transcribing
transcription
transferring
transformer
transfusion
transistor
transition
transitive
transitory
translating
translation
translator
translucent
transmission
transmitted
transmitter
transmitting
transparent
transpiring
transposing
transversal
transvestite
trapezoid
traveller
travelling
traversing

* * * * * *

tabulating
tabulation
tabulator
tachometer
tactically
tantalising
zing
Tanzania
tapioca
tarantula
Tasmania

theatrical ly
thematically

tobacconist
totality

trafficator
tragically
trajectory -ies
trampolining
tranquilliser
zer
tranquillity
transatlantic
transcendental
transferable
transformation
transistorise d
ze
transitional ly
transitory
transmutation
transparency -ies
transpiration
transportation
transubstantiation

tyrannical ly
tyrannosaurus es / -i

for Scots: a -r is on page 235

In these words you can hear the vowel sound a as in cat

T

* *

tranquil ly
***transact** make a deal
transcribe d
***transect** cut across
transept
transfer red
transfix es
transfixed
transform ed
transit
translate
transmit ted
transpire d
transplant
transport
transpose d
transverse
trapdoor
trapper
trapping
travel led
traveller
travelling
traverse d

In these words the first letter 'a' is neutral.

tattoo ed
trachea
tradition
traditional ly
trajectory -ies
trapeze
trapezium

for Scots: a -r is on page 235

U

*

* *

* * *

Uganda
unhappy -ier, -iest

* * * * *

unanimous ly
unhappily
unhappiness

V

*

valve d
van
-**vase**
-**vast**
vat

Here the first 'a' is a neutral vowel.

vacate
vacating
vacation
vagina
validity
vanilla
variety -ies

* *

vaccine
vacuum ed
valiant
valid
valley
valour
value d
vampire
vandal
vanish es
vanished
vanquish es
vanquished
-**vantage**

* * *

vaccinate
vacillate
vacuole
vagabond
vaginal
valentine
valiant
validate
valium
valuable
valuing
vandalise d
ze
vanity -ies
vaseline
Vatican

veranda / verandah

-**vibrato**

* * * * *

vaccination
vacillating
vacillation
validation
valuable
valuation
vandalism

vernacular

vocabulary -ies

vulgarity -ies

for Scots: a -r is on page 235

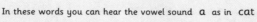

In these words you can hear the vowel sound a as in cat

W

*

*rack ed stretch to the limits / framework with bars / cogged bar
*rap knock / speech music
*rapped knocked / performed rap
*rapt entranced

wag ged
***wax** ed grow larger or stronger / plastic substance

whack ed
***whacks** more than one whack

***wrack** seaweed
***wrap** cover by winding or folding
***wrapped** covered
-wrath

* *

*rapping knocking / performing rap

wacky -ier, -iest
wagging
waggle d
wagon
wagtail

wrangle d
wrangling
wrapper
***wrapping** covering

* * *

* * * *

Y

*

yank ed
yap ped

* *

yapping

* * *

* * * *

for Scots: a -r is on page 235

Z

*

zap ped

* *

zapping

* * *

Zambia

-Zimbabwe

* * * *

*

* *

abreast

***accept** take something offered

address es
addressed
adept

***affect** alter
afresh

again
against

ahead

allege d

amend

annexe d
any

append

arrest

ascend
***ascent** climb
***assent** agree
assess es
assessed

attempt
attend

avenge d

*effect result / bring about

*except not including

* * *

acceptance
accepting
accession

adventure

aesthetic ally

affected
affection

agenda
aggression
aggressive
aggressor

alleging
allegro
already

amendment

annexing
anyhow
anymore
anyone
anything
anyway
anywhere

appendix -ces
apprentice d

ascending
ascension
assemble d
assembling
assembly -ies
assessment

attempted
***attendance** those present / rate of attending
attendant
***attendants** servants
attended
attention
attentive

authentic ally

avenging

* * * * * *

accelerate
accelerating
acceleration
accelerator
acceptable
accessibility
accessible
accessory -ies
acetylene

adrenalin
adventurous

aesthetically

affectionate
affectionately

allegedly

America
American

anemone
anybody

appendicitis
apprenticeship
apprenticing

authentically

for Scots: e -r is on page 242

*

beck
bed ded
beg ged
belch es
belched
***bell** instrument
***belle** beauty
belt
bench es
bend
[bent]
best
bet ted
[bet]

bled
blend
bless es
blessed
[blest]

***bread** food
***breadth** width
breast
***breath** air passing in and out of lungs
***bred** produced young / reared

* *

beckon ed
bedclothes
bedding
bedrock
bedroom
bedside
bedtime
befell
befriend
beggar
begging
behead
beheld
Belgian
Belgium
bellow ed
belly -ies
benchmark ed
bending
benzene
bereft
***beret** flat, round cap
***berry** -ies fruit
beset
[beset]
betted
better
betting
bevel led
beverage

blessed
blessing

breakfast
breastbone
breathless
brethren

***bury** -ies place deep down
buried

* * *

Belarus
benefit ed
besetting
bestseller
bevelling
beverage

breathalyse d
ze
breathtaking

burial

* * * * *

beneficial ly
beneficiary -ies
benefited
benefiting
benevolent

breathalyser
zer
breathalysing
zing

Here the first letter 'e' has a short 'i' sound.

B*E*HAVING WORDS

became	belong ed
because	belonging s
become	beloved
[became]	below
[become]	bemuse d
becoming	bemusing
befall	beneath
[befell]	benign
[befallen]	bereave d
before	bereavement
beforehand	beseech es
begin	beseeched
[began]	[besought]
[begun]	beside
beginner	besides
beginning	besiege d
behalf	besieging
behave d	besotted
behaving	bestow ed
behaviour	betray ed
behavioural	betrayal
behind	between
behold	betwixt
[beheld]	beware
belated ly	bewilder ed
belief	bewilderment
believe d	bewitch es
believer	bewitched
believing	beyond

for Scots: e -r is on page 243

C

*

***cell** unit
Celt
***cent** money / hundred
***cents** money

***check**ed stop / test
chef
***cheque** order to bank
chess
chest

cleansed
clef
cleft
clenches
clenched

crêche
crêpe
crept
cresses
crest

***Czech** Czechoslovakian

kelp
kept
ketch es

*scent perfume / smell
*scents more than one scent

*sell exchange for money
*sense understandable pattern
*sent made to go

for Qu . . .
see page 47

* *

cadet
caresses
caressed
cassette

***cellar** underground storage room
cellos
Celtic
cement
***censer** pan for burning incense
***censor** judge of what may not be published
***census** official count
centaur
centrally
centre
centring
***cession** giving up ownership

checking
checklist
chemist
cherishes
cherished
cherry-ies
chestnut

cleansing
clever

collect
commenced
compelled
compresses
compressed
condemned
condensed
confesses
confessed
connect
consent
contempt
contend
content
contest
correct

credited
crescent
crevice

* * *

celebrate
celery
celestial
cellophane
cellular
celluloid
cellulose
Celsius
cemetery-ies
censorship
centigrade
centipede
centrally
century-ies
cerebral
cerebrum

chemically
chemistry

cleanliness
clerical

collecting
collection
collectively
collector
commencing
compelling
complexion
compression
compressor
concentric
conception
conceptually
concession
condenser
condensing
confession
confessor
confetti
congested
congestion
conjectured
connected
connecting
connection
connector
consensus
contention
contestant
convection
convector
convention
corrected
correction
correctly

* * * * * *

celebrated
celebrating
celebration
celebrity-ies
celestial
centenary-ies
centimetre
centrifugally
centurion
cerebellum
ceremonially
ceremony-ies

chemically
cholesterol

collectively
commemorate
commemoration
competitive
competitiveness
competitor
complexity-ies
conceptually
confectioner
confectionery
confessional
congenitally
conjecturing
consecutive
contemporary-ies
contemptible
contemptuous
conventionally
cosmetically

credibility
crematorium

Czechoslovakia

kinetically

for Scots: e -r
is on page 244

C

* *

Kelvin / kelvin
kennel
kestrel
ketchup
kettle

*seller person who sells
*senses means of gaining information
*sensor detecting device
*session meeting / period

* * *

cosmetic ally
cosmetics

credential
credible
credited
creditor
crescendo s

kinetic ally

Here the first letter 'e' has a short 'i' sound.

cremate
cremation
cremating
crevasse

for Qu . . . see page 47

for Scots: e -r is on page 244

D

*

dead
deaf
dealt
death
debt
deck ed
den
***dense** closely packed / stupid
dent
***dents** more than one dent
depth
desk

dread ed
dreamt
dredge d
dregs
drench es
drenched
dress
dressed

dwell ed
[dwelt]

* *

deaden ed
deadline
deadlock
deadly -ier, -iest
deafen ed
deafer
deafest
debit ed
debris
debtor
debut / début
decade
deckchair
defect
defence
defend
deflect
delta
deluge d
demo s
denim
Denmark
dental
dentist
depend
depot
depress es
depressed
descant
descend
***descent** way down
desert
desktop
desperate
despot
detect
detest
devil led
dexterous / dextrous

* * *

deafening
debited
December
deception
deceptive
decimal
decorate
dedicate
defective
defector
defendant
defender
defensive
deference
deficit
definite
deflection
delegate
delicate
deluging
democrat
demonstrate
denigrate
density -ies
***dependant** person who depends
***dependants** people who depend
depended
***dependence** reliance
***dependent** relying / hanging
depending
depression
depressive
deputy -ies
derelict

* * * * * *

decimetre
declaration
decorated
decoration
decorative
decorator
dedicated
dedication
defamation
deferential ly
definitely
definition
degradation
delegation
delicacy -ies
delicatessen
deliquescent
delphinium
democratic ally
demographic ally
demolition
demonstrating
demonstration
denigrating
dependable
dependency -ies
deposition
deprivation
derivation
desiccated
desiccation
designated
designating
desolation

for Scots: e -r is on page 245

In these words you can hear the vowel sound e as in elephant

D

* *

digest
direct
dispense d
dissect
*__dissent__ disagreement
distress es
distressed

dreaded
dreadful ly
dredger
dredging
dresser
dressing

dweller
dwelling

* * *

*__descendant__ offspring
descended
*__descendent__ moving down
designate
desolate
desperate ly
destiny -ies
destitute
detection
detective
detector
detention
*__deterrence__ prevention by causing fear
deterrent
*__deterrents__ more than one deterrent
detonate
detriment
devastate
develop ed

digestion
dilemma
dimension
directed
direction
directive
directly
director
discredit ed
discretion
dishevelled
dispelling
dispenser
dispensing
displeasure
dissension
dissenter
distressing

domestic ally

dreadfully

dyslexic / dyslectic

* * * * * *

desperately
desperation
despotism
destination
detonating
detonator
detrimental
devastated
devastating
devastation
developer
developing
development
developmental ly

digestible
directory -ies
discredited
discrepancy -ies
disseminate
dissemination

domestically
domesticate

dyslexia

for Scots: e -r is on page 245

Here the first letter 'e' has a short 'i' sound.

D**E**LIGHTFUL WORDS

debate
debating
decamp ed
decay ed
decease d
deceit ful ly
deceive d
deceiving
decide
deciding
deciduous
decipher ed
decision
decisive
declare d
declaring
decline d
declining
decree d
decry -ies
decried
deduce d
deducing
deduct ion
deductive
defeat ed
defer red
deferring
defiance
defiant
deficiency -ies
deficient
define d
defining
deform ed
defy -ies
defied

degree
delay ed
delete
deleting
deletion
deliberate ly
delicious
delight ed
delightful ly
delirious
deliver ed
deliverance
delivery -ies
delusion
demand ed
demanding
demean ed
demise
demob bed
democracy -ies
demolish es
demolished
demonstrative
denial
denomination
denominator
denote
denoting
denounce d
denouncing
denunciation
deny -ies
denied
depart ure
department
deploy ed
deployment

deport
deposit ed
depositing
depreciate
depreciating
depreciation
deprive d
depriving
derail ed
derailment
derivative
derive d
deriving
derogatory
describe d
describing
description
descriptive
desert ed
deserve d
deserving
design ed
designer
desirable
desire d
desiring
despair ed
despatch es
despatched
despise d
despising
despite
despondency
despondent
dessert
destroy ed
destroyer

destruction
destructive
detach es
detached
detain ed
deter red
detergent
deteriorate

deteriorating
deterioration
determination
determine d
determining
deterring
detract
device

devise d
devising
devoid
devote d
devotion
devour ed
devout

E

*

ebb ed

edge d

egg ed

elf [elves]
elm
else

end

etch es
etched

* *

*accept take something offered

*affect alter

any

echo ed
eczema

eddy -ies
eddied
edging
edit ed

***effect** result / bring about
effort

ego

eject

elbow ed
elder
eldest
elect
elsewhere

embed ded
ember
emblem
empire
empress es
empty -ies
emptied

enclave
ending
endless
engine
ensign
entail ed
enter ed
entrails
entrance
entrench es
entrenched
entry -ies
envoy
envy -ies
envied
enzyme

epic

See also E on page 65

for H . . . see page 40

for I . . . see page 41

* * *

aesthetic ally

anyhow
anymore
anyone
anything
anyway
anywhere

ebony

eccentric ally
ecstasy -ies
ecstatic ally
Ecuador
eczema

edible
edifice
edited
editor
educate

effective
effervesce d
effigy -ies
effortless

egoist / egotist

ejector

elderly
election
elector
electric ally
electrode
electron
elegance
elegant
element
elephant
elevate
eleven th
eloquence
eloquent

embargo es
embargoed
embassy -ies
embedded
embellish es
embellished
embezzle d
embryo s
emerald
emery

* * * * * * * *

aesthetically

anybody

eccentrically
economic
economical ly
economics
ecstatically
ecumenical ly

editorial ly
educated
educating
education
educational ly
educator
Edwardian

effectively
effectiveness
effervescence
effervescent
effervescing
efficacy -ies

egoism / egotism
egoistic / egotistic

electoral ly
electorate
electrical ly
electrician
electricity
electrocute
electrocution
electrolyse d
ze
electrolysing
zing
electrolysis
electrolyte
electrolytic ally
electromagnetic ally
electronic ally
electronics
electrostatic ally
elementary
elevated
elevation
eligible
elocution

for Scots: e -r is on page 245

In these words you can hear the vowel sound e as in elephant

E

SHORT VOWEL e

* *

erect
errand
error

escort
esquire
essay
essence

etching
ethics
ethnic ally

event
ever
every

excel led
***except** not including
***excerpt** selected passage
excess es
excise
exempt
exhale d
exhort
exile d
exit
expect
expel led
expense
expert
exploit
export
express es expressed
extend
extent
extra
extract

* * *

emigrant
emigrate
eminence
eminent
empathy
emperor
emphasis [emphases]
emphasise d
ze
emphatic ally
emptiness

endeavour ed
endocrine
enemy -ies
energy -ies
engineer ed
entering
enterprise
entertain ed
entity -ies
***envelop** ed surround
***envelope** letter holder
envious

epilogue
episode
epitaph
epithet

equinox es
equity

erection

escalate
escapade
Eskimo s
esplanade
espresso / expresso
essential ly
estimate
estuary -ies

etcetera
ethernet
ethical ly
ethnical ly
etiquette

eventual
evergreen
everyday
everyone
everything
everywhere
evidence
evident

* * * * * * *

embarkation
embryonic ally
emigration
emissary -ies
emphatically
empirical ly

energetic ally
engineering
entertainer
entertainment
enveloping
enviable

epicyclic ally
epidemic ally
epilepsy
epileptic ally

equatorial
equilibrium
equitable

escalator
especially
essentially
estimated
estimating
estimation

etcetera
ethically
ethnically
etymological ly
etymology

eventually
everlasting
everybody
evidently

excavating
excavation
excellency -ies
exceptional ly
excitation
exclamation
executing
execution
executioner
executive
exemplary

See also E on page 65

for H . . . see page 40

for I . . . see page 41

for Scots: e -r is on page 245

In these words you can hear the vowel sound e as in elephant

E

Here the first letter 'e' has a short 'i' sound.

E XCITING WORDS

ecclesiastical ly
eclipse d
eclipsing
ecologist
ecology
edit
edition
efficient
Egyptian
elaborate
elaborating
elaboration
elapse d
elastic ally
elasticity
elated
elation
elicit ed
eliciting
eliminate
eliminating
elimination
Elizabethan
ellipse
elliptical ly
elope d
eloping
elucidate
elude
eluding
elusive
emancipate
emancipation
embankment
embark ed
embarrass es
embarrassed
embarrassing
embarrassment
embroider ed
embroidery
emerge d
emergence
emergency -ies
emerging
emission
emit ted
emitting
emotion
emotional ly
emotive
employ ed
employee
employer
employment
empower ed
emulsion ed
enable d
enabling
enact
enamel led
enamelling
enamour ed
encamp ed
encase d
encasing
enchant
enchanting
encircle d
encircling
enclose d

enclosing
enclosure
encounter ed
encourage d
encouragement
encouraging
encroach es
encroached
encyclopedia
endanger ed
endear ed
endearment
endorse d
endorsing
endow ed
endurance
endure d
enduring
enfold
enforce d
enforcement
enforcing
engage d
engagement
engaging
engrave d
engraving
engross es
engrossed
engulf ed
enhance d
enhancing
enjoy ed
enjoying
enjoyment
enlarge d
enlarging
enlighten ed
enlist
enormous ly
enough
enquire d
enquiring
enquiry -ies
enrage d
enraging
enrich es
enriched
enrol led
enrolment
enslave d
enslaving
ensure d
ensuring
entangle d
entangling
enthusiasm
enthusiast
enthusiatic ally
entire ly
entitle d
entitlement
entitling
entrancing
entrust
enumerate
enumerating
environment al ly
environmentalism
environmentalist
envisage d

envisaging
epitome
equality
equate
equation
equator
equip ped
equipment
equipping
equivalence
equivalent
erase d
eraser
erasing
erode
eroding
erosion
erotic ally
erratic ally
erroneous ly
erupt ed
eruption
escape d
escaping
escarpment
establish es
established
establishment
estate
estrange d
eternal ly
evacuate
evacuating
evacuation
evacuee
evade
evading
evaluate
evaluating
evaluation
evaporate
evaporating
evaporation
evasion
evasive
evict
evoke d
evoking
evolve d
evolving
exacerbate
exact ly
exaggerate
exaggerating
exaggeration
exalt
exam ination
examine d
examining
example
exceed
exceeding ly
exchange d
exchanging
excitable
excite d
excitedly
excitement
exciting
exclaim ed
exclude

* * *

excavate
excellence
excellent
excelling
exception
excessive
exchequer
execute
exemption
***exercise** practice / use
***exercise** d take exercise / use
exhaling
exodus
***exorcise** d cast out devil
expectant
expected
expelling
expensive
expertise
exporter
expressing
expression
expressive
expresso / espresso
exquisite
extended
extending
extension
extensive
external ly
extravert / extrovert

* * * * * *

exhibition
exhortation
expectancy -ies
expectantly
expectation
expedition
expeditious
expendable
expenditure
experiment
experimental ly
experimentation
experimenter
explanation
exploitation
exploration
exponential ly
exposition
expressionism
externally
extraversion /
extroversion
extremity -ies
exultation

for Scots: e -r is on page 245

See also E on page 65

for H . . . see page 40

for I . . . see page 41

excluding
exclusion
exclusive ly
excrete
excreting
excretion
excursion
excuse d
excusing
exert ion
exhaust ed
exhaustion
exhibit ed
exhibiting
exist ed
existence
exorbitant
exotic ally
expand ed
expandable
expanding
expanse

expansion
expansive
expedient
experience d
experiencing
explain ed
explanatory
explicit
explode
exploding
exploratory
explore d
explorer
exploring
explosion
explosive
exponent
expose d
exposing
exposure
expulsion
exquisite

exterior
exterminate
extermination
external ly
extinct ion
extinguish ed
extinguisher
extract ion
extractor
extraneous
extraordinarily
extraordinary
extrapolate
extrapolating
extravagance
extravagant
extravaganza
extreme ly
extremist
extrusion
exuberance
exuberant

In these words you can hear the vowel sound e as in elephant

F

*

fed
fell
***felled** cut down
***felt** did feel / type of cloth
fen
fence d
fend
fetch es
fetched
fête

fleck ed
fled
flesh ed
flex es
flexed

French
fresh
fret ted
friend

phlegm

for th . . . see page 52

* *

feather
fellow
fencing
fennel
ferment
ferret ed
ferry -ies
ferried
fester ed
festive
***feta** cheese
***fetter** ed chain

fledgeling / fledgling
Flemish

foretell
forget
forwent / forewent

freckles
Frenchman [Frenchmen]
frenzy -ies
frenzied
Fresnel
fretful ly
fretsaw
fretted
fretting
friendly
friendship

pheasant

* * *

February
federal ly
fellowship
feminine
feminist
ferreted
ferreting
festival

flexible
fluorescence
fluorescent

forensic
forever
forgetful ly
forgetting

Frenchwoman
[Frenchwomen]
frenetic ally
freshwater
fretfully
friendliness

phonetic ally

Here the first letter 'e' has a short 'i' sound.
ferocious ferocity

* * * * *

February
federally
federation
femininity
feminism
festivity -ies

fidelity

flexibility
fluorescence
fluorescent

forgetfully
forget-me-not

frenetically

phonetically

for Scots: e -r is on page 246

G

*

***gel** semi-solid mixture
gem
get
[got]

glen

guess es
***guessed** did guess
***guest** person invited

*jell set as a jelly
jest
jet ted

The 'e' is neutralised.
geranium
gregarious
guerilla / guerrilla

* *

gazelle

gender
general ly
generous
gentile
gentle
gently
gesture d
getting

ghetto es / s

jealous
jelly -ies
jellied
jemmy -ies
jester
jetted
jetty -ies

* * *

gelatine / gelatin
general ly
generalise d
ze
generate
generic
generous
genetic ally
gentleman
gentlemen
genuine
gestation
gesturing
getaway

jealousy -ies
jellyfish
jeopardy
jettison ed

* * * * * *

generalisation
zation
generalise d
ze
generalising
zing
generally
generation
generator
generosity
genetically
genuinely
geriatric
gesticulate

for Scots: e -r is on page 246

H

SHORT VOWEL *e*

*

head
health
hedge d
held
hell
helm
help ed
hem med
hemp
hen
hence

* *

headache
head-dress es
headed
header
heading
headlamp
headland
headlight
headline d
headphones
headscarf -ves
heady -ier, -iest
healthcare
healthy -ier, -iest
heather
heaven
heavy -ier, -iest
heckle d
heckling
hectare
hectic ally
hedgehog
hedgerow
hedging
hefty -ier, -iest
heifer
hello
helmet ed
helper
helpful ly
helping
helpless
hemming
henceforth
herald
***heron** large bird
***Herren** title for German men
herring
herself

himself

* * *

haematite / hematite
haemorrhage / hemorrhage d

headier
headiest
headlining
headmaster
headmistress es
headquarters
headteacher
headwaters
healthier
healthiest
heavenly
heavier
heaviest
heavily
heaviness
heavyweight
hectically
heftier
heftiest
helical ly
heliport
helmeted
helpfully
helplessly
helplessness
hemisphere
heptathlon
heraldry
heresy -ies
heretic
heritage
***heroin** drug
***heroine** female hero
hesitant
hesitate
hexagon

horrendous

hysterics

* * * * * *

hectically
helically
helicopter
helter-skelter
hepatitis
hereditary
heredity
heretical ly
heroism
hesitantly
hesitation
heterogeneous
heterosexual
hexagonal ly

hysterical ly

for Scots: e -r is on page 247

Here the first letter 'e' has a short 'i' sound.

heroic heroically

In these words you can hear the vowel sound e as in elephant

I

*

**

immense
impelled
impresses
impressed

incensed
indent
inept
infect
inject
inspect
instead
intend
***intense** extreme
intent
***intents** purposes
invent
invest

itself

***

immensely
impeller
impelling
impending
impregnate
impression
impressive

incensing
incentive
inception
incessant
indebted
indented
indentured
infection
infectious
inflection
ingestion
inherent
inherited
injection
inspection
inspector
intensely
intensive
intention
intestine
invention
inventive
inventor
investment
investor

**** **

identifier
identity -ies

illegible

immeasurable
immensity
impeccable
impeccably
impediment
impenetrable
imperative
impetuous
impregnable
impregnating
impressionable
impressionism
impressionist

incredible
incredibly
indefinitely
inedible
ineptitude
inevitable
inevitably
inflexible
inflexibly
inheritance
inherited
inheriting
insecticide
insensitive
integrity
intelligence
intelligent
intelligible
intelligibly
intensify -ies
intensified
intensity -ies
intentional ly
interrogate
interrogation
investigate
investigating
investigation
investigator

irregular
irregularity -ies
irrelevance
irrelevant
irreparable
irreparably

for E . . .
see page 36

for Scots: e -r
is on page 247

In these words you can hear the vowel sound e as in elephant

J

*

*gel semi-solid mixture
gem

*jell set as a jelly
jest
jet ted

*for dr . . .
see page 34*

* *

gender
general ly
generous
gentile
gentle
gently
gesture d

jealous
jelly -ies
jellied
jemmy -ies
jester
jetted
jetty -ies

* * *

gelatine / gelatin
general ly
generalise d
ze
generate
generic
generous
genetic ally
gentleman
gentlemen
genuine
gestation
gesturing

jealousy -ies
jellyfish
jeopardy
jettison ed

* * * * * *

generalisation
zation
generalise d
ze
generalising
zing
generally
generation
generator
generosity
genetically
geriatric
gesticulate

*for Scots: e -r
is on page 248*

K

*

kelp
kept
ketch es

knelt

*for C . . .
see page 33*

*for Qu . . .
see page 47*

* *

Kelvin / kelvin
kennel
Kenya
kestrel
ketchup
kettle

* * *

kinetic ally

* * * * *

kinetically

*for Scots: e -r
is on page 248*

In these words you can hear the vowel sound e as in elephant

L

*

***lead** metal
***leant** did lean
leaped / leapt
***led** showed / shown the way
ledge
left
leg ged
lend
*[lent] did lend
length
lens es
***Lent** the 40 days before Easter
less
lest
let
[let]
let's

* *

lament
lapel
leather ed
lectern
lecture d
ledger
left-hand
left-wing
legend
leggings
leisure d
lemon
lender
lending
lengthen ed
lengthy -ier, -iest
lentil
leopard
leper
***lessen** ed make less
lesser
***lesson** period of instruction
letter ed
letting
lettuce
level led
levy -ies
levied

* * *

Lebanese
Lebanon
lecturer
lecturing
legacy -ies
legendary
legislate
lemonade
leprechaun
leprosy
lesbian
lessening
lethargy
letterbox es
lettering
levelling
lexical
lexicon

libretto [libretti]
lieutenant

* * * *

legendary
legislation
legislative
legislator
legislature
levitation

longevity

for Scots: e -r is on page 248

Here the first letter 'e' has a short 'i' sound.

legality -ies
legato
legitimacy -ies
legitimate
lethargic

M

*

meant
melt
[molten]
men
mend
mesh es
meshed
mess es
messed
met

* *

many

meadow
measure d
***medal** award /
memento
***meddle** d interfere
***meddler** person who interferes
meddling
medicine
***medlar** fruit
medley
mellow ed
melon
melted
melting
member
membrane
memo
memoirs
menace d
mental ly
mention ed
mentor
menu
merit ed
merry -ier, -iest
message
***messes** more than one mess / does mess
Messieurs
***Messrs** plural of 'Mr'
messy -ier, -iest
***metal** mineral substance
metalled
method
metric ally
***mettle** courage

misdealt
misled
misspell ed
[misspelt]
misspend
[misspent]

* * *

majestic ally

measurement
measuring
mechanise d
ze
meddlesome
medical ly
medicine
meditate
megabyte
megaphone
megaton
melody -ies
membership
memento es / s
memorable
memorise d
ze
memory -ies
meniscus es / -i
menopause
menstruate d
mentally
merited
meriting
merrily
merriment
mesmerise d
ze
messaging
messenger
metaphor
Methodist
metrical ly
metricate
metronome
Mexican
Mexico

momentum

* * * * * * *

majestically
malevolent

measurable
mechanising
zing
mechanism
medically
medication
medieval
meditating
meditation
Mediterranean
melancholy
Melanesia
melanoma
memorable
memorandum
memorising
zing
meningitis
menopausal
menstruating
menstruation
mentality -ies
mesmerising
zing
metabolic
metabolism
metallurgy
metamorphic
metamorphosis -es
Methodism
methodological ly
methodology -ies
methylated
metrically
metricating
metrication
metropolitan

millennium [millennia]

molecular

for Scots: e -r is on page 249

Here the first letter 'e' has a short 'i' sound.

mechanic ally
medicinal ly
melodic al ly
melodious
memorial
meniscus es / -i
meridian
methodical ly
meticulous
metropolis es
mnemonic

N

*	* *	* * *	* * * * *
knelt	**necklace**	**nebula**	**necessarily**
	nectar	**nebulous**	**necessary**
necked	**neglect**	**necessary**	**necessity**-ies
nest	**nephew**	**nectarine**	**neglectfully**
netted	**nestle**d	**negative**	**negligible**
next	**nestling**	**neglectful**ly	**nepotism**
	netball	**negligence**	**nevertheless**
	nether	**negligent**	
	netted	**Netherlands**	**numerical**ly
	netting	**networking**	
	nettled		
	netware	**November**	
	networked		
	never	**numeric**al	
	Noel		

for Scots: e -r is on page 249

Here the first letter 'e' has a short 'i' sound.

negate
negation
negotiable
negotiate
negotiating
negotiation
negotiator

O

*	* *	* * *	* * * * *
	object	already	authentically
	obsesses		
	obsessed	authentically	**objectionable**
			objectively
	offence	**objection**	**objectivity**
	offend	**objective**	**obscenity**-ies
		obsession	**obsessional**ly
	oppresses	**obsessive**	
	oppressed		**ostensible**
		offender	**ostensibly**
		offensive	
		oppression	
		oppressive	
		oppressor	

for Scots: e -r is on page 249

P

SHORT VOWEL *e*

*

peck ed
peg ged
pelt
pen ned
pence
pest
pet ted

phlegm

pledge d

press es
pressed

* *

peasant
pebble
***pedal** foot lever
pedalled
***peddle** d carry and try to sell
peddler
peddling
pegboard
pegging
pellet
pelvic
pelvis
penance
pencil led
pendant
pending
penguin
pennant
***penne** pasta
penning
***penny** -ies old coin
pension ed
pepper ed
peptic
percent / per cent
perfect
peril
perish es
perished
perplex es
perplexed
pester ed
pestle
petal led
***petrel** sea-bird
***petrol** fuel
petting
petty -ier, -iest

pheasant

pleasant
pleasure
pledging
plenty

possess es
possessed

* * *

parental
pathetic ally

pedalling
pedalo s
pedestal
pedigree
pelican
penalty -ies
pendulum
penetrate
penniless
pensioner
pentagon
pentathlon
peppermint
percentage
perception
perceptive
perceptual ly
peregrine
perfection
perilous
periscope
perpetual ly
perplexing
perspective
pessimist
pesticide
petrify -ies
petrified
petticoat

phonetic ally

pleasantly
plentiful ly
plethora

possession
possessive
potential ly

***precedence** priority
precedent
***precedents** previous examples
precipice
predator
predatory
predicate
preferably
preference
pregnancy -ies
prejudice d

* * * * * *

parenthesis
[parentheses]
pathetically

pedestrian
penetrating
penetration
penicillin
***peninsula** land almost surrounded by water
***peninsular** of or like a peninsula
perceptible
perceptually
perennial ly
perfectionist
perishable
peristalsis
perpetually
pessimism
pessimistic ally

phonetically

pleasurable
plentifully

potentially

predatory
preferably
preferential ly
premiership
preparation
preposition
prepositional ly
Presbyterian
presentable
presentation
preservation
presidency -ies
presidential ly
professional ly
professionalism
progressively
propensity -ies
prophetically

pterodactyl

for Scots: e -r is on page 250

In these words you can hear the vowel sound e as in elephant

P

**

precious
preface
preference
pregnant
prelude
premier
premise
***presence** being
present
present
***presents** gifts
pressing
pressure d
prestige
presto
pretence
pretend
prevent
profess es
professed
progress es
progressed
project
propel led
prospect
protect
protest

***

premature
premier
premiership
premises
presented
presenting
presently
president
pressuring
prestigious
pretended
pretentious
prevalence
prevalent
prevention
preventive
procession
profession
professor
progression
progressive
projectile
projection
projector
propeller
propelling
prophetic ally
prospective
prospector
prospectus es
protected
protection
protective
protector

for Scots: e -r is on page 250

The first letter 'e' in these words is a neutral short vowel. It is pronounced like the 'i' in 'pig'.

PH***E***NOMENAL WORDS

peculiar
peculiarity -ies
peninsula
peninsular
perimeter
peripheral ly
periphery -ies
peroxide
petition ed
petroleum
phenomenal ly
phenomenon
[phenomena]
precaution
precede d
preceding
precipitate
precipitating
precipitation
predominant ly
prefer red
preferring
preliminary -ies
prepare d
preparing
prescribe d
prescribing
prescription
preservative
preserve d
preserving
preside
presiding
presumably
presume d
presuming
presumptuous
prevail ed
prevailing

Q

*

quell ed
quench es
quenched
quest

**

quelling
question ed
quintet

***

***questioner** person who asks
***questionnaire** set of questions

****

questionable

R

SHORT VOWEL *e*

*

***read** looked at and understood
realm
***red** colour
ref
rend
[rent]
rent
***rest** repose / ones left over
***retch**es try to vomit
retched
***rev** rotation per minute
***Rev** the Reverend
***rex / Rex** king

wreck ed
*wrecks does smash / more than one wreck
wren
wrench es
wrenched
*wrest seize
*wretch unhappy creature

* *

ready -ier, -iest
rebel led
recess es
recessed
reckless
reckon ed
record
rector
rectum
redden ed
redder
reddest
reddish
redhead
redskin
redwood
reference d
reflect
refresh es
refreshed
refuge
refuse
reggae
regret ted
reject
relent
relic
relish es
relished
remnant
render ed
renege d
rental
repel led
repent
repress es
repressed
reptile
request
rescue
resent
resin
respect
respite
rested
restful
resting
restless
revel led
revenge d
reverence
***reverend** deserving respect
***Reverend** title
***reverent** feeling or showing reverence

rosette

* * *

readier
readiest
readily
readiness
rebelling
rebellion
rebellious
reception
receptive
receptor
recession
recessive
recipe
recognise d
ze
recollect
recommend
reconcile d
rectangle
rectify -ies
rectified
rectory -ies
redemption
referee
reference d
referencing
reflected
reflection
reflector
reflexive
reformer
refreshment
refugee
regiment
register ed
registrar
registry -ies
regretful ly
regretted
regretting
regular
regulate
rejection
relative
relegate
relentless
relevance
relevant
remedy -ies
remedied
remember ed
remembrance
reminisce d
Renaissance
rendition
reneging
renovate d

* * * * * *

receptacle
receptionist
recitation
recitative
recognisable
zable
recognising
zing
recognition
recollection
recommendation
reconciliation
reconciling
recreation
recreational
rectangular
rectifier
rectifying
referencing
referendum
reformation
regimental ly
registration
regretfully
regularity -ies
regularly
regulating
regulation
regulator
regulatory
relatively
relativity
relegating
relegation
remembering
reminiscence
reminiscent
reminiscing
renovated
renovating
renovation
repertory -ies
repetition
repetitive
replication
representation
representative
represented
representing
reputable
reputation

for Scots: e -r is on page 251

In these words you can hear the vowel sound e as in elephant

R

* *

wreckage
wrestle d
wrestler
wrestling
wretched

* * *

repartee
repellent
repelling
repentance
repertoire
repertory -ies
replica
represent
repression
repressive
requiem
rescuing
resemblance
resemble d
resembling
resentful ly
resentment
reservoir
***residence** house
resident
***residents** occupiers
residue
resolute
resonance
resonant
respectful ly
respective
restaurant
résumé
retention
retentive
retina
retrograde
revelling
revelry -ies
revenging
revenue
reverence
***reverend** deserving respect
***Reverend** title
***reverent** feeling or showing reverence
reversal

rhetoric

* * * * * *

resentfully
reservation
residential
resignation
resolution
respectable
respectfully
respectively
respiration
respiratory
restoration
resurrection
retribution
retrospective
retroviral
retrovirus
revelation
revolution
revolutionary -ies

for Scots: e -r is on page 251

Here the first letter 'e' has a short 'i' sound.

R***E*** FRESHING WORDS

rebound
rebuke d
rebuking
recall ed
recede d
receding
receipt
receive d
receiver
receiving
recipient
reciprocal ly
reciprocate
recital
recite
reciting
reclaim ed
recline d
reclining
recoil ed
record ed
recorder
recording
recount
recourse
recover ed
recovery -ies
recruit ment
recuperate
recur red
recurrence
recurrent
recurring
reduce d
reducing
reduction
redundancy -ies
redundant
refer red
referral
referring
refine d
refinery -ies
refining
reform ed
refract ion
refractive
refrain ed
refrigerator
refund
refusal
refuse d
refute
refuting
regain ed

regard ed
regardless
regatta
rehearsal
rehearse d
rejoice d
rejoicing
rejoin ed
relate d
relating
relation
relationship
relax es
relaxed
release d
releasing
reliability
reliable
reliance
relief
relieve d
relieving
religion
religious
relinquish es
relinquished
reluctance
reluctant ly
rely -ies
relied
remain ed
remainder
remaining
remark ed
remarkable
remind ed
reminder
remote
removable /
removeable
removal
remove d
removing
renew ed
renewal
renown ed
repair ed
repay
[repaid]
repeal ed
repeat ed
repeating
replace d
replacement
replacing

reply -ies
replied
report ed
reporter
repose d
reposing
reprieve d
reprisal
reproach es
reproached
republic an
repudiate
repudiating
repulsive
repute
require d
requirement
requiring
research es
researched
researcher
reserve d
reserving
resign ed
resist ance
resistor
resolve d
resolving
resort
resource d
resourceful
resources
resourcing
respire d
respond
response
responsibility -ies
responsible
responsive
restore d
restoring
restrain ed
restraint
restrict ion
restrictive
result ed
resultant
resulting
resume d
resuscitate
resuscitation
retain ed
retard ed
retire d
retirement

retiring
retort
retreat
retrieval
retrieve d
retrieving
return ed
returnable
returning
reveal ed

reverberate
reverberating
reversal
reverse d
reversible
reversing
review ed
revise d
revising
revision

revival
revive d
reviving
revolt
revolve d
revolver
revolving
revue
revulsion
reward

In these words you can hear the vowel sound e as in elephant

*

*cell unit
Celt
*cent money / hundred
*cents money

chef

said
says

***scent** perfume / smell
***scents** more than one
scent

sect
***sects** religious groups
self
***sell** exchange for money
[sold]
send
[sent]
***sense** understandable pattern
sensed
***sent** made to go
set
[set]
***sex**es male / female
sexed

shed
[shed]
shelf [shelves]
shelled
shelved
shredded

sketches
sketched

sledged
slept

smelled
[smelt]

speck
sped
spelled
[spelt]
spend
[spent]
spread
[spread]
☛

* *

*cellar underground storage room
Celtic
cement
*censer pan for burning incense
*censor judge of what may not be published
*census es official count
centaur
central ly
centre d
centring
*cession giving up ownership

sceptic
sceptred
scheduled

second
section
sector
segment
seldom
select
selfish
***seller** person who sells
semblance
senate
sending
señor
***senses** means of gaining information
sensing
***sensor** detector
sensually
sentenced
sentry-ies
sepal
separate
septic
***session** meeting / period
setback
setted
settee
setter
setting
settled
settler
settling
set-up
seventh
severed
several
☛

* * *

celebrate
celery
celestial
cellophane
cellular
celluloid
cellulose
Celsius
cemetery -ies
censorship
centigrade
centipede
centrally
century -ies
cerebral
cerebrum

sceptically
scheduling

secateurs
secession
secondary -ies
second-hand
secondly
secretary -ies
secular
sedative
sediment
segregate
selected
selecting
selection
selective
selector
sellotape
semibreve
seminar
senator
señora
sensation
sensible
sensitive
sensory
sensually
sensuous
sentencing
sentiment
sentinel
separate
September
sepulchre
sequentially
serenade
sesame
settlement
☛

* * * * * *

celebrated
celebrating
celebration
celebrity -ies
celestial
centenary -ies
centimetre
centrifugal ly
centurion
cerebellum
ceremonial ly
ceremony -ies

scepticism

secondary -ies
secretarial
secretary -ies
sedimentary
segmentation
segregating
segregation
selectively
self-reliant
self-sufficient
semicircle
semicircular
semicolon
semiconductor
semi-detached
semi-final
semiquaver
semolina
señorita
sensationally
sensibility -ies
sensitivity -ies
sentimentally
separated
separately
separating
separation
sequentially
serenading
serenity
seventieth
severity -ies
sexuality -ies
sexually

sincerity
☛

for Scots: e -r is on page 252

In these words you can hear the vowel sound e as in elephant

S

*

squelch es
squelched

stealth
stem med
stench es
***step** pace / stage
***steppe** dry, treeless plain
stepped
stet
strength
stress es
stressed
stretch es
stretched

sweat
swell
[swollen]
swept

Here the first letter 'e' has a short 'i' sound.

scenario s
seclude d
secrete
secreting
secretion
secure d
securing
security -ies
seduce d
seducing
seduction
seductive
semantic ally
semantics
sequoia
severe ly
specific ally

* *

sexist
sextet
sexual ly
sexy -ier, -iest

shedding
shellfish
shelter ed
shelving
shepherd
sheriff
sherry -ies
shredded
shredder
shredding

sketchy -ier, -iest

sledging
slender

smelter

special ly
speckle d
spectre
spectrum [spectra]
speller
spelling
spending
splendid
splendour
spreading
spreadsheet

steady -ies
steadied
stealthy -ier, -iest
stellar
stemming
stencil led
stepping
sterile
steroid
strengthen ed
stretcher

subject
subtend
success es
suggest
suppress es
suppressed
suspect
suspend
suspense

sweater

* * *

seventeen th
seventy -ies
several
severance
sexism
sexual ly

skeleton

spaghetti
specialise d
ze
specialist
specially
specify -ies
specified
specimen
spectacle
spectacles
spectator
speculate
spherical ly

steadily
steadiness
stealthier
stealthiest
stencilling
stepbrother
stepdaughter
stepfather
stepmother
stepsister
stereo s
sterilise d
ze
stethoscope
strenuous

subjected
subjection
subjective
successful ly
succession
successive
successor
suggested
suggesting
suggestion
suggestive
suppression
surrender ed
suspected
suspension

symmetric al
synthetic ally
systemic ally

* * * * * * *

specialisation
zation
specialising
zing
speciality -ies
specification
spectacular ly
speculating
speculation
speculative
spherically

stegosaurus es / -i
stereophonic ally
stereoscopic ally
stereotype
stereotypical ly
sterilising
zing

successfully
suggestible
susceptibility -ies
susceptible

symmetrical ly
synthetically
systemically

for Scots: e -r is on page 252

T

*

tell
[told]
tempt
tenth
tend
***tense** form of verb / stretched tight
tensed
tent
tenth
***tents** more than one tent
test
text

Thames
theft
them
then
thence
threaded
threat

tread
[trod]
[trodden]
trekked
trenches
trend

twelfth
twelve

* *

technique
techno
teddy-ies
telling
telly-ies
tempered
tempest
template
temple
tempos
tenant
tendered
tendon
tendril
***tenner** ten pound note
tennis
tenoned
***tenor** male voice
tensing
tension
tepid
terraced
terrain
terror
tested
testing
testis [testes]
tethered
textbook
textile
textual
textured

themselves
threadbare
threaded
threatened
threshold

treadle
treasured
trebled
trebling
trekking
trellised
trembled
trembling
tremor
trendy-ier, -iest
trestle

twenty-ies

* * *

technically
technician
tectonic
telecom
telegram
telegraphed
telephoned
telescoped
televised
temperament
temperate
temperature
temporary
temptation
tenancy-ies
tendency-ies
tenderness
tenement
tentacle
tentative
tenuous
terracing
terrapin
terrible
terribly
terrier
terrify-ies
terrified
territory-ies
terrorised
ze
terrorist
tessellate
testament
testicle
testify-ies
testified
tetanus
textually

therapist
therapy-ies

together
torrentially

treacherous
treachery-ies
treasurer
treasury-ies
tremendous

twentieth

* * * * ***

pterodactyl

technically
technologically
technology-ies
telecommunications
telegraphy
telepathically
telepathy
telephoning
telephonist
telephoto
telescoping
televising
television
temperamentally
temperature
temporarily
temporary
tentatively
terrarium
terrestrially
terrifying
territorially
territory-ies
terrorising
zing
terrorism
tessellating
tessellation
testimonial
testimony-ies
tetrahedron
textually

therapeutically

torrentially

trajectory-ies
tremendously

for Scots: e -r is on page 253

Here the first letter 'e' has a short 'i' sound.

terrific ally thematic ally thesaurus es / -i

In these words you can hear the vowel sound e as in elephant

U

*	* *	* * *	* * * *
	unless	**unhelpful**	**unspecified**

V

*	* *	* * *	* * * * * * *
Venn	**vector**	**vegetable**	**vasectomy** -ies
vent	**Velcro**	**venison**	
vest	**velvet**	**ventilate**	**vegeburger**
vet ted	**vending**	**ventricle**	**vegetable**
vex es	**vendor**	**venturing**	**vegetarian**
vexed	**vengeance**	**verify** -ies	**vegetarianism**
	venom	verified	**vegetation**
	venture d	**veteran**	**Venezuela**
	venue		**ventilating**
	very		**ventilation**
	vessel		**ventilator**
	vested		**ventriloquist**
	vestry -ies		**verification**
	veteran		**veterinary**
	vetted		
	vetting		

for Scots: e -r is on page 254

In these words the first 'e' is a neutral vowel.

velocity -ies   Venetian   veranda / verandah

W

*

*rest repose / ones left over
*retch es try to vomit
retched
*rex / Rex king

wealth
web bed
wed ded
[wed]
wedge d
weft
***weld** join metal by heat
well
***welled** gushed
Welsh
wench es
went
wept
west
***wet** ted, ter, test make wet / not dry
[wet]

whelk
whelp ed
when
whence
***whet** ted sharpen

wreck ed
***wrecks** does smash / more than one wreck
wren
wrench es
wrenched
***wrest** seize
***wretch** es unhappy creature

* *

waistcoat

wealthy -ier, -iest
weapon
***weather** conditions outside / survive bad weather
weathered
webbing
webcam
webcast
webpage
website
wedded
wedding
wedging
Wednesday
welcome d
welfare
well-known
Welshman [Welshmen]
western
westward
***wether** neutered ram
wetsuit
***wetted** made wet
wetter
wettest
***wetting** making wet

***whether** if
***whetted** sharpened
***whetting** sharpening

wreckage
wrestle d
wrestler
wrestling
wretched

* * *

weathercock
weathering
weatherman
[weathermen]
weathervane
webmaster
welcoming
wellbeing
wellington
westerly
West Indies

whenever

* * * *

weatherwoman
[weatherwomen]

for Scots: e -r is on page 255

X

*

* *

X-ray

* * *

* * * * *

xenophobia
xenophobic

In these words you can hear the vowel sound e as in elephant

Y

*	* *	* * *	* * * *
yeah	**yelling**	**yesterday**	**yellowhammer**
yell ed	**yellow**		
yelp ed	**Yemen**		
yen			
yep	**yourself**		
yes	**yourselves**		
yet			

for Scots: e -r is on page 255

Z

*	* *	* * *	* * * * *
Zen	**zealot**		xenophobia
zest	**zealous**		xenophobic
	zebra		
	zenith		
	zephyr		

*

**

abyss es

acquit ted

admit ted
adrift

affix es
affixed
afflict

amid
amidst
amiss

assist

***

abysmal ly

acidic
acquittal
acquitted
acquitting
acrylic

addicted
addiction
addictive
addition
admission
admittance
admitted
admitting

affliction

ambition
ambitious

arisen

***assistance** help
assistant
***assistants** helpers

attribute

**** *

ability -ies
abysmally

acidity

additional ly
administer ed
administrate
administrating
administration
administrator

affiliate
affiliating
affiliation

agility

alliteration
alliterative

anticipate
anticipating
anticipation

applicable

arithmetic

assimilate
assimilating
assimilation
astigmatism

attributed
attributing

auxiliary -ies

for Scots: i -r is on page 242

*

***been** past form of 'be'

bib
bid
[bade]
[bid]
[bidden]
big
bill
***billed** did bill
***bin** container
binge
bit
bitch es
bitched

blink ed
bliss
blitz ed

brick ed
bridge d
brim med
bring
[brought]
brink
brisk

***build** construct
[built]

* *

became
because
become
[became]
[become]
befall
[befell]
[befallen]
before
befriend
begin
[began]
[begun]
behalf
behave d
behead
beheld
behind
behold
[beheld]
belief
believe d
belong ed
beloved
below
bemuse d
beneath
benign
bereave d
[bereft]
beseech es
beseeched
[besought]
beset
[beset]
beside
besides
besiege d
besought
bestow ed
betray ed
between
betwixt
beware
bewitch es
bewitched
beyond

* * *

becoming
befallen
beforehand
beginner
beginning
behaving
behaviour
believing
belonging
belongings
beloved
bemusing
bereavement
besetting
besieging
besotted
bewilder ed

biblical
bickering
bikini
bilberry -ies
bishopric
bitterly
bitterness

blissfully

bricklayer
bricklaying
brigadier
brilliant ly

busier
busiest
busily
businessman
[businessmen]

* * * * *

beatitude
behavioural
belatedly
belligerent
benevolent
bewilderment

bibliography -ies
binocular
binoculars

Bolivia

brilliantly

businesswoman
[businesswomen]

for Scots: i -r is on page 243

* *

bicker ed
bidden
bidder
bidding
bigger
biggest
bilious
billiards
billion
billow ed
binging
bingo
biscuit
bishop
***bitten** past form of 'bite'
bitter
***bittern** bird
bizarre

blinkered
blinkers
blissful ly
blister ed
blizzard

Brazil
breeches
brickwork
bridging
brigade
brilliance
brilliant
brimming
bringing
briskly
bristle d
bristling
***Britain** country
British
***Briton** British person
brittle

builder
building
business
busy -ies
busied
busy -ier, -iest

for Scots: i -r is on page 243

In these words you can hear the vowel sound i as in pig

*

chick
chid
chill ed
chimp
chin
chink
chintz
chip ped

cinch es

click ed
cliff
cling
[clung]
clink ed
clip ped

crib bed
cringe d
crisp
crypt

cyst

kick ed
kid ded
kids
kill ed
kiln
kilt
kin
king
kink ed
kiss ed
kit ted
kith

* *

cement

chicken ed
chicklit
chickpea
chidden
chiffchaff
chiffon
chilblain
children
*Chile country
*chilli hot spice
*chilly -ier, -iest cold
chimney
chipboard
chipmunk
chipping
chisel led
christen ed
christening
Christian
Christmas

cigar
cinder
cirrus
cistern
citrus
city -ies
civic
civil ly

clinic ally
clipper
clipping

commit ted
conflict
conscript
consist
convict
convince d

create
cremate
cribbing
cricket
crimson
crinkle d
crinkly
cripple d
crippling
crisscross ed
critic ally
critique
crystal

* * *

capricious

celestial
ceramic

charisma
chickenpox
chicory
chimpanzee
chiselling
chivalrous
chivalry
christening
chrysalis

cigarette
*cilia more than one
cilium
ciliary
cilium [cilia]
cinema
cinnamon
citizen
civilian
civilise d
ze
civilly

clickable
clinical ly
clinician
clitoris

cognition
collision
commission ed
commitment
committed
committee
committing
condition ed
conscription
consider ed
consistent
consisting
constriction
continual ly
continue d
contribute
conviction
convincing

* * * * *

calligraphy
capillary -ies
captivity

celebrity -ies
celestial
certificate

Christianity
chrysanthemum

ciliary
citizenship
civilian
civilisation
zation
civilising
zing

clinically

commissioner
conditional ly
conditioner
configuration
coniferous
considerable
considerate
consideration
consistency -ies
consistently
conspicuous
conspiracy -ies
conspirator
constituency -ies
constituent
contingency -ies
continual ly
continuance
continuation
continuing
continuous ly
continuum
contributed
contributing

*for Qu . . .
see page 83*

*for Scots: i -r
is on page 244*

In these words you can hear the vowel sound i as in pig

* *

cuisine

***cygnet** young swan
***cymbals** discs to clash
cystic

kebab

kick-off
kidded
kidding
kidnap ped
kidney
killer
killing
kindle d
kindling
kingdom
king-size
kinky -ier, -iest
kinship
kipper
kissing
kitchen
kitted
kitten
kitting

for Qu . . .
see page 83

*signet seal / ring

*symbols signs

* * *

created
creating
creation
creative
creator
cremating
cremation
crescendo s
cricketer
criminal ly
crinoline
critical ly
criticise d
ze
crystalline
crystallise d
ze

cylinder
cynical ly
Cypriot
cystitis

kidnapper
kidnapping
kilogram
kimono s
kinetic ally
kingfisher

*sillier more silly

* * * * *

creativity
criminally
criminology
critically
criticising
zing
criticism
crystallisation
zation
crystallising
zing

curricular
curriculum [curricula]

cylindrical
cynically
cynicism

kilometre
kindergarten
kinetically

for Scots: i -r
is on page 244

In these words you can hear the vowel sound i as in pig

*

did
dig ged
[dug]
dim med
din
ding
dip ped
disc / disk
dish es
dished
ditch es
ditched

drift
drill ed
drink
[drank]
[drunk]
drip ped

* *

debate
decamp ed
decay ed
decease d
deceit
deceive d
decide
declare d
decline d
decrease d
decree d
decry -ies
decried
deduce d
deduct
defeat
defect
defence
defend
define d
deflect
deform ed
defy -ies
defied
degree
delay ed
delete
delight
demand
demean ed
demise
demob bed
denote
denounce d
deny -ies
denied
depart
depend
depict
deploy ed
deport
depress es
depressed
deprive d
derail ed
derive d
descend
*__descent__ way down
describe d
*__desert__ leave
deserve d
design ed
desire d
despair ed
*__despatch__ es send off
despatched

* * *

deceitful ly
deceiving
December
deception
deceptive
deciding
decipher ed
decision
decisive
declaring
declining
decreasing
deducing
deduction
deductive
defeated
defective
defector
defendant
defender
defensive
defiance
defiant
deficient
defining
deflection
deleting
deletion
deliberate
delicious
delighted
delightful ly
delinquent
deliver ed
delusion
demanded
demeanour
demolish es
demolished
denial
denoting
denouncing
department
departure
*__dependant__ person who depends
*__dependants__ people who depend
depended
*__dependence__ reliance
*__dependent__ relying / hanging
depending
deployment

* * * * * *

decapitate
decapitating
deceitfully
deciduous
deficiency -ies
deliberate
deliberately
deliberating
delightfully
delinquency
delirious
deliverance
delivery -ies
democracy -ies
demonstrative
demoralise d
ze
demoralising
zing
denomination
denominator
denunciation
dependable
dependency -ies
deposited
depositing
depreciate
depreciating
depreciation
derivative
desirable
despicable
deteriorate
deteriorating
deterioration
determination
determining
developer
developing
development
dictatorial ly
dictatorship
dictionary -ies
differential
differentiate
differentiating
differentiation
differently
difficulty -ies
digestible
digitally

for Scots: i -r is on page 245

* *

despise d
despite
*__dessert__ sweet dish
destroy ed
detach es
detached
detain ed
detect
deter red
detest
detract
*__device__ gadget / plan
*__devise__ d invent / work out
devoid
devote
devour ed

dickey / dicky
dictate
diction
didn't
differ ed
difference
different
diffuse d
digest
digger
digging
digit
dimmer
dimming
dimple d
*__dinghy__ -ies small boat
*__dingy__ -ier, -iest dull
dinner
diphthong
dipper
dipping
dipstick
direct
disarm ed
discard
discern ed
discharge d
disclose d
disco s
discount
discourse
*__discreet__ careful not to embarrass
*__discrete__ separate
*__discus__ es heavy disc to throw in games
*__discuss__ es debate
*__discussed__ debated

* * *

deposit ed
depression
depressive
depriving
deriving
descendant
descended
describing
description
descriptive
deserted
deserving
designer
desiring
despising
destroyer
destruction
destructive
detachment
detection
detective
detector
detention
detergent
determine d
*__deterrence__ prevention by causing fear
deterrent
*__deterrents__ more than one deterrent
deterring
develop ed
devoted
devotion

dictating
dictation
dictator
dictionary -ies
difference
different
differently
difficult
diffusing
diffusion
digestion
digital ly
dignify -ies
dignified
dignity -ies
dilemma
dimension
diminish es
diminished
diploma
diplomat

* * * * * *

dilapidated
diphtheria
diplodocus
diplomacy
diplomatic ally
directory -ies
disability -ies
disablement
disadvantage d
disagreeable
disagreement
disappearance
disappointment
disapproval
disapproving
disarmament
disassemble d
disciplinarian
disciplinary
discouraging
discovery -ies
discredited
discrepancy -ies
discriminate
discriminating
discrimination
disgracefully
disinfectant
disintegrate
disintegrating
disloyally
disloyalty
disobedience
disobedient
disorganise d
ze
disposition
disproportionate ly
disqualify -ies
disqualified
dissatisfaction
dissatisfy -ies
dissatisfied
disseminate
dissimilar
dissolution
distillation
distinguishable
distractible
distributing
distribution
distributive
distributor

for Scots: i -r is on page 245

* *

disdain ed
disease d
disgrace d
disguise d
***disgust** strong dislike
dishcloth
dishes
dislike d
dislodge d
disloyal ly
dismal ly
dismay ed
dismiss ed
dismount
disown ed
***dispatch** es despatch / message
dispatched
dispel led
dispense d
disperse d
displace d
display ed
displease d
dispose d
disprove d
[disproven]
dispute
disrupt
dissect
***dissent** disagreement
dissolve d
***distal** *farthest from point of attachment*
distance d
distant
***distil** led make pure
distinct
distort
distract
distraught
distress es
distressed
district
distrust
disturb ed
disused
dither ed
ditto
divan
diverge d
diverse
divert
divide
divine d
divorce d
dizzy -ier, -iest
☛

* * *

directed
direction
directive
directly
director
disable d
disabling
disagree d
disappear ed
disappoint
disapprove d
disaster
disastrous
disbelief
discharging
disciple
discipline d
disclosure
discomfort
discontent
discordant
discothèque
discourage d
discover ed
discredit ed
discretion
discussing
discussion
disgraceful ly
disgracing
disgruntle d
disgruntling
disgusting
dishearten ed
dishevelled
dishonest
dishwasher
disinfect
disliking
dislodging
disloyally
disloyalty
dismally
dismantle d
dismantling
dismissal
dismissing
disobey ed
disorder ed
dispelling
dispenser
dispensing
dispersing
displacement
displacing
displeasing
displeasure
☛

* * * * * *

diversification
diversify -ies
diversified
diversity
divinity -ies
divisibility
divisible
divisional

dysentery
dyslexia

for Scots: i -r is on page 245

In these words you can hear the vowel sound i as in pig

* *

dribble d
dribbling
drifted
driftwood
drinker
drinking
dripping
driven
drizzle d
drizzling

dwindle d
dwindling

* * *

disposal
disposing
disproven
disproving
disputing
disregard
disruption
disruptive
dissension
dissenter
***dissidence** disagreeing with those in power
dissident
***dissidents** people who are against the system
dissolving
distancing
distillate
distilling
distinction
distinctive
distinguish es
distinguished
distortion
distraction
distractor
distressing
distribute
disturbance
disturbing
divided
dividend
dividers
dividing
division
divisor
divorcee
divorcing

dynasty -ies
dysentery
dyslexic / dyslectic
dystrophy -ies

for Scots: i -r is on page 245

In these words you can hear the vowel sound i as in pig

E

SHORT VOWEL i

*

* *

*accept take something offered

*affect alter

éclair
eclipse d

***effect** result / bring about

eject

elapse d
elect
élite
ellipse
elope d
elude

embark ed
embed ded
embrace d
embroil ed
emerge d
emit ted
employ ed
empower ed

enact
encamp ed
encase d
enchant
enclose d
encroach es
encroached
endear ed
endorse d
endow ed
endure d
enfold
enforce d
engage d
England
English
engrave d
engross es
engrossed
engulf ed
enhance d
enjoy ed
enlarge d
enlist
enough
enquire / inquire d

* * *

eccentric ally
eclipsing

edition

effective
efficient

Egyptian

ejector

elaborate
elastic ally
election
electors
electric ally
electrode
electron
eleven th
***elicit** ed draw out
élitist
eloping
eluding
***elusive** hard to find

embankment
embargo es
embargoed
embarrass es
embarrassed
embedded
embedding
embellish es
embellished
embezzle d
embody -ies
embodied
embracing
embroider ed
emergence
emerging
emission
emitted
emitting
emotion
emotive
emphatic ally
employee
employer
employment
empower ed
emulsion ed

enable d
enabling
enamel led
enamour ed

* * * * ****

eccentrically
ecclesiastical ly
ecology
economy -ies

effectively
effectiveness
efficiency
efficiently

elaborate
elaboration
elastically
elasticity
electoral ly
electorate
electrical ly
electrician
electricity
electrocute
electrolyse d
ze
electrolysis
electrolyte
electrolytic ally
electromagnetic ally
electronic ally
elicited
eliciting
eliminate
eliminating
elimination
élitism
Elizabethan
elliptical ly
elucidate

emancipate d
emancipating
emancipation
embarrassing
embarrassment
embroidery
emergency -ies
emotional ly
emphatically
empirical ly

for H . . .
see page 71

for I . . .
see page 72

In these words you can hear the vowel sound i as in pig

* *

enrage d
enrich es
enriched
enrol led
enslave d
*__ensure__ d make certain
entail ed
entire
entrance d
entrench es
entrenched
entrust / intrust

equate
equip ped

erase d
erect
erode
erupt

escape d
escort
estate
esteem ed
estrange d

evade
event
evict
evoke d
evolve d

exact
exalt
exam
exceed
excel led
*__except__ not including
excess es
exchange d
excite
exclaim ed
exclude
excrete
excuse d
exempt
exert
exhaust
exhort
exist

* * *

encasing
enchanting
encircle d
encircling
enclosing
enclosure
encounter ed
encourage d
endanger ed
endearment
endeavour ed
endorsing
endurance
enduring
enforcement
enforcing
engagement
engaging
Englishman
[Englishmen]
engraving
enhancing
enigma
enjoying
enjoyment
enlarging
enlighten ed
enormous
enquiring / inquiring
enquiry / inquiry -ies
enraging
enrolling
enrolment
enslaving
*__ensuring__ making certain
entangle d
entangling
entirely
entitle d
entrancing
envelop ed
envisage d

equation
equator
equipment
equipping

eraser
erasing
erection
eroding
erosion
erotic ally
erratic ally
erupted
eruption

* * * * * * *

enamelling
encouragement
encyclopedia
Englishwoman
[Englishwomen]
enormously
enthusiasm
enthusiast
enthusiastic ally
entitlement
enumerate
enumerating
enveloping
environment
environmental ly
environmentalism
environmentalist
envisaging

epitome

equality
equivalence
equivalent

erotically
erratically
erroneous ly

especially
essentially
establishment

etcetera
eternally

evacuate
evacuation
evacuee
evaluate
evaluation
evangelism
evangelist
evaporate
evaporation
eventually

exacerbate
exaggerate
exaggeration
examination

for H . . .
see page 71

for I . . .
see page 72

* *

expand
expanse
expect
expel led
expense
explain ed
explode
exploit
explore d
expose d
express es
expressed
extend
extent
extinct
extract
extreme
exult

*inshore near the shore
*insure d protect against loss

* * *

escaping
escarpment
essential ly
establish es
established

etcetera
eternal ly

evading
evasion
eventual ly
evoking
evolving

exactly
examine d
example
excellent
excelling
exception
excessive
exchanging
exchequer
excited
excitement
exciting
excluding
exclusion
exclusive
excreting
excretion
excursion
excusing
exemption
exertion
exhausted
exhaustion
exhibit ed
existed
existence
exotic ally
expanded
expanding
expansion
expansive
expectant
expected
expelling
expensive
explaining
explicit
exploding
explorer
exploring
explosion
explosive

* * * * * * *

exceedingly
exceptional ly
excitedly
exclamation
exclusively
excruciating
executive
exemplary
exhibited
exhibiting
exhilarating
exorbitant
exotically
expandable
expectantly
expediency
expedient
expenditure
experience d
experiencing
experiment
experimental ly
explanatory
exploratory
exterior
exterminate
externally
extinguisher
extraordinarily
extraordinary
extraneous
extrapolate
extravagance
extravagant
extravaganza
exuberance
exuberant

for H . . .
see page 71

for I . . .
see page 72

In these words you can hear the vowel sound i as in pig

E

* * *

exponent
exposing
exposure
expressing
expression
expressive
expulsion
exquisite
extended
extending
extension
extensive
external ly
extinction
extinguish es
extinguished
extraction
extractor
extremely
extremist
extrusion

*illicit illegal
*illusive deceptive

*insuring protecting against loss

for H . . . see page 71

for I . . . see page 72

F

*

fib bed
fifth
fig
fill ed
film ed
filth
***fin** what fish use to swim and balance
finch es
***Finn** citizen of Finland
finned
fiord / fjord
***fish** es creature(s) with tail and fins
fished
fist
fit ted
fix es
fixed
fizz es
fizzed

for th . . . see page 90

* *

fibbing
fiction
fiddle d
fiddler
fiddling
fiddly
fidget ed
fifteen th
fifty -ies
figure d
filler
fillet
filling
filly -ies
***filter** ed pass through
filthy -ier, -iest
finale
finance d
finger ed
***finish** es end
finished
Finland
***Finnish** language spoken by Finns / of or from Finland

* * *

familiar

ferocious

***fiancé** man engaged to be married
***fiancée** woman engaged to be married
fiasco s
fictional
fictitious
fidgeted
fidgeting
fidgety
fiesta
fiftieth
filament
filthiest
filtration

* * * * * *

facilitate
facilitating
facility -ies
familiarity
fastidious

ferocity
fertility

fidelity
figurative
financially
financier

frenetically

phenomena
phenomenal ly
phenomenon
philatelist

for Scots: i -r is on page 246

F

SHORT VOWEL i

*

flick ed
flinch es
fling
[flung]
flint
flip ped
flit ted

fridge
frill ed
fringe d
frisk ed

*phish ed attempt
internet fraud

for th . . .
see page 90

* *

fiord / fjord
fiscal
***fisher** man who fishes
fishes
***fishing** trying to catch
fish
fission
***fissure** d crack
fitness
fitted
fitting
fixture
fizzle d
fizzy -ier, -iest

flicker ed
flimsy -ies
flipper
flipping
flitted
flitting

forbid
[forbade / forbad]
[forbidden]
forgive
[forgave]
[forgiven]

friction
frigate
frigid
Frisbee
fritter ed
frizzy -ier, -iest

fulfil led

*philtre love-potion
*phishing attempting
internet fraud
physics
physique

* * *

finale
financial ly
fingernail
fingerprint
fingertip
finicky -ier, -iest
finishing
fisherman [fishermen]
fishery -ies
fixation

flamingo es / s

forbidden
forbidding
forgiven
forgiveness
forgiving

frenetic ally
frivolous
fruition

fulfilling
fulfilment

physically
physician
physicist

* * * * * * *

philosopher
philosophical ly
philosophy -ies
physically
physiological ly
physiology
physiotherapist
physiotherapy

for Scots: i -r
is on page 246

In these words you can hear the vowel sound i as in pig

G

*

gift
gig
***gild** paint with gold
[gilt]
gills
***gilt** gilded
gin
gist
give
[gave]
[given]

glib
glimpse d
glint

grid
***grill** ed cook by direct heat / bars for cooking / food so cooked
***grille** protecting set of bars in door or window
grim
grin ned
grip ped
grit ted

***guild** association
***guilt** responsibility for doing wrong

gym

jib bed
jig ged
jilt
*jinks lively behaviour
*jinx es cause bad luck
jinxed

* *

giggle d
giggling
gilded
***gilder** person who gilds
gimlet
gimmick
ginger ed
gingham
gipsy / gypsy -ies
giraffe
given
giver
giving

glimmer ed
glimpsing
glisten ed
glitter ed

grenade
griddle
gridlock ed
grimace d
grimly
grinning
gripping
***grisly** -ier, iest horrible
gristle
gritting
gritty -ier, iest
grizzle d
grizzling
***grizzly** -ier, iest grey / bear

***guilder** old Dutch coin
guilty -ier, -iest
***guinea** twenty one old shillings
***Guinea** West African country
guitar

gymnast
gymslip
gypsy / gipsy -ies

jibbing
jiffy
jigging
jiggle d
jigsaw
jihad
jingle d
jingling

* * *

genetic ally

gibberish
Gibraltar
gigabyte
gingerbread
gingerly

glycerine

***gorilla** ape

grimacing

***guerrilla / guerilla** agent of political violence
guillemot
guillotine d
guinea-pig
guitarist

gymkhana
gymnastics
gymnosperm

* * * * * *

gelatinous
genetically
geographic al ly
geography -ies
geological ly
geology
geometric al ly
geometry -ies
geranium

gregarious

guillotining

gymnasium

for Scots: i -r is on page 246

In these words you can hear the vowel sound i as in pig

H

*

hid
hill
hilt
***him** that male individual
hinge d
hint
hip
his
hiss ed
hit
[hit]
hitch es
hitched

***hymn** song with verses sung in church

* *

hiccup ped
hidden
hijab
hillside
hilltop
himself
hinder ed
hindrance
Hindu
hip-hop
hippy -ies
hissing
hither
hitting

hymnal

* * *

habitual ly

heroic ally

hiccupping
hickory
hideous
historic ally
history -ies
hitherto

holistic ally
horrific ally

hypnosis
hypnotic ally
hypnotise d
ze
hypocrite
hysterics

* * * * * *

habitually

hereditary
heredity
heroically

higgledy-piggledy
hilarious
Himalayas
Hinduism
hippopotamus es / -i
historian
historical ly

holistically
horrifically
hostility -ies

hypnotically
hypnotising
zing
hypnotism
hypocrisy
hypocritical ly
hysteria
hysterical ly

*

if

ill

imp

***in** not outside
inch es
inched
ink
***inn** small hotel

is

it
itch es
itched
***its** belonging to it
***it's** it is

for E . . .
see page 65

for H . . .
see page 71

* *

*ensure d make certain

igloo
ignite
ignore d

illness es

image d
immense
immerse d
immune
impact
impair ed
impart
impasse
impede d
impel led
impinge d
implore d
imply -ies
implied
import
impose d
impress es
impressed
imprint
improve d
impulse
impure

inbox es
incense d
incest
***incite** encourage strong feeling or action
incline d
include
income
increase d
incur red
indeed
indent
in-depth
index es [indices]
indexed
indict
indie
indoor
indoors
induce d
indulge d
inept
inert

* * *

*allusion reference

*elicit ed draw out
*elusive hard to find
*ensuring making certain

idiom
idiot

igneous
ignition
ignorance
ignorant
ignoring

***ileum** part of intestine
***ilium** [ilia] part of hip-bone
illegal ly
***illicit** illegal
***illusion** false belief or appearance
***illusive** deceptive
illustrate

imagery
imagine d
imaging
imbalance
imitate
immature
immediate
immensely
immersing
immersion
immigrant
immigrate
imminent
immobile
immoral
immortal ly
immunise d
ze
impartial ly
impasto
impatience
impatient
impeachment
impeding
impeller
impelling
imperfect
impetus es
implement
implicate
implicit
imploring

* * * * * * *

idiomatic ally
idiotic ally

iguanodon

illegally
illegible
illiterate
illogical ly
illuminate
illumination
illustrating
illustration
illustrative
illustrator
illustrious

imaginary
imagination
imaginative
imagining
imitating
imitation
immaculate
immeasurable
immediate ly
immensity
immigration
immortality
immortally
immovable
immunisation
zation
immunising
zing
immunity
impartially
impassable
impatiently
impeccable
impediment
impenetrable
imperative
imperceptible
imperial ly
imperialism
impermeable
impersonal
impersonate
impersonation
impertinent
impervious
impetuous

for Scots: i -r
is on page 247

I

* *

infant
infect
infer red
infirm
inflame d
inflate
inflict
influx es
inform ed
infringe d
ingot
inhale d
inject
injure d
inland
in-law
inlet
inmate
innate
inner
innings
input
inquest
inquire / enquire d
insane
inscribe d
insect
insert
*inshore near the shore
inside
*insight understanding
insist
inspect
inspire d
instal led / install ed
*instance example
instant
*instants moments
instead
instinct
instruct
insult
*insure d protect against loss
intact
intake
intend
*intense very strong
intent
*intents purposes
inter red
interest
into
intrigue d
intrude
intrust / entrust

* * *

impolite
importance
important
imposing
impotence
impotent
impregnate
impression
impressive
imprison ed
impromptu s
improper
improvement
improving
improvise d
impudence
impudent
impulsive

incarnate
incensing
incentive
incessant
*incidence rate of happening
incident
*incidents events
incision
incisor
inciting
inclining
included
including
inclusion
inclusive
incoming
incomplete
incorrect
increasing
incurring
indebted
indecent
indented
indenture d
India
Indian
indicate
indictment
indifferent
indignant
indigo
indirect
indiscreet
indistinct

* * * * * *

implacable
implementation
implication
impossibility
impossible
impoverish ed
impractical
impregnable
impregnating
impressionable
impressionism
impressionist
imprisonment
improvisation
improvising
impunity
impurity -ies

inability
inaccessible
inaccuracy -ies
inaccurate
inadequate ly
inadvertent ly
inappropriate
inattentive
inaudible
inaugural
inauguration
incapable
incidental ly
inclination
incognito
incompatible
incomprehensible
inconceivable
incongruity -ies
incongruous
inconsistent
inconvenience
inconvenient
incorporate d
incorporating
increasingly
incredible
incredibly
incubation
incubator
incurable
indecisive
indefensible
indefinite ly
independence
independent
indestructible
indeterminate

for E . . . see page 65

for H . . . see page 71

for Scots: i -r is on page 247

**

invade
invent
inverse
invert
invest
invite
invoice d
invoke d
involve d
inward
inwards

Iran
Iraq

Islam
isn't
Israel
issue d
isthmus

itself

for E . . .
see page 65

for H . . .
see page 71

***

inducing
induction
inductive
indulgence
indulgent
indulging
industry -ies
inertia
infamous
infancy
infantile
infantry
infection
infectious
inference
inferring
infinite
inflaming
inflating
inflation
inflection
influence d
informal ly
informant
informer
infra-red
infrequent
infringement
ingenious
inhabit ed
inhaler
inhaling
inherent
inherit ed
inhibit
inhuman
initial led
injection
injuring
injury -ies
injustice
innermost
innkeeper
***innocence** freedom from guilt
innocent
***innocents** people who have done no wrong
innovate
inquiring / enquiring
inquiry / enquiry -ies
inscribing
inscription

for Scots: i -r
is on page 247

**** ***

indicated
indicating
indication
indicator
indifferent
indigenous
indigestible
indigestion
indignation
indiscretion
indiscriminate ly
indispensable
individual ly
individualism
individuality
indivisible
Indonesia
industrial ly
industrialisation
zation
industrialise d
ze
industrialist
industrious
inedible
ineffective ly
ineffectual ly
inefficiency
inefficient ly
ineptitude
inequality -ies
inevitable
inevitably
inexpensive ly
inexperienced
infatuate d
infatuation
inferior
inferiority
infinitely
infinitive
infinity
infirmary -ies
inflammable
inflammation
inflammatory
inflationary
inflexible
influential ly
influenza
informally
information
informative
infrastructure
infuriate
infuriating

In these words you can hear the vowel sound i as in pig

I

* * *

insecure
insertion
insider
insipid
insisted
insistence
insofar
insolence
insolent
inspection
inspector
inspiring
installing
instalment /
installment
instantly
instinctive
institute
instruction
instructive
instructor
instrument
insulate
insulin
insulting
insurance
***insuring** protecting against loss
integer
integral
integrate
intensely
intensive
intention
interact
intercept
interchange
intercourse
interested
interesting
interface
interfere d
interim
interlock ed
interlude
internal ly
internet
interpret ed
interrupt
intersect
intersperse d
interval
intervene d
interview ed

for Scots: i -r
is on page 247

* * * * * *

ingenious
ingenuity
ingredient
inhabitant
inhabited
inhabiting
inheritance
inherited
inheriting
inhibition
inhospitable
iniquity
initialling
initially
initiate
initiating
initiative
injurious
innovation
innovative
innumerable
inoculate
inoculation
inorganic ally
inquisition
inquisitive
insanitary
insanity
inscrutable
insecticide
insensitive
insidious ly
insignificant
insoluble
insomnia
inspiration
installation
instantaneous
institution al
instrumental ly
insufficient ly
insulating
insulation
insulator
insuperable
integrating
integration
integrity
intellectual ly
intelligence
intelligent
intensify -ies
intensified
intensity -ies
intentional ly

for E . . .
see page 65

for H . . .
see page 71

***

intestine
intimate
intranet
intricate
intriguing
intrinsic
introduce d
introvert
intruder
intruding
intrusion
intrusive
invaded
invader
invading
invalid
invasion
invention
inventive
inventor
inventory -ies
inversely
inversion
inverted
investment
investor
invited
invoicing
invoking
involvement
involving
inwardly

Iraqi
irrigate
irritate

Islamic
Israel
Israeli
issuing

Italian
italic
Italy

**** **

interaction
interactive
interception
interchangeable
interested
interesting ly
interference
interfering
interior
intermediate
interminable
intermission
intermittent
internally
international ly
interpolate
interpolating
interpretation
interpreted
interpreter
interpreting
interrogate
interrogating
interrogation
interrogative
interrupted
interruption
intersection
interspersing
intervening
intervention
interwoven
intestinal ly
intimacy -ies
intimidate
intimidating
intolerable
intolerance
intonation
intoxicate
intoxicating
intoxication
intransitive
intravenous
introducing
introduction
introductory
introversion
intuition
intuitive
invaluable
invariably

for E . . .
see page 65

for H . . .
see page 71

for Scots: i -r
is on page 247

In these words you can hear the vowel sound i as in pig

I

SHORT VOWEL i

* * * * * * *

inventory -ies
invertebrate
investigate
investigating
investigation
investigator
invincible
invisible
invitation
involuntarily

Iranian
irrational ly
irregular
irregularity -ies
irrelevance
irrelevant
irreparable
irresistible
irrespective ly
irresponsible
irrigating
irrigation
irritability
irritable
irritating
irritation

italicise d
ze
italicising
zing
iteration
itinerant
itinerary

for E . . .
see page 65

for H . . .
see page 71

for Scots: i -r
is on page 247

J

*

gin
gist

gym

jib bed
jig ged
jilt
***jinks** lively behaviour
***jinx** es cause bad luck
jinxed

* *

ginger ed
gipsy / gypsy -ies
giraffe

gymnast
gymslip
gypsy / gipsy -ies

jibbing
jiffy
jigging
jiggle d
jigsaw
jihad
jingle d
jingling

* * *

genetic ally

gibberish
Gibraltar
gingerbread
gingerly

gymkhana
gymnastics
gymnosperm

* * * * * * *

gelatinous
genetically
geographic al ly
geography -ies
geological ly
geology
geometric al ly
geometry -ies
geranium

gymnasium

for dr . . .
see page 61

In these words you can hear the vowel sound i as in pig

K

*

kick ed
kid ded
kids
kill ed
kiln
kilt
kin
king
kink ed
kiss ed
kit ted
kith

***knit** ted loop together with needles [knit]

*nit egg of louse / nitwit

for C . . . see page 59

for Qu . . . see page 83

* *

kebab

kick-off
kidded
kidding
kidnap ped
kidney
killer
killing
kindle d
kindling
kingdom
king-size
kinky -ier, -iest
kinship
kipper
kissing
kitchen
kitted
kitten
kitting

knickers
knitted
knitting

* * *

kidnapper
kidnapping
kilobyte
kilogram
kimono s
kinetic
kingfisher

* * * * * *

kilometre
kinaesthetic ally
kindergarten

knickerbocker

for Scots: i -r is on page 248

In these words you can hear the vowel sound i as in pig

L

*

lick ed
lid
lift
***limb** part of body / branch
***limn** draw the outline
limp ed
link ed
***links** connections / golf course
lip
lisp ed
list
lit
live d

lynch es
lynched
***lynx** es animal

* *

liberal ly
Libya
lichen
***licker** creature that licks
licorice / liquorice
lifted
lifting
lift-off
lily -ies
limit ed
limpet
linen
linger ed
linguist
linkage
linking
linseed
lintel
lipid
lipstick
liquid
***liquor** alcoholic drink
listed
listen ed
listener
listening
listing
listless
litmus
litter ed
little
liver
livid
living
lizard

lyric ally
lyrics

* * *

legato
lethargic

liberal ly
liberate
liberty -ies
libretto [libretti]
licorice / liquorice
ligament
limited
limiting
lineage
linear
linguistic ally
linguistics
liniment
liquefy -ies
liquefied
liquidate
listener
listening
literal ly
literate
literature
lithium
lithosphere
liturgy -ies
liverish
livery -ies

lyrical ly

* * * * * *

legitimacy -ies
legitimate

liberalism
liberally
liberation
limitation
linguistically
linoleum
liquidating
liquidation
liquidity -ies
listeria
literacy
literally
literary
literature
Lithuania
litigation

lyrically

M

*

midge
midst
***mil** measuring unit
milk ed
***mill** building equipped for grinding or manufacturing / move in a confused mass
milled
***mince** cut into small pieces
minced
mink
mint
***mints** more than one mint
Miss
miss es
***missed** did miss
***mist** thin fog
mitt
mix es
mixed

myth

* *

miaow
mickey
midday
middle
midfield
midget
midnight
midpoint
midway
midwife
mildew ed
milkman [milkmen]
miller
millet
million
mimic ked
mineral
mingle d
mingling
minim
minnow
minstrel
minute
mirage
mirror ed
mischief
misdeal
[misdealt]
mishap
misjudge d
mislay
[mislaid]
mislead
[misled]
missile
missing
mission
misspell ed
[misspelt]
misspend
[misspent]
mistake
[mistook]
[mistaken]
mistress es
mistrust
misuse d
mitten
mixture

Monsieur [Messieurs]

Mr
Mrs

***mystic** deeply hidden / spiritual explorer
***mystique** air of secrecy

* * *

magician
malicious
malignant

meander ed
mechanic ally
medallion
melodic ally
melodious
memento es / s
meniscus es / -i

middle-class
midfielder
midsummer
militant
military
militia
milligram
milliner
millionaire
millipede
mimicking
mimicry
mineral
miniature
minibus es
minimal ly
minimise ed
ze
minimum
minister ed
ministry
Minorca
minuend
miracle
mischievous
miserable
misery -ies
misfortune
misgivings
misjudging
misleading
missionary -ies
mistaken
mistaking
mistletoe
misusing
mitigate

mnemonic

myriad
mystery -ies
mystical
mystify -ies
mystified
mythical

* * * * *

manipulate
manipulation

mechanical ly
medicinal ly
melodically
melodious
memorial
menagerie
meridian
methodical ly
meticulous
metropolis es

military
millennium [millennia]
millilitre
millimetre
millionairess es
mineralogy
minestrone
minimising
zing
ministerial
minority -ies
miraculous ly
misbehaviour
miscellaneous
miserable
misogynist
misogyny
missionary -ies
misunderstand
[misunderstood]
misunderstanding
mitigating

mobility

mysterious ly
mysticism
mythology -ies
myxomatosis

for Scots: i -r is on page 249

In these words you can hear the vowel sound i as in pig

N

*

*knit ted loop together with needles [knit]

nib
nil
nip ped
***nit** egg of louse / nitwit

nymph

* *

knickers
knitted
knitting

neglect
nibble d
nibbling
nickel
nickname
nimble
nipping
nipple
nitwit

* * *

mnemonic

negation
neglectful ly

nutrition
nutritious

* * * * *

knickerbocker

nativity -ies

necessity -ies
neglectfully
negotiable
negotiate
negotiating
negotiation
negotiator

Nicaragua

nutritional
nutritionist

O

*

* *

omit ted

* * *

official ly

Olympic

omission
omitted
omitting

opinion

* * * * * *

auxiliary -ies

obituary -ies
obligatory
obliterate
obliterating
oblivion
oblivious
obsidian

officially

original ly
originality
originate
originating

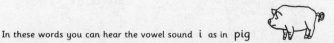

P

*

*fish es creature(s) with tail and fins

***phish** ed attempt internet fraud

pick ed
pig ged
pill
pin ned
pinch es pinched
pink ed
pip ped
piss ed
pit ted
pitch es pitched
pith

prick ed
***prince** son of king
print
***prints** more than one print

* *

*filter ed pass through
*fishing trying to catch fish

permit ted
persist

***philtre** love-potion
***phishing** attempting internet fraud
physics
physique

pianist
piano s
picket
picking
pickle d
pickling
pickup
picky -ier, -iest
picnic
***picture** painting, drawing or photo
pictured
***pidgin** mixture of two languages
***pigeon** bird
pigging
piglet
pigment
pigtail
pilchard
pilgrim
pillar
pillow ed
pimple d
pincers
ping-pong
pinion
pinning
pinpoint
pipit
pipping
pissing
***pistil** part of flower
***pistol** small handgun
piston
***pitcher** large jug
pitchfork
pitching
piteous
pitfall
pitta / pita
pitting
pity -ies pitied
☛

* * *

Pacific
pavilion

peculiar
permission
permitted
permitting
pernicious ly
persistence
persistent ly
petition ed

Philippines
physical ly
physician
physicist

pianist
piano s
piccolo s
pictogram
pictograph
picturesque
pilgrimage
pinafore
pincushion
pinnacle
piranha
pirouette d
piteous
pitiful ly
pivoted
pivoting

position ed

precaution
preceded
preceding
precisely
precision
precocious
prediction
preferring
preparing
prescription
presented
presenting
prestigious
presumptuous
pretended
pretentious
prettier
prettiest
prevailing
prevention
preventive
☛

* * * * * * *

parishioner
participant
participate
participating
participation
particular ly

peculiar ly
peculiarity -ies
pedestrian
***peninsula** land almost surrounded by water
***peninsular** of / like a peninsula
perimeter
peripheral ly
periphery -ies
permissible
perniciously
persistently
petroleum

phenomena
phenomenal ly
phenomenon [phenomena]
philatelist
philosopher
philosophical ly
philosophy -ies
physically
physiological ly
physiology
physiotherapist
physiotherapy

pianoforte
pictorial ly
pirouetting
pistachio s
pitifully
pituitary

political ly
polyphony

precipitate
precipitating
precipitation
predictable
predominant ly
preliminary -ies
preoccupation
☛

In these words you can hear the vowel sound i as in pig

P

**

pivot ed
pixel
pixie
pizza

precede
precise
predict
prefer red
prepare d
prescribe d
present
preserve d
preside
presume d
pretence
pretend
pretty -ier, -iest
prevail ed
prevent
prickle d
prickly
primrose
princess es
printed
printer
printing
prism
prison
prisoner
pristine
privet
privy

pygmy -ies

***

primitive
***principal** chief
principally
***principle** rule for action
principled
prisoner
privacy
privilege d
prodigious
proficient
prohibit ed
prolific ally
provincial
provision
provisions

pyjamas
pyramid
Pyrenees
pyrites

*****

presentable
presumably
presumptuous
principally
proficiency -ies
prohibited
prohibiting
prohibitive
proliferate
proliferating
proliferation
prolifically
provisional ly
proximity

publicity

Q

*

quick
quid
quill
quilt
quin
quince
quip ped
quit ted
[quit]
quiz zed

**

quibble d
quibbling
quicker
quickest
quickly
quinine
quintet
quipping
quitted
quitting
quiver ed

***

quicksilver
quintuplet
quizmaster

****

for Scots: i -r is on page 251

R

SHORT VOWEL i

*

***real** genuine

rib bed
rich es
rid ded
[rid]
ridge d
rift
rig ged
***rill** small stream
rim med
***ring** ed circle
***ring** sound
[rang]
[rung]
rink
rinse d
rip ped
risk ed

*wring twist
[wrung]
wrist
writ

* *

react
really
rebel led
rebound
rebuke d
recall ed
receipt
receive d
recess es
recessed
recite
reclaim ed
recoil ed
record
recount
recruit
recur red
redeem
reduce d
refer red
refine d
reflect
reform ed
refract
refrain ed
refresh es
refreshed
refund
refuse d
regain ed
regard
regret ted
rehearse d
reject
rejoice d
rejoin ed
relate
relax es
relaxed
release d
relent
relief
relieve d
rely -ies
relied
remain ed
remark ed
remind
remote
remove d
renege d
renew ed
renown ed
repaid
repair ed
repay
[repaid]

* * *

reaction
reactor
reagent
realise d
ze
rebelling
rebellion
rebellious
rebuking
receding
receiver
receiving
reception
receptive
receptor
recession
recessive
recital
reciting
recorded
recorder
recording
recover ed
recruitment
recurrence
recurrent
recurring
redemption
reducing
reduction
redundant
referral
referring
refining
reflected
reflection
reflector
reflexive
reformer
refraction
refreshment
refusal
refusing
regarded
regarding
regardless
regatta
regretful ly
regretted
regretting
rehearsal
rehearsing
rejection
rejoicing

* * * * * *

rapidity

reactionary -ies
realising
zing
realism
realistic ally
reality -ies
receptacle
receptionist
recipient
reciprocal ly
reciprocate
reciprocating
recovery -ies
recuperate
redundancy -ies
refinery -ies
refrigerate
refrigeration
refrigerating
refrigerator
regretfully
relationship
reliability
reliable
reluctantly
remarkable
remembering
removable /
removeable
repetitive
republican
repudiate
repudiating
resentfully
respectable
respectfully
respectively
responsibility -ies
responsible
resuscitate
resuscitating
resuscitation
retaliate
retaliating
retaliation
returnable
reverberate
reversible

rhetorical ly
rhythmically

In these words you can hear the vowel sound i as in pig

* *

repeal ed
repeat
repel led
repent
replace d
reply -ies
replied
report
repose d
repress es
repressed
reprieve d
reproach es
reproached
repute
request
require d
research es
researched
resent
reserve d
resign ed
resist
resolve d
resort
resource d
respect
respire d
respond
response
restore d
restrain ed
restraint
restrict
retrieve d
result
resume d
retain ed
retard
retire d
retort
retreat
return ed
reveal ed
revenge d
reverse d
review ed
revise d
revive d
revolt
revolve d
reward

rhythm
rhythmic ally

* * *

related
relating
relation
releasing
relentless
reliance
relieving
religion
religious
relinquish es
relinquished
reluctance
reluctant
remainder
remaining
remember ed
remembrance
reminded
reminder
remission
remittance
removal
removing
Renaissance
reneging
renewal
repeated
repeating
repellent
repelling
repentance
replacement
replacing
reported
reporter
reposing
repression
repressive
reprieving
republic
repulsive
requirement
requiring
researcher
resemblance
resemble d
resembling
resentful ly
resentment
reserving
resistance
resistor
resolving
resources
resourcing

* * * *

ridiculing
ridiculous
rigidity
rigorously
ritually

* *

ribbing
ribbon
richer
richest
richly
richness
riddance
ridded
ridden
ridding
riddled
riddling
***rigger** person who rigs
rigging
rigid
***rigor** rigid state
***rigour** severe conditions
rimming
***ringer** person who rings / close likeness
ringing
ringtone
ripping
rippled
rippling
risen
risky-ier, -iest
ritually
river
riveted / ted

wriggle d
wriggling
*wringer clothes dryer with rollers
wrinkle d
wrinkling
written

* * *

respectfully
respective
respiring
resplendent
respondent
responsive
restoring
restraining
restriction
restrictive
resultant
resulted
resulting
resuming
retarded
retention
retentive
retirement
retiring
retrieval
retrieving
returning
reversal
reversing
revising
revision
revival
reviving
revolver
revolving
revulsion
rewritten

rhythmically

rickety
ricochetted / ed
ridiculed
rigorous
ringleader
riskier
riskiest
ritually
riverside
riveted / rivetted
riveting / rivetting

*

cinch es

cyst

schist
scrimp
scrip
script

shift
shin ned
ship ped
shit
shrill
shrimp
shrink
[shrank]
[shrunk / shrunken]

***sic** written in this way
***sick** unwell
sieve d
sift
silk
sill
silt
sin ned
since
sing
[sang]
[sung]
***sink** slowly go down / basin in kitchen
[sank] [sunk / sunken]
sip ped
sit
[sat]
six th

skid ded
skill ed
skim med
skimp ed
skin ned
skip ped
skit

slick
slid
slim med
sling
[slung]
slink
[slunk]
slip ped
slit
[slit]

* *

cement

chiffon

cigar
cinder
cirrus
cistern
citrus
city -ies
civic
civil ly

*cygnet young swan
*cymbals discs to clash
cystic
***Scilly** Isles
scissors
scribble d
scribbling
scripture

seclude
secrete
secure d
select
settee
severe

shilling
shimmer ed
shingle
shipment
shipping
shipwreck ed
shipyard
shiver ed
shrinkage
shrivel led

sibling
sickening
sickness
sieving
signal led
***signet** seal / ring
***silly** -ier, -iest lacking sense
silver ed
simmer ed
simple
simpler
simplest
simply

* * *

celestial
ceramic

chivalrous
chivalry

cigarette
*cilia more than one
cilium
ciliary
cilium [cilia]
cinema
cinnamon
citizen
civilian
civilise d
ze
civilly

cylinder
cynical ly
Cypriot
cystitis

sadistic ally

scriptural ly

secession
secluded
secluding
secretion
secreting
selected
selecting
selection
selective
selector
semantic ally
semantics
sequential ly
sequoia
severely

shipbuilding
shivering
shrivelling

Sicily
sickening
signalling
signature
signify -ies
signified

* * * * * *

celebrity -ies
celestial
certificate

ciliary
citizenship
civilian
civilisation
zation
civilising
zing

cylindrical
cynically
cynicism

sadistically
salinity
satirical ly

scenario
schizophrenia
schizophrenic ally

security -ies
selectively
semantically
sequentially
severity -ies

significance
significant ly
similarity -ies
similarly
simplicity
simplification
simplistically
simulating
simulation
simultaneous ly
sincerity
singularity -ies
sister-in-law
situated
situation

solicitor
solidify -ies
solidified
solidity
soliloquy -ies
sophisticated
sophistication

for Scots: i -r is on page 252

*

smith

sniff ed
snip ped

sphinx es
spill ed
[spilt]
spin
[span]
[spun]
spit
[spat]
[spit]
splint
split
[split]
sprig
spring
[sprang]
[sprung]
sprint

squib
squid
squint

stick
[stuck]
stiff
still ed
stilts
sting
[stung]
stink
[stank]
[stunk]
stint
stitch es
stitched
strict
string
[strung]
strip ped

swift
swill ed
swim
[swam]
[swum]
swing
[swung]
☛

* *

sincere
sinew
sinful ly
singer
singing
single d
singling
singly
sinning
sipping
siskin
sissy -ies
sister
sitcom
sitter
sitting
sixpence
sixteen th
sixty -ies
sizzle d
sizzling

skidded
skidding
skilful ly
skillet
skimming
skinhead
skinning
skinny -ier, -iest
skipper
skipping
skittle

slimming
slipper ed
slippery
slipping
slipstone
slither ed
slitting

smitten

sniffle d
sniffling
snigger ed
snippet
snivel led

sphincter
spilling
spinach
spindle
spinner
spinning
spinster
☛

* * *

silhouette
silica
silicon
***sillier** more silly
silliest
silverware
silvery
similar
simile
simplify -ies
simplified
simplistic ally
simulate
sincerely
sinfully
Singapore
singular
sinister
sixtieth

skilfully

slippery

smithereens

snivelling

specific ally
spiritual ly

statistic ally
statistics
stimulant
stimulate
stimulus [stimuli]
stinginess

submission
submissive
submitted
submitting
subscription
subsistence
succinctly
sufficient
suspicion
suspicious ly

Switzerland
swivelling

sycamore
syllabic ally
syllable
syllabus [syllabuses / syllabi]
☛

* * * * * *

specifically
spirituality
spiritually

stability
statistical ly
stimulating
stimulation

subsidiary -ies
sufficiently
suspiciously

syllabically
syllabification
symbiosis
symbiotic ally
symbolically
symbolising
zing
symbolism
symmetrical ly
sympathetic ally
symphonically
symposium [symposia]
symptomatic ally
synchronising
zing
syncopated
syncopation
synonymous
synthesiser
zer
synthesising
zing
synthetically
systematic ally
systemically

for Scots: i -r is on page 252

*

swish es
swished
Swiss
switch es
switched

***sync** happening at the same time

* *

spirit
spitting
splinter ed
splitting
springboard
springtime
sprinkle d
sprinkler
sprinkling
sprinter

squirrel

sticker
sticking
sticky -ier, -iest
stiffness
stigma
stillness
stingy -ier, -iest
stipple d
stippling
stirrup
stitches
stitching
stricken
strictly
stridden
stringent
stringy -ier, -iest
stripper
stripping
striptease
striven

submit ted
subsist
succinct

swiftly
swimmer
swimming
swimsuit
swindle d
swindling
swinging
switching
swivel led
swivelling

symbol
***symbols** signs
symptom
syndrome
syntax
syringe d
syrup
system

* * *

symbolic ally
symbolise d
ze
symmetric al
symmetry -ies
sympathise d
ze
sympathy -ies
symphonic ally
symphony -ies
synagogue
synchromesh
synchronise d
ze
syndicate
synonym
synoptic
syntactic
synthesis [syntheses]
synthesise d
ze
synthetic ally
syphilis
Syria
syringing
syrupy -ier, -iest
systemic ally

for Scots: i -r is on page 252

T

*

thick
thin ned
thing
think
[thought]
this
thrift
thrill ed

tick ed
till
tilt
tin ned
tint
tip ped
tit

trick ed
trim med
trip ped

twig ged
twin ned
twinge
twist
twit
twitch es
twitched

* *

terrain

thicket
thickness
thimble
thinker
thinking
thinner
thinning
thistle
thither
thrifty -ier, -iest
thriller
thriven

ticket
tickle d
tickling
ticklish
tiller
timber
timid
tinder
tingle d
tingling
tinkle d
tinkling
tinning
tinsel
tipping
tiptoe d
tissue
titter ed

tribune
tribute
trickle d
trickling
tricky -ier, -iest
trigger ed
trillion
trimming
trimmings
trinket
triple d
triplet
tripling
tripping

twiddle d
twiddling
twigging
twinkle d
twinkling
twinning
twisted
twisting
twitter ed

* * *

terrific ally

thematic ally

tiara
tiddlywinks
timpani

tradition
tremendous
tributary -ies
trickery
trilogy -ies
Trinidad
Trinity
trivial

typical ly
tyrannise d
ze
tyranny -ies

* * * * * *

telegraphy
telepathy
telephonist
terrestrial ly
terrifically

theatrical ly
thematically
theodolite
theological ly
theology -ies
theoretical ly

traditional ly
tremendously
tribulation
tributary -ies
trigonometric
trigonometry
triviality -ies

Tunisia

typically
tyrannical ly
tyrannising
zing
tyrannosaurus es / -i

for Scots: i -r is on page 253

In these words you can hear the vowel sound i as in pig

U

*

* *

until
uplift

* * *

unwilling

* * * *

unthinkable
unwillingness
unwittingly

V

*

* *

vicar
vicious
victim
victor
victual
vigil
vigour
villa
village
***villain** wicked person
***villein** free villager in medieval times
villus [villi]
vineyard
vintage
virile
visage
viscose
vision
visit ed
visual ly
vivid
vixen

* * *

vanilla

Venetian
vermilion

vibrato
vicarage
victimise d
ze
victory -ies
video s
Vietnam
vigilance
vigilant
vigorous
villager
vindicate
vinegar
viola
virulent
visible
visibly
visionary -ies
visited
visiting
visitor
visual ly
visualise d
ze
vitamin
vitreous
vivacious

volition

* * * * * *

validity

velocity -ies

vicissitude
vicinity
victimisation
zation
victimising
zing
Victorian
victorious
videotape d
videotaping
Vietnamese
vigilante
vigorously
visibility
visionary -ies
visualisation
zation
visualise d
ze
visualising
zing
visually

for Scots: i -r
is on page 254

W

*

*ring ed circle
*ring sound
[rang]
[rung]

whelk
***which** that / which one
whiff ed
***Whig** former political party
whim
***whin** gorse / type of hard rock
whip ped
***whish** ed make a whishing sound
whisk ed
whist
***whit** little bit
whiz zed

wick
width
***wig** ged hairpiece
will ed
wilt
***win** gain what you aim for
[won]
wince d
winch es
winched
wind
wing ed
wink ed
***wish** es want it to be true
wished
wisp
***wit** humour / humorous person
***witch** woman said to use magic
with

***wring** twist
[wrung]
wrist
writ

* *

*ringer person who rings / close likeness

whimper ed
whinny -ies
whinnied
whippet
whipping
whisker ed
***whiskey** (Irish or American)
***whisky** -ies (Scotch)
whisper ed
whistle d
whistling
***whither** to which place
Whitsun
whittle d
whittling
whizzing

wicked
wicker
wicket
widow ed
wigging
wiggle d
wiggling
wigwam
wiki
wilful ly
willing
willow
wincing
windfall
windmill
window
windpipe
windscreen
windsurf ed
windward
windy -ier, -iest
winger
wingspan
winkle d
winkling
winner
winning
winter ed
wintry
wisdom
wishful
wishing
wistful ly

* * *

whichever
whispering

wilderness es
wilfully
willingly
willingness
windier
windiest
windowpane
window-sill
windsurfer
windsurfing
wintertime
wishfully
wistfully
withdrawal
wittier
wittiest

* * * *

Wikipedia
witticism

for Scots: i -r is on page 255

W

* *

witchcraft
withdraw
[withdrew]
withdrawal
withdrawn
*__wither__ ed become dry and shrivelled
withhold
[withheld]
within
without
withstand
[withstood]
witness ed
witty -ier,-iest
wizard
wizened

women

wriggle d
wriggling
*__wringer__ clothes dryer with rollers
wrinkle d
wrinkling
written

for Scots: i -r is on page 255

Z

*

zinc
zip ped

* *

zigzag ged
zipper
zipping
zither

* * *

zigzagging
Zimbabwe

* * * *

A

SHORT VOWEL o

*

*-**all** every one
-**alms**

*-**aught** anything at all

*-**awe** fear and wonder
*-**awed** made to feel awe
*-**awl** boring tool

*odd unusual

*-or marks choice

*-ought should

for H . . .
see page 102

* *

-**abroad**
abscond

across

adopt

agog

allot ted
-**almost**
aloft
along
-**alright**
-**also**
*-**altar** holy table
*-**alter** ed change
-**although**
-**always**

anon

-**appal** led
-**applaud**
-**applause**

assault

-**auburn**
-**auction** ed
-**audit**
*-**auger** tool
*-**augur** suggest for the future
*-**August** month
*-**august** impressive
-**aura** s / -ae
*-**aural** ly by the ear
-**austere**
-**author**
-**autumn**

-**awesome / awsome**
*-**awful** ly dreadful
-**awkward**

*-offal less valuable meat

*-oral ly by the mouth

* * *

abolish es
abolished

acknowledge d

adoption

-**albeit**
allotment
allotted
allotting
-**almighty**
alongside
-**already**
-**alternate**

apostle
-**appalling**

astonish es
astonished

atomic

-**audible**
-**audience**
-**auditor**
-**auditory**
*-**aurally** by the ear
-**aurora**
-**Austria**
-**authentic** ally
-**authorise** d
ze
-**autograph** ed

-**awfully**

*-orally by the mouth

for Scots: o -r
is on page 256

* * * * * * * *

abdominal
abominable
abominate
abominating

accommodate
accommodating
accommodation
acknowledgement /
acknowledgment
acknowledging
acropolis [acropoles]

-**alteration**
-**alternating**
-**alternative** ly
-**alternator**
-**altogether**

anonymous

apologetic ally
apologise d
ze
apologising
zing
apology -ies
apostrophe
approximate ly
approximating
approximation

astonishment
astrology
astronomer
astronomy

atrocity -ies

-**auditorium**
-**auditory**
Australia
-**authentically**
-**authorising**
zing
-**authority** -ies
-**autobiographical** ly
-**autobiography** -ies
-**autocracy** -ies
-**autocratic** ally
-**automatic** ally
-**automation**
-**automobile**
-**autonomic**
-**autonomous**
-**auxiliary** -ies

In these words you can hear the vowel sound o as in dog

B

SHORT VOWEL o

*

*-**bald** lacking hair
-**balk / baulk** ed
*-**ball** round object / dance
*-**balled** made into a ball
*-**balm** ointment
-**baulk / balk** ed
*-**bawl** yell
*-**bawled** did yell

blob
***bloc** group of allied countries
***block** ed stop / solid squared-off object
blog ged
***blond** man with fair hair
***blonde** woman with fair hair
blot ted

bob bed
bog ged
***bomb** explosive device
bombed
bond
boss es
bossed
botch es
botched
-**bought**
box es
boxed

-**brawl** ed
-**brawn**
-**broad**
bronze d
broth
-**brought**

* *

-**ballpoint**
-**ballroom**
-**balmy** -ier, -iest
balsa
balti
Baltic
baroque
-**basalt**
-**bauxite**

because
-**befall**
[befell]
-[befallen]
belong ed
-**besought**
beyond

blancmange
blockade
blockboard
blocking
blogger
blogging
blossom ed
blotted
blotter
blotting

bobbing
bodice
body -ies
bodied
boggy -ier, -iest
bombard
bomber
bombshell
bondage
bonfire
bonnet
bonny -ier, -iest
borrow ed
bossy -ier, -iest
botching
bother ed
bottle d
bottling
bottom ed
boxer
boxing
boxplot

-**brawny** -ier, -iest
-**broadcast**
-[broadcast]
-**broadside**
bronchial
bronco

* * *

-**befallen**
belonging
belongings
besotted

bodily
bombardment
bombastic ally
borrowing
Bosnia
botanist
botany
Botswana
bottleneck

-**broadcaster**
-**broadcasting**
broccoli
bronchitis
brontosaur

* * * * *

barometer

binocular
binoculars
biographer
biography -ies
biologist
biology

bombastically

brontosaurus es / -i

In these words the first letter 'o' is a neutral vowel. It sounds like the 'o' in 'occurring'.

Bolivia
bonanza
botanical
brocade

for Scots: o -r is on page 257

In these words you can hear the vowel sound o as in dog

C

*

*-call ed shout / name
-calm ed
*-caught got / trapped
-caulk ed
*-cause bring about / reason
-caused
*-caw hard bird cry
*-cawed did caw
*-caws does caw

-chalk ed
chop ped

*-clause words in sentence / part of written agreement
-claw ed
*-claws curved nails or limbs
clock ed
clod
clot ted
cloth

*-coarse rough
cob
cock ed
*cod fish
*col gap between mountains
cop ped
*cops the police
*copse small wood
*-cord string
*-core central part / take out the core from
*-cored did core
*-corps group
cost
[cost]
*cot baby's bed
cough ed
*-course track / direction / part of meal / of course

-crawl ed
crock ed
croft
crop ped
cross es
crossed

**

-calling
-cauldron
-causal ly
-causing
-caustic ally
-caution ed
-cautious

chocolate
*choler anger
chopper
chopping
choppy -ier, -iest
chopsticks
*-choral for or by a choir
chronic ally

clockwise
clotted
clotting

cobbler
cobweb bed
cocker
cockerel
cockle
Cockney
cockpit
cockroach es
cocksure
cocktail
codfish
coffee
coffin
*collage picture made by sticking on items
*collar ed band or ring round a neck or shaft / seize by the neck
colleague
collect
*college educational establishment
collie
collier
column ed
combat ted
combine
comet
comic
comma
comment
commerce
common
Commons
commune

***

cauliflower
-causally
-causation
-caustically
-cautiously

chloroform ed
chlorophyll
cholera
chorister
chronically
chronicle d
chronicling

cochlea
cockatoo
cockerel
cognition
cognitive
colliery -ies
colonise d
ze
colonist
colony -ies
colossal ly
columnist
combatted
combatting
combining
comedy -ies
comical ly
commentary -ies
commonly
commonplace
commonwealth
communal ly
communist
comparable
compensate
competence
competent
*complement something that completes
complicate
*compliment expression of praise or politeness
composite
comprehend
compromise

**** ***

cauliflower
-caustically

choreographer
choreography
chronically
chronological ly
chronology

-claustrophobia
-claustrophobic

colonisation
zation
colonising
zing
colossally
combination
comically
commentator
commodity -ies
communally
communism
commutative
commutator
comparable
compensating
compensation
competition
*complementary making up a whole
complicated
complicating
complication
*complimentary expressing praise
composition
compositor
comprehensible
comprehension
comprehensive
compromising
computation al
concentrating
concentration
concertina
condemnation
condensation
confidential ly
confidentiality
confidently
confirmation
confiscating
confrontation

for Qu . . . see page 109

for Scots: o -r is on page 258

In these words you can hear the vowel sound o as in dog

* *

compact
complex es
compost
compound
comrade
concave
concept
concert
concoct
concord
concourse
concrete
condom
conduct
conflict
Congo
congress
conic
***conker** horse chestnut
***conquer** ed defeat
conquest
conscience
conscious
conscript
console
constant
contact
content
contents
contest
context
contour ed
contract
contrast
convent
converse
convert
convex
convict
convoy
copper
copping
copy -ies
copied
***coral** substance formed from bones of sea creatures
***corral** enclosure for horses and cattle
cosmic ally
costly -ier, -iest
costume d
cottage
cotter ed
cotton ed

-crawling

* * *

concentrate
concentric
concoction
concreting
conference
***confidant** person trusted to keep secrets
***confidants** people trusted to keep secrets
***confidence** self-belief
***confident** very sure
confiscate
confluence
congregate
congruence
congruent
conical
conifer
conjugate
connoisseur
conqueror
consciously
consciousness
consecrate
consequence
consequent
consonant
constantly
constitute
consulate
contemplate
continent
contraband
contradict
contrary
convalesce d
copulate
copyright
coronary -ies
coroner
correspond
corridor
cosmetic ally
cosmetics
cosmically
cosmonaut
costuming
cottoning

crockery
crocodile
cross-section

Kosovo

* * * * * *

conglomerate
conglomeration
congregating
congregation
conjugating
connotation
conquistador
conscientious
consecrating
consecration
consequently
conservation
consolation
consolidation
constellation
consultation
constipated
constipation
constitution al
constitutional ly
contemplating
contemplation
continental ly
continuity -ies
contraception
contraceptive
contradiction
contribution
controversial ly
controversy -ies
convalescence
convalescent
conversation
copulating
copulation
coronary -ies
coronation
correlation
***correspondence** exchange of letters / similarity
correspondent
***correspondents** those sending letters or reports
corresponding ly
corrugated
cosmetically
cosmically

cross-sectional

kilometre

for Qu . . . see page 109

for Scots: o -r is on page 258

In these words you can hear the vowel sound o as in dog

* *

cropping
crossbar
crossfade
crosshatch ed
crossing
crossroads
crossword
crotchet

for Qu . . .
see page 109

for Scots: o -r
is on page 258

In these words the first letter 'o' is a neutral vowel. It sounds like the 'o' in 'occurring'.

C**O**RRECT WORDS

cholesterol
chorale
cocoon ed
collapse d
collapsible
collapsing
collect ing
collection
collective ly
collector
collide
colliding
collision
colloquial ly
cologne
colonial ly
colonialism
combat ted
combatting
combine d
combining
combustible
combustion
comedian
comedienne
command er
commandment
commemorate
commemoration
commence d
commencing
commercial ly
commission ed
commissioner
commit ted
commitment
committee
committing
commodity -ies
commotion
communal ly
commune d
communicate
communication
communing
communion
community -ies
commutative
commute
commuter
commuting
companion
compare d
comparing
comparison
compartment
compassion ate
compatible
compel led
compelling
compete
competing
competitive ness
competitor
compile d
compiling
complacency
complacent
complain ed
complaint
complete ly
completing
completion
complexion
complexity -ies
comply -ies
complied
component
compose d
composer
composing
composure
compress es
compressed
compression
compressor
comprise d
comprising
compulsion
compulsive
compulsory
compute
computer ised
computing
conceal ed
concede
conceit ed
conceive d
conceiving
concentric
conception
conceptual ly
concern ed
concerning
concerto s
concession
concise
conclude
concluding
conclusion
conclusive
concurrent
concuss es
concussed
concussing
concussion
condemn ed
condense d
condenser
condensing
condition ed
conditional ly
conducive
conduct
conduction
conductor
confectioner
confectionery
confer red
conferring
confess es
confessed
confession al
confessor
confetti
confide
confiding
confine d
confining
confirm ed
conflict
conform ed
conformist
conformity
confront
confuse d
confusing
confusion
congenital ly
congested
congestion
congratulate
congratulating
congratulations
coniferous
conjecture d
conjecturing
conjunction
connect ed
connecting
connection
connector
conscription
consecutive
consensus
consent
conservatory -ies
conservatism
conservative
conserve d
conserving
consider ed
considerable
considerate
consideration
consist ing
consistency -ies
consistent ly
console d
consoling
conspicuous
conspiracy -ies
conspirator
conspire d
conspiring
constabulary -ies
constituency -ies
constituent
constrain ed
constraint
construct ed
construction al
constructive
consult ed
consultancy -ies
consultant
consume d
consumer
consuming
consumption
contagious
contain ed
container
contaminate
contamination
contemporary -ies
contempt
contemptible
contemptuous
contend
content
contention
contest ant
contingency -ies
continual ly
continuance
continuation
continue d
continuing
continuous ly
continuum
contract ion
contractor
contractual ly
contralto s
contraption
contrary
contrast
contribute d
contributing
control led
controller
controlling
convection
convector
convenience
convenient ly
convention
conventional ly
converge d
convergent
converging
converse d
conversely
conversing
conversion
convert ible
convey ed
conveyor /
conveyer
convict ion
convince d
convincing
convulse d
convulsing
convulsion
convulsive
correct ed
correction
correctly
corrode
corroding
corrosion
corrosive
corrupt ion

D

*

-daub ed
-dawn ed

dock ed
dodge d
dog ged
doll ed
don ned
dong ed
dot ted

***-draw** pull / sketch
[drew]
-[drawn]
***-drawer** sliding container
-drawl ed
drop ped

* *

-daughter
-dawdle
-dawdling

demob bed

dislodge d
dissolve d
-distraught

doctor ed
doctrine
dodgem
dodging
dodgy -ier, -iest
dogging
doghouse
doldrums
dollar
dollop
dolly -ies
dolphin
donkey
donning
dotcom
dotplot
dotted
dotting

-drawback
-drawbridge
-drawing
droplet
dropout
dropping

* * *

demolish es
demolished
deposit ed
despondent

dishonest
dislodging
dissolving

doctrinal ly
document
doggedly
dogmatic ally
dominant
dominance
dominate
domino es

* * * * *

democracy -ies
demonstrative
denomination
denominator
deposited
depositing
derogatory
despondency

dichotomy -ies
dishonourable
disqualify -ies
disqualified

doctrinally
docu-drama
documentary -ies
documentation
dogmatically
dolphinarium
dominating
domination

dromedary -ies

In these words the first letter 'o' is a neutral vowel. It sounds like the 'o' in 'occurring'.

domain domestic ally domesticate

for Scots: o -r is on page 259

E

*

* *

encore d

evolve d

exalt
-exhaust

* * *

embody -ies
embodied

envelope

erotic ally

evolving

exalted
-exhausted
-exhaustion
exotic ally

* * * * *

ecologist
ecology
economist
economy -ies

entrepreneur ial
entrepreneurship

equality

erotically

exotically
exploratory

for I . . . see page 102

for Scots: o -r is on page 259

In these words you can hear the vowel sound o as in dog

F

*

-**fall**
[fell]
-[fallen]
false
fault
*-**faun** goat-god
*-**fawn** young deer / colour / try to win favour
*-**fawned** did fawn

-**flaunt**
-**flaw** ed
flock ed
***flocks** more than one flock of animals
flog ged
flop ped
floss ed

fog
***fond** showing love
font
-**fought**
fox es
foxed

-**fraud**
-**fraught**
frock
frog
from
frond
frost
froth ed

*phlox flowering plant

for th . . .
see page 113

* *

-**falcon**
-**fallen**
-**falling**
-**fallout**
falter ed
faulty -ier, -iest

-**flawless**
flogging
flopping
floppy -ier, -iest
floral
florist

fodder
foggy -ier, -iest
foghorn
follow ed
folly -ies
fondle d
fondling
forage d
forehead
foreign
forest
forgone / foregone
forgot
fossil
foster ed
foxglove
foxy -ier, -iest

frogman [frogmen]
frolic ked
frostbite
frosty -ier, -iest
frothy -ier, -iest

phosphate

* * *

*-**fiancé** man engaged to be married
*-**fiancée** woman engaged to be married

foggiest
follower
following
foraging
foreigner
forestry
forgotten
fossilise d
ze

-**fraudulent**
frolicking
frostbitten

phosphorus

* * * * * *

ferocity

fossilising
zing

phenomena
phenomenal ly
phenomenon
[phenomena]
philosopher
philosophical ly
philosophy -ies
photographer
photography

for Scots: o -r
is on page 260

In these words the first letter 'o' is a neutral vowel. It sounds like the 'o' in 'occurring'.

forensic forever forget-me-not

In these words you can hear the vowel sound o as in dog

G

SHORT VOWEL o

*

*-**gall** cheek / bitterness / sore / swelling
*-**Gaul** ancient region of Europe
-**gaunt**
-**gauze**

genre

gloss es
glossed

*-**gnaw** keep biting
*-**gnawed** did gnaw

god
God
golf ed
gone
gong
gosh
got
goth

*nod ded move the head down and up
*-nor and not

* *

-**galling**
-**gaudy** -ier, -iest
-**gauntlet**

genre

globule
glossy -ies

gobble d
***gobbling** greedily eating
goblet
***goblin** evil spirit
goddess es
goggles
golfer
golly
gosling
gospel
gossip ed
Gothic

grotto es / s
grotty -ier, -iest
grovel led
grovelling

* * *

galoshes

geography

-**Gibraltar**

globular
glockenspiel
glossary -ies

godparents
golliwog
gossiping

grovelling

* * * *

geography -ies
geology
geometry -ies

for Scots: o -r is on page 261

In this word the letter 'o' is a neutral vowel.

gorilla

H

*

*-**hall** large room / passage
halt
*-**haul** drag / amount gained
-**hauled**
-**haunch**es
-**haunt**
*-**hawk** bird / carry and try to sell / clear the throat noisily
-**hawked**

hob
***hock** leg joint / wine / pawn
hogged
honked
hopped
hot

* *

-**halter**
-**haughty**-ier, -iest
-**haulage**
-**haunches**
-**hawthorn**

hobbled
hobbling
hobby -ies
hockey
hogging
Holland
hollowed
holly
homage
honest
Hong Kong
honoured
hopper
hopping
hopscotch
horrid
horror
hospice
hostage
***hostel** place to stay in
***hostile** unfriendly
hotch-potch
hotter
hottest
hovel
hovered

* * *

-**haughtily**

historically

holiday
hollyhock
holocaust
hologram
holograph
homograph
homonym
homophone
honestly
honesty
honourable
horoscope
horrible
horribly
horrify-ies
horrified
hospital
hovercraft

hypnotically

* * * * *

historically

holography
***homogeneous** of the same kind throughout
***homogenous** of the same genetic origin
honorary
honourable
horizontally
horrifying
hospitable
hospitalised
ze
hospitalising
zing
hospitality
hostility-ies

hypnotically
hypocrisy
hypothesis [hypotheses]

In these words the 'o' is neutral.
horizon horrendous horrific ally

for Scots: o -r is on page 261

I

*

* *

-**install**ed / **install**ed
involved

* * *

immoral
impromptus
improper

-**installing**
-**instalment** / **installment**
involvement

* * * * * *

illogically

impossibility
impossible
impoverished

-**inaugural**
-**inauguration**
incongruous
inoculate
inoculation
insoluble
insomnia
intolerable
intolerance
intoxicate
intoxication
involuntary

for E . . . see page 99

for Scots: o -r is on page 262

J

*

-**jaunt**
-**jaw** ed

job bed
jog ged
jolt
jot ted

for dr . . .
see page 99

**

-**jaunty** -ier, -iest
-**jawing**

jobbing
jobless
jockey ed
jockstrap
jodhpurs
jogger
jogging
jolly -ies
jollied
jostle d
jostling
jotted
jotter
jotting

***

geography

-Gibraltar

jocular

****

geography
geology
geometry

for Scots: o -r
is on page 262

K

*

knob
knock ed
***knot** ted tied fastening / hard part of wood / sea mile (per hour)

*-naught / nought zero

*not used in denial, negation, refusal
*-nought / naught zero

**

knocker
knockout
knotted
knotting
***knotty** -ier, -iest full of knots
knowledge

*-naughty -ier, -iest badly behaved

***

Kosovo

****

kilometre

knowledgeable

In these words the letter 'o' is a neutral vowel.

Korea Korean

for C . . .
see page 96

for Qu . . .
see page 109

for Scots: o -r
is on page 262

L

*

-launch es
-launched
***-law** laws enforced in a country
-lawn

lob bed
***loch** Scottish word for 'lake'
***lock** fastening device
locked
lodge d
loft
log ged
long ed
lop ped
***-lore** traditions and facts
loss es
lost
lot

* *

-launcher
-launder ed
-laundry -ies
laurel
-lawful ly
-lawyer

lobbing
lobby -ies
lobbied
lobster
locker
locket
locus [loci]
lodger
lodging
lodgings
lofty -ier, -iest
logging
logic ally
longer
longest
longing
long-term
lopping
lorry -ies
lotto
lozenge

* * *

laconic ally
-launderette
-lawfully

logical ly
lollipop
longitude
lottery -ies

* * * * * *

laboratory -ies
laconically

logarithm
logically
longevity
longitudinal ly

for Scots: o -r is on page 263

In these words you can hear the vowel sound o as in dog

M

*

*mall public walk / walk lined with shops
malt
*-maul ed handle roughly / heavy mallet
-mauve

mob bed
mock ed
mod
*moll gangster's girl
mop ped
mosque
moss es
moth
motte

* *

Malta

mobbing
mocha
model led
modelling
moderate
modern
modest
module
mollusc
monarch
mongoose s
monsoon
monster
monstrous
mopping
*moral ly concerning right and wrong
*morale confidence
morrow
mossy -ier, -iest
motley
mottled
motto es / s

* * *

melodic ally

mnemonic

moccasin
mockery -ies
modelling
moderate
modernise d / ze
modesty
modify -ies
modified
modular
molecule
monarchy -ies
monastery -ies
monitor ed
monochrome
monologue
monotone
monoxide
monument
moralise d / ze
morally
Morocco
mosquito es

* * * * * * *

mahogany
majority -ies

melodically
methodical ly
metropolis es

misogynist
misogyny

moderation
moderato
modernisation / zation
modernising / zing
modification
modifier
modulation
molecular
monochromatic ally
monogamous
monolithic
monopolise d / ze
monopoly -ies
monotheism
monotonous
monstrosity
monumental ly

mythology -ies

In these words the first letter 'o' is a neutral vowel. It sounds like the 'o' in 'occurring'.

Mohammed	momentum	morality
molasses	moraine	morose

for Scots: o -r is on page 263

N

*

*-gnaw keep biting
*-gnawed did gnaw

knob
knock ed
*knot ted tied fastening / hard part of wood / sea mile (per hour)

*-naught / nought zero

*nod ded move head down and up
*-nor and not
*not used in denial, negation, refusal
notch es
notched
*-nought / naught zero

* *

knocker
knockout
knotted
knotting
*knotty -ier, -iest full of knots
knowledge

*-naughty -ier, -iest badly behaved

nodding
nodule
nonsense
nonstop
nostril
novel
novice
noxious
nozzle

* * *

-naughtier
-naughtiest
-naughtiness
-nausea
-nauseous
-nautical ly

neurotic ally

nocturnal ly
nominal ly
nominate
nominee
nonchalant
nonfiction / non-fiction
nostalgia
nostalgic ally
novelist
novelty -ies

* * * * *

knowledgeable

-nautically

neurotically

nocturnally
nominally
nomination
nonconformist
nostalgically
notwithstanding

for Scots: o -r is on page 263

O

SHORT VOWEL O

*

*-all every one
-alms

*-aught anything at all

*-awe fear and wonder
*-awed made to feel awe
*-awl boring tool

***odd** unusual

of
off

on

opt

*-**or** marks choice

*-**ought** should

ox [oxen]

* *

-almost
-alright
-also
*-altar holy table
*-alter ed change
-although
-always

-auburn
-auction ed
-audit
*-auger tool
*-augur suggest for the future
*-August month
*-august impressive
-aura s / -ae
*-aural ly by the ear
-austere
-author
-autumn

-awesome / awsome
*-awful ly dreadful
-awkward

honest
honour ed

object
oblong

occult
o'clock
octane
octave

oddly
oddment

***offal** less valuable meat
offer ed
offering
office
off-line
offset
offshore
offside
offspring
offstage
often

olive

omelette
☛

* * *

-albeit
-almighty
-already
-alternate

-appalling

-audible
-audience
-auditor
-auditory
*-aurally by the ear
-aurora
Austria
-authentic ally
-authorise d
ze
-autograph ed

-awfully

honestly
honesty
honourable

obnoxious
obsolete
obstacle
obvious

occupant
occupy -ies
occupied
octagon
October
octopus es / -i
ocular
oculist

oddity -ies

offering
offertory -ies
officer

ominous
omnibus

oncoming
ongoing
onlooker

opera
operate
ophthalmic
opossum
opposite
☛

* * * * * * * *

-alteration
-alternating
-alternative ly
-alternator
-altogether

-auditorium
-auditory
Australia
-authentically
-authorising
zing
-authority -ies
-autobiographical ly
-autobiography -ies
-autocracy -ies
-autocratic ally
-automatic ally
-automation
-automobile
-autonomic
-autonomous
-auxiliary -ies

entrepreneur ial
entrepreneurship

honorary
honourable

objectively
objectivity
obligation
observation
obsolescence
obsolescent
obviously

occupation al
occupier
octagonal

offertory -ies

onomatopoeia
☛

for H . . .
see page 102

for Scots: o -r
is on page 264

In these words you can hear the vowel sound o as in dog

O

* *

on-line
onset
onslaught
onto
onward
onwards

opera
opted
optic ally
opting
option
opus es [opera]

*-**oral** ly by the mouth
orange

osprey
ostrich es

otter

oxen
oxide

* * *

optical ly
optician
optimal ly
optimist
optimum
optional

oracle
*-**orally** by the mouth
orangeade
orator
oratory
origin

oscillate
osmium
osmosis
ossicle

oxidise d
ze
oxygen

* * * * * *

operated
operatic ally
operating
operation
operational ly
operating
operator
opportunist ic
opportunity -ies
opposition
optically
optimally
optimism
optimistic ally

orientate
orientation
orienteering

oscillation
ostensible
ostensibly
ostinato

oxidation
oxidisation
zation
oxidising
zing
oxyacetylene

for H . . . see page 102

for Scots: o -r is on page 264

In these words the first letter 'o' is a neutral vowel. It sounds like the 'o' in 'occurring'.

ORIGINAL WORDS

obedience
obedient
obey ed
obituary -ies
object ion
objectionable
objective
obligatory
oblige d
obliging
oblique
obliterate
obliterating
oblivion
oblivious
obscene
obscenity -ies
obscure d
obscuring
obscurity -ies
observable
observant
observatory -ies
observe d
observer
observing
obsess ed
obsession al ly
obsessive
obsidian
obstruct ion
obstructive
obtain ed
obtuse
occasion
occasional ly
occur red
occurrence
occurring
offence
offend
offender
offensive
official ly
omission
omit ted
omitting
opinion
opponent
oppose d
opposing
oppress es
oppressed
oppression
oppressive
oppressor
original ly
originality
originate
originating

In these words you can hear the vowel sound o as in dog

P

SHORT VOWEL o

*

*flocks more than one flock of animals

-**palm** ed
-**paunch** es
*-**pause** brief gap / hesitate
-**paused**
*-**paw** foot of animal
*-**pawed** examined by paw
-**pawn**
*-**pawned** left in return for loan
*-**paws** feet of animal

***phlox** flowering plant

plot ted

***pod** ded form pods / casing
pomp
***pond** pool
*-**poor** badly off
pop ped
*-**pore** tiny hole / study closely
posh
pot ted
*-**pour** flow out
*-**poured** did pour

-**prawn**
prod ded
prompt
prong ed
prop ped

-**psalm**

* *

-**palfrey**
palsy -ied
-**pausing**
-**pawpaw**

phosphate

plotted
plotting

pocket
podcast
podded
podding
podgy -ier, -iest
polish es
polished
polka
pollen
pompom
pompous
poncho s
ponder ed
pontoon
popcorn
poplar
poplin
popping
poppy -ies
porridge
possum
posture d
pothole
potted
potter
potting

problem
prodded
prodding
produce
product
***profit** ed gain
project
prolong ed
promise d
promptly
proper
***prophet** inspired religious leader
propping
prospect
prosper ed
prostate
prostrate
proverb
province
proxy -ies

* * *

peroxide

phosphorus

-**plausible**

podgier
podgiest
policy -ies
politics
pollinate
poltergeist
polygon
polythene
ponderous
***populace** common people
popular
populate
***populous** full of people
positive
possible
possibly
postulate
posturing
pottery -ies
poverty

-**precaution**
probable
probably
prodigal
prodigy -ies
profited
profiting
progeny
promenade
prominence
prominent
promising
promontory -ies
propagate
properly
property -ies
***prophecy** -ies statement about a future event
***prophesy** -ies make a statement about the future
prophesied
prosecute
prosperous
prostitute
Protestant
providence
provident

* * * * * *

pathology

personification
personify -ies
personified

phenomena
phenomenal ly
phenomenon
[phenomena]
philosopher
philosophical ly
philosophy -ies
photographer
photography

politician
pollination
polyester
Polynesia
polynomial
polyphonic ally
polystyrene
polytechnic
polytheism
polyurethane
pomegranate
popularity
populating
population
possibility -ies
postulating

predominant ly
probability -ies
problematic al ly
proclamation
productivity
profitability
profitable
promiscuity
promontory -ies
propaganda
propagating
proposition
prosecuting
prosecution
prosecutor
prosperity
prostitution
provocation
provocative
proximity

for Scots: o -r is on page 265

In these words you can hear the vowel sound o as in dog

P

In these words the first letter 'o' is a neutral vowel. It sounds like the 'o' in 'occurring'.

PR**O**FOUND WORDS

phonetic ally
photographer
photography
polarity -ies
police
policeman
[policemen]
policewoman
[policewomen]
policing
polite ly
political ly
pollutant
pollute
polluting
pollution
polyphony
position ed
possess es
possessed
possession

possessive
potato es
potential ly
probation
procedure
proceed ing
proceedings
procession
proclaim ed
procure d
procuring
prodigious
produce d
producer
producing
production
productive
profane
profess es
professed
profession

professional ly
professionalism
professor
proficiency -ies
proficient
profound
profuse
profusion
progression
progressive ly
prohibit ed
prohibiting
prohibitive
project
projectile
projection
projector
proliferate
proliferating
prolific ally
promote

promoter
promoting
promotion
pronounce d
pronouncement
pronouncing
pronunciation
propel led
propeller
propelling
propensity -ies
proportion al ly
proportionate ly
propos
proposal
propose d
proposing
proprietor
propulsion
prospect
prospective

prospector
prospectus es
protected
protection
protective
protector
protest
protractor
protrude
protruding
provide
provided
providing
provincial
provision
provisional ly
provisions
provoke d
provoking

Q

*

quash es
quashed

* *

quadrant
quagmire
quandary -ies
quantum
quarrel led
quarry -ies
quarried

* * *

quadrangle
quadratic
quadriceps
quadruped
quadruple d
quadruplet
quadrupling
qualify -ies
qualified
quality -ies
quandary -ies
quantify -ies
quantified
quantity -ies
quarantine
quarrelling

* * * * *

quadrilateral
qualification
qualifier
qualitative
quantitative

R

*

-raw

rob bed
rock ed
rod ded
romp ed
***rot** ted decay

wrath
wrong ed
*-wrought made to fit

* *

-recall ed
resolve d
respond
response
revolt
revolve d

rhomboid
rhombus

robber
robbing
robin
rocker
rocket
rocky -ier, -iest
rodded
rodding
***rollick** act with enjoyment
***rollock / rowlock** pivot for oar
rosin ed
roster
rostrum s [rostra]
rotted
rotten
rotting
***rowlock / rollock** pivot for oar

wrongful ly
wrongly

* * *

rendezvous
resolving
respondent
responsive
revolver
revolving

robbery -ies
rockery -ies
rollicking
rottweiler

wrongdoing
wrongfully

* * * * * *

responsibility -ies
responsible

rhetorical ly

for Scots: o -r is on page 266

In these words the first letter 'o' is a neutral vowel. It sounds like the 'o' in 'occurring'.

romance d   romancing   romantic ally

In these words you can hear the vowel sound o as in dog

*

-psalm

salt
-**sauce**
*-**saw** looked at / cutting tool
*-**sawed** did saw
-[sawn]

-**scald**
scoff ed
scone
Scot
scotch ed
Scotch
-**scrawl** ed

-**shawl**
shock ed
shod
shone
shop ped
shot

slog ged
slop ped
slosh es
sloshed
slot ted

-**small**
smock ed
smog

snob
snot

*-**soar** fly high
*-**soared** flew high
sob bed
sock ed
***sod** turf
soft
solve d
song
*-**sore** painful
-**sought**

-**spawn** ed
spot ted
-**sprawl** ed

squad
squash es
squashed
squat ted
-**squawk** ed

* *

-**salty** -ier, -iest
-**saucepan**
-**saucer**
-**saucy** -ier, -iest
-**sauna**
-**saunter** ed
sausage
-**sawdust**

scholar
scoffing
Scotland
Scotsman [Scotsmen]
Scottish

shoddy -ier, -iest
shoplift
shopper
shopping
shotgun

-**slaughter** ed
slogging
slopping
sloppy -ier, -iest
slotted
slotting

-**smaller**
-**smallest**
-**smallpox**
-**small-scale**

snobbish
snotty -ier, -iest

sobbing
soccer
socket
sodden
soften ed
softer
softly
software
soggy -ier,-iest
solace
solder ed
solemn
solid
solvent
solving
sombre
sonic
sonnet
sorrow ed
sorry -ier, -iest
sovereign

* * *

-**saucily**

scholarly
scholarship
Scotswoman
[Scotswomen]

shopkeeper

snottier
snottiest

soldering
solemnly
solenoid
solidly
solitary
solitude
soluble
sombrero s
sonorous
sovereignty -ies
soviet

sponsorship

stockbroker
stockmarket
-**strawberry** -ies
strontium

swastika

symbolic ally
symphonic ally
synoptic

* * * * *

solidarity
solubility
sostenuto

spontaneity
spontaneous ly

symbolically
symphonically
synonymous

for Scots: o -r is on page 267

In these words you can hear the vowel sound o as in dog

*

*-**stalk** stem / hunt / walk stiffly
-**stalked**
-**stall** ed
-**staunch** es
-staunched
***stock** ed supply
stodge
stop ped
-**straw**
strong

swab bed
swamp ed
swan
swap ped
***swat** slap with a flat object
*-**sword** weapon
***swot** study hard

* *

sponsor ed
spotlight
spotted
spotting
spotty -ier, -iest
sprocket

squabble d
squabbling
squadron
squalid
squalor
squander ed
squatted
squatter
squatting

-**stalker**
*-**stalking** hunting / walking stiffly
-**stalling**
-**stalwart**
stockade
***stocking** ed covering for legs and feet / providing
stocky -ier, -iest
stodgy -ier, -iest
stoppage
stopper
stopping
stopwatch es
-**strawberry** -ies
stronger
strongest
stronghold
strongly

swabbing
swallow ed
swapping
***swatted** did swat
***swatting** slapping with a flat object
***swotted** did swot
***swotting** studying hard

for Scots: o -r is on page 267

In these words the first letter 'o' is a neutral vowel. It sounds like the 'o' in 'occurring'.

society -ies
solicitor
solidify -ies
solidified
solidity
soliloquy -ies
solution
Somalia
sophisticated
sophistication
soprano s
sporadic ally

T

*

*-**talk** speak
-talked
-**tall**
*-**taught** instructed
-**taunt**
*-**taut** tight

-**thaw** ed
thongs
-**thought**
throb bed
throng ed

tongs
top ped
*-**torque** turning force / necklace
toss es
tossed
***tot** young child / small amount / add

trod
trot ted
trough ed

* *

-**talking**
-**taller**
-**tallest**
-**tawny** -ier, -iest

-**thoughtful** ly
throbbing
throttle d

***tocsin** alarm bell
toddle d
toddler
toddling
toffee
toggle
toggling
tomboy
tomcat
tonic
tonsil
topic
topping
topple d
toppling
topsoil
torrent
toxic
***toxin** poison

-**trauma** s [traumata]
trodden
trolley
trombone
tropic ally
trotted
trotting

* * *

-**talkative**

tectonic

-**thoughtfully**

toboggan
tolerance
tolerant
tolerate
tomahawk
tommy-gun
tomorrow
topical

-**traumata**
-**traumatic**
tropical ly

* * * *

theodolite
theology -ies
thermometer

tolerable
tolerating
toleration
tonsillitis / tonsilitis
topography
topology
topsy-turvy

tropically

for Scots: o -r is on page 268

In these words the first letter 'o' is a neutral vowel. It sounds like the 'o' in 'occurring'.

tobacco s
tobacconist
tomato es
torrential ly

U

*

* *

upon

* * *

* * * *

V

*	* *	* * *	* * * * *
***vault** gymnastic leap / underground room / arched roof	**vodka**	**volatile**	**velocity** -ies
	volley ed	**volcano** es / s	
	voltage	**volcanic** ally	**volatility**
	volume	**voluntary**	**volcanically**
***volt** unit of electrical force	**vomit** ed	**volunteer** ed	**voluntarily**

In these words the letter 'o' is a neutral vowel.

vocabulary -ies vocation vocational ly

W

*	* *	* * *	* * * *
*rot ted decay	**wadding**	-**wallflower**	-**walkie-talkie**
	waddle d	-**wallpaper** ed	-**watercolour**
waft	**waddling**	**wandering**	
*-**walk** ed go in steps	**waffle** d	**warranty** -ies	**whatsoever**
-**wall** ed	**waffling**	**warrior**	
waltz es	-**walker**	**washable**	
waltzed	-**walking**	**watchfully**	
wan	**wallet**	-**waterfall**	
wand	-**wallflower**	-**waterfowl**	
want	**wallow** ed	-**waterproof** ed	
was	-**walnut**	-**watershed**	
wash es	-**walrus**	-**watertight**	
washed	**wander** ed	-**waterway**	
wasp	**wanted**	-**watery**	
watch es	**wanting**		
watched	**wanton**	**whatever**	
***watt** unit of electric power	**warrant**		
	warren	-**withdrawal**	
***watts** units of electric power	**washer**		
	***washers** means of washing / sealing rings	**wrongdoing**	
		wrongfully	
***what** that or those which / which / how much / I do not understand	***washes** cleans with water		
	washing		
	wasn't		
***what's** what is	**watchdog**		
	watchful ly		
***wok** cooking pan	**watching**		
	watchman [watchmen]		
wrath	**watchword**		
wrong ed	-**water** ed		
*-**wrought** made to fit			
	-**withdraw** [withdrew]		
	-**withdrawal**		
	-**withdrawn**		
	wobble d		
	wobbling		
	wobbly		
	wonky -ier, -iest		
	wrongful ly		
	wrongly		

for Scots: o -r is on page 269

In these words you can hear the vowel sound o as in dog

for Scots: o -r is on page 269

Y

*	* *	* * *	* * * *
yacht -**yawn** ed	**yachting** **yoghourt / yoghurt / yogurt** **yonder**		

Z

*	* *	* * *	* * * *
	zombi / zombie		**zoology**

A

SHORT VOWEL **u** SHORT VOWEL **oo**

*

* *

above
abrupt

-**adjourn** ed
adjust
adult

affront
-**afoot**

among
amongst

-**assure** d

august

* * *

abruptly
abundance
abundant

accomplice
accomplish es
accomplished
accustom ed

adjuster
adjustment

another

assumption
-**assurance**
-**assuring**

* * * * *

accompaniment
accompany -ies
accompanied
accomplishment

adultery

for Scots: ur & ir are on page 242

B

*

blood
bluff ed
blunt
blush es
blushed

-**book** ed

-**brook** ed
brunt
brush es
brushed

buck ed
bud ded
budge d
buff ed
bug ged
bulb
bulge d
bulk
-**bull**
bum med
bump ed
bun
bunch es
bunched
bung ed
bunk ed

* *

because
become
[became]
[become]
begun
beloved

bloodshed
bloodstream
bloody -ier,-iest
blubber ed
blunder ed
bluntly

-**bookcase**
-**booking**
-**booklet**
-**bookmark** ed
-**bookshelf** [bookshelves]
-**bookshop**
***borough** town or district with an MP
-**bosom**
-**bourgeois**

brother
Brussels

* * *

becoming
beloved

bloodthirsty

-**bookseller**
-**bourgeoisie**

brotherhood

buccaneer ed
bucketful
bucketing
-**Buddhism**
budgerigar
budgetary
budgeting
buffalo es
-**bulldozer** ed
-**bulletin**
bumblebee
bungalow
Burundi
buttercup
butterfly -ies
buttermilk
butterscotch

* * * * * *

brother-in-law

budgerigar
budgetary
Bulgaria
-**bureaucracy** -ies
-**bureacratic** ally

for Scots: ur & ir are on page 243

-or oo as in woodpecker 

In these words you can hear the sound u as in duck 

B

*

bus es
-**bush** es
-bushed
***bussed** carried by bus
***bust** upper part of body / break / arrest
***but** except / instead / yet
***butt** large cask / person made fun of / thick end of tool or weapon / push with head
buzz es
buzzed

* *

bubble d
bubbling
bucket ed
buckle d
buckling
-**Buddha**
-**Buddhist**
budding
buddy -ies
budget ed
budgie
budging
buffer ed
***buffet** ed push roughly
***buffet** self-service meal
buffing
bugging
buggy -ies
bulbous
bulky -ier, -iest
-**bulldog**
-**bullet**
-**bullfrog**
-**bullock**
-**bullseye**
-**bully** -ies
-bullied
-**bulrush** es
bumming
bumper
bundle d
bundling
bungle d
bungling
bunion
bunker ed
bunny -ies
Bunsen
***burgh** borough in Scotland
burrow ed
-**bushel**
busker
bustle d
bustling
-**butcher** ed
butler
***butted** pushed with head
***butter** ed spread with butter
buttocks
button ed
buttress es
buttressed
butty -ies
buzzard
buzzer

for Scots: ur & ir are on page 243

-or oo as in woodpecker

In these words you can hear the sound u as in duck

C

SHORT VOWEL u SHORT VOWEL oo

*

chuck ed
chug ged
chum med
chump
chunk ed

club bed
cluck ed
clump ed
clung
clutch es
clutched

come
[came]
[come]
-cook ed
-could

-crook
crumb
crunch es
crunched
crush es
crushed
crust
crutch es
crux es [cruces]

cub
cuff ed
cult
cup ped
-cure d
cut
[cut]

* *

chuckle d
chuckling
chugging
chumming
chunky -ier, -iest
chutney

clubhouse
clumsy -ier, -iest
cluster ed
clutter ed

colour ed
comeback
comfort
coming
compass es
concuss es
concussed
conduct
confront
conjure d
construct
consult
convulse d
-cooker
-cookie
-cooking
corrupt
-couldn't
country -ies
couple d
coupling
courage
cousin
cover ed

-crooked
crumble d
crumbling
crumpet
crumple d
crumpling
crunchy -ier, -iest
crutches

* * *

chunkier
chunkiest

colander / cullender
colourful ly
colouring
colourless
combustion
comfortable
comfortably
comforting
company -ies
compulsion
compulsive
concurrent
concussing
concussion
conduction
conductor
conjunction
conjurer / conjuror
constable
constructed
construction
constructive
consultant
consulted
consumption
convulsion
convulsive
-cookery
corruption
countryman
[countrymen]
countryside
-courier
covenant
coverage
covering

crustacean

cul-de-sac
culinary
culminate
cultivate
cultural ly
cumbersome
-curator
-curio
-curious
currency -ies
currently
custody
customary
customer
cutlery

* * * * *

circumference

colourfully
combustible
comfortable
comfortably
compulsory
constructional
consultancy -ies

culinary
culminating
culmination
cultivation
culturally
-curiosity -ies
-curiously
custodial
customary

for Scots: ur & ir are on page 244

-or oo as in woodpecker

In these words you can hear the sound u as in duck

* *

-**cuckoo**
cuddle d
cuddling
culprit
culture d
cunning
cupboard
cupful
cupping
-**curate**
-**curing**
***currant** fruit
***current** flowing
stream / present
curry -ies
curried
-**cushion** ed
custard
custom
customs
cutback
cutter
cutting

for Scots: ur & ir
are on page 244

Here the first syllable vowel sounds are neutral.

courageous curricular curriculum [curricula]

D

SHORT VOWEL u SHORT VOWEL oo

*

does
***done** finished
***dost** old form of 'do', used with 'thou'
doth
dove

drug ged
drum med
drunk

duck
***ducked** did duck
***duct** tube or pipe
dug
dull ed
dumb
dump ed
***dun** grey-brown
dunce
dung
dusk
***dust** particles of earth or waste matter
Dutch

* *

deduct

discuss es
***discussed** debated
***disgust** strong dislike
disrupt
distrust

doesn't
double d
doubling
doubly
dozen

drugging
drummer
drumming
drumstick
drunkard
drunken

duchess es
duckling
duffel / duffle
dugout
dummy -ies
dumpling
dungeon
-**during**
dustbin
duster
dusty -ier, -iest

* * *

deduction
deductive
destruction
destructive

discomfort
discourage d
discover ed
discussing
discussion
disgruntle d
disgruntling
disgusting
disruption
disruptive

drunkenness

dungarees

* * * * *

denunciation

discouraging
discovery -ies

for Scots: ur & ir are on page 245

E

*

for I . . . see page 123

* *

-**endure** d
engulf ed
enough
*-**ensure** d make certain
entrust

erupt

-**euro**
-**Europe**

*-insure d protect against loss

* * *

emulsion ed

encourage d
-**endurance**
-**enduring**
*-**ensuring** making certain

erupted
eruption

expulsion

*-insuring protecting against loss

* * * *

encouragement
encouraging

-**European**

for Scots: ur & ir are on page 245

-or oo as in woodpecker

In these words you can hear the sound u as in duck

*

flood
fluff ed
flung
flush es
flushed
flux es

-**foot**

front

fudge d
-**full**
fun
fund
fuss es
fussed

* *

flooded
flooding
floodlight
floodlit
flourish es
flourished
fluffy -ier, -iest
-**fluoride**
-**fluorine**
flurry -ies
flurried
fluster ed
flutter ed

-**football**
-**footer**
-**foothill**
-**foothold**
-**footing**
-**footnote**
-**footpath**
-**footstep**
-**forsook**

frontier
frustrate

fudging
-**fulcrum**
-**fulfil** led
-**full-back**
-**fuller**
-**fullest**
-**fullness**
-**full-scale**
-**full-time**
-**fully**
fumble d
fumbling
function ed
funding
funfair
fungi
***fungous** spongy or in other ways like a fungus
***fungus** type of plant
funnel led
funny -ier, -iest
furrow ed
-**fury** -ies
fuzzy -ier, -iest

* * *

fluctuate
-**fluorescence**
-**fluorescent**

-**footballer**
forthcoming

frontier
frustrating
frustration

-**fulfilling**
-**fulfilment**
functional ly
functioning
funnelling
funnier
funniest
-**furious**

* * * * *

fluctuating
fluctuation
-**fluorescence**
-**fluorescent**
-**fluoridation** /
fluoridisation
zation

functionality -ies
functionally
fundamental ly
-**furiously**

*for th . . .
see page 133*

*for Scots: ur & ir
are on page 246*

-or oo as in woodpecker 

In these words you can hear the sound u as in duck 

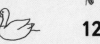

G

SHORT VOWEL **u** SHORT VOWEL **oo**

*

glove d
glum
glut

-**good**
-**goods**
-**gourd**

grub bed
grudge
gruff
grunt

gulf
gull ed
gulp ed
gum med
gun ned
gush es
gushed
gust
gut ted
guts

* *

gazump ed

glutton

-**goodbye**
-**goodness**
-**goodnight**
-**goodwill**
-**gooseberry** -ies
-**gourmet**
govern ed

grubbing
grubby -ier, -iest
grudging
grumble d
grumbling
grumpy -ier, -iest

gudgeon
gullet
gulley / gully -ies
gulling
gumboil
gumming
gunfire
gunman [gunmen]
gunner
gunning
gunshot
guppy -ies
-**guru** s
gusto
gusty -ier, -iest
gutter
gutting
guzzle d
guzzling

* * *

gluttony

-**good-looking**
-**gooseberry** -ies
government
governor

grudgingly

gullible
gunpowder
guttering
guttural ly

* * * * *

governmental ly

gutturally

for Scots: ur & ir are on page 246

-or **oo** as in woodpecker 

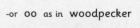

In these words you can hear the sound **u** as in duck 

H

*

-**hood**
-**hook** ed

hub
huff
hug ged
hulk
hull
hum med
hump ed
hunch es
hunched
hung
hunk
hunt
hush es
hushed
husk
hut
hutch es

* *

honey ed
-**hoodie / hoody** -ies
-**hoummos / hommus / hummous / hummus / houmous / humus**

hubbub
huddle d
huddling
hugging
hulky -ier, -iest
hullo
humble d
humbling
humming
hundred
hundredth
hunger ed
hungry -ier, -iest
hunted
hunter
hunting
-**hurrah!**
-**hurray!**
hurry -ies
hurried
husband
husky -ies
hustle d
hustling

* * *

honeybee
honeycomb
honeydew
honeymoon

hummingbird
Hungary
hungrier
hurricane
hurriedly
hurrying

* * * *

honeysuckle

hullabaloo
Hungarian

for Scots: ur & ir are on page 247

I

*

* *

*-ensured make certain

indulge d
instruct
insult
*-**insure** d protect against loss
intrust / entrust

* * *

*-ensuring making certain

impulsive

induction
inductive
indulgence
indulgent
indulging
injunction
injustice
instruction
instructive
instructor
insulting
-**insurance**
*-**insuring** protecting against loss

* * * * * * *

illustrious

-**impurity** -ies

-**incurable**
industrial ly
industrialisation
zation
industrialise d
ze
industrialist
industrious
-**infuriate**
-**injurious**

for E . . . see page 120

for Scots: ur & ir are on page 247

-or oo as in woodpecker

In these words you can hear the sound u as in duck

J

SHORT VOWEL u   SHORT VOWEL oo

*

judge d
jug ged
jump ed
junk
just
jut ted

* *

judgement / judgment
judging
juggle d
juggler
juggling
jumble d
jumbling
jumper
jumping
junction
juncture
jungle
-juror
-jury -ies
justice
justly
jutting

* * *

juggernaut
jugular
justify -ies
justified
juxtapose d

* * * * *

-jurisdiction
-jurisprudence
justifiable
justifiably
justification
juxtaposing
juxtaposition

for dr . . .
see page 120

K

*

for C . . .
see page 118

* *

knuckle d
knuckling

kung fu

* * *

* * * *

for Scots: ur & ir
are on page 248

-or oo as in woodpecker 

In these words you can hear the sound u as in duck 

*

-look ed
love d

luck
lug ged
lugs
lull ed
lump ed
lunch es
lunched
lung
lunge d
-lure d
lush
lust

* *

London
-lookout
lovely -ier, -iest
lover
loving

lucky -ier, -iest
luggage
lugging
***lumbar** lower back
***lumber** junk / timber / move awkwardly
lumbered
lumpy -ier, iest
luncheon ed
lunchtime
lunging
luscious
lustre
lusty -ier, -iest

* * *

Londoner
lovable
loveliest
lovingly

luckier
luckiest
luckily
lullaby -ies
lumbago
lumberjack
Luxembourg / Luxemburg
luxury -ies

* * * *

luxuriant
luxurious

for Scots: ur & ir are on page 248

-or oo as in woodpecker

In these words you can hear the sound u as in duck

*

monk
month
-**moor** ed

much
muck ed
mud
muff ed
mug ged
mulch es
mum
mumps
munch es
munched
mung
mush
musk
must

* *

-**manure** d
-**mature** d

misjudge d
-**mistook**
mistrust

Monday
money ed
mongrel
monkey ed
monthly
-**mooring**
-**moorland**
-**Moslem / Muslim**
mother ed

muddle d
muddling
muddy -ier, -iest
mudguard
***muffin** teacake
***muffing** missing a shot or catch
muffle d
muffling
mugger
mugging
muggy -ier, -iest
mulberry -ies
mumble d
mumbling
mummy -ies
mundane
***muscat** wine / grape
***muscle** body tissue
muscled
muscling
mushroom ed
***musket** gun
-**Muslim / Moslem**
***muslin** fine thin cotton
***mussel** shellfish
mustang
***mustard** plant with hot-tasting seeds
muster
***mustered** called together
mustn't
musty -ier, -iest
mutter ed
mutton
muzzle d
***muzzling** putting a muzzle on

* * *

misjudging

monetary
motherhood

mulberry -ies
multiple
multiply -ies
multiplied
multitude
muscatel
muscular

Here the 'ou' is a neutral vowel.
moustache

* * * * * *

-**maturity**

monetary
mother-in-law
mother-of-pearl

multicultural ly
multilateral ly
multimedia
multi-million
multinational
multiplicand
multiplication
multiplicative
multiplicity
multiplier
musculature

for Scots: ur & ir are on page 249

-or oo as in woodpecker 

In these words you can hear the sound u as in duck 

N

*

***none** not any
-nook

nudge d
null
numb ed
***nun** woman in convent
nut

* *

knuckle d
knuckling

-neural
-neuron / neurone

nothing

nudging
nugget
number ed
nutmeg
nutty -ier, -iest
nuzzle d
nuzzling

* * *

nonetheless
nourishment

nullify -ies
nutcracker

* * * * * **

-neurological ly
-neurologist
-neurology

for Scots: ur & ir are on page 249

O

*

once
***one** 1
oops

*won gained

for H . . . see page 123

* *

august

-obscure d
obstruct

one-off
oneself
one-way
onion

other

oven

* * *

-obscuring
obstruction
obstructive

occurrence

otherwise

* * * *

-obscurity -ies

for Scots: ur & ir are on page 249

-or oo as in woodpecker

In these words you can hear the sound u as in duck

P

SHORT VOWEL **u** SHORT VOWEL **oo**

*

plucked
plugged
***plum** fruit
***plumb** lead weight on a cord / do work of plumber
plumbed
plumped
plunged
pluses
plush

***-poor** badly off
***-pore** tiny hole / study closely
***-pour**ed flow out

pub
puffed
pug
-pulled
pulped
pulsed
pumped
punned
punches
punched
punk
punt
pup
***-pure** unmixed
***pus** liquid from poisoned place
-pushes
-pushed
***-puss**es cat
***-put** place
-[put]
***putt** hit golf ball gently / throw weight

* *

plover
plugging
plumber
plumbing
plundered
plunging
-plurally

-poorer
-poorest
-poorly

-procured

publicly
publishes
published
-pudding
puddled
puddling
puffin
-pulley
-pulpit
pulsar
pulsing
pumice
pumpkin
punctually
punctured
pungent
punishes
punished
punning
puppet
puppy-ies
-purely
-pushchair
-pussy-ies
putted
putter
***-putting** placing
***putting** doing putts
putty-ies
puttied
puzzled
puzzling

* * *

percussion
percussive

-pluralist
-plurally

presumptuous
-procuring
production
productive
propulsion

publican
publicised
publicly
publisher
publishing
-pullover
punctually
punctuate
puncturing
punishment
-purify-ies
-purified
-Puritan / puritan
-purity

* * * * *

-pluralism

presumptuous
pronunciation

publication
publicising
publicity
pulmonary
punctually
punctuating
punctuation
-purification
-puritanical
-puritanism

for Scots: ur & ir are on page 250

Q

*

* *

Qur'an / Koran

* * *

* * * *

-or oo as in woodpecker 

In these words you can hear the sound u as in duck 

R

*

-rook
-room
***rough** uneven / harsh / crude
roughed

rub bed
ruck
***ruff** collar
rug
rum
rump
run
[ran]
[run]
***rung** step of ladder / sounded
runt
rush es
rushed
rusk
rust
rut ted

*wrung twisted

* *

refund
result

roughage
roughen ed
roughly

rubber
rubbing
rubbish
rubble
rucksack
rudder
ruddy -ier, -iest
ruffle d
ruffling
Rugby
rugged
rugger
rumba
rumble d
rumbling
rummy
rumpus es
runner
running
runny -ier, -iest
runway
rupture d
rushing
Russia
Russian
rustic
rustle d
rustling
rusty -ier, iest
rutted
rutting

* * *

recover ed
recurrence
recurrent
reduction
redundant
reluctance
reluctant
republic
repulsive
resultant
resulted
resulting
revulsion

-rookery -ies

ruffian
runaway
runner-up
rupturing

* * * * *

recovery -ies
redundancy -ies
reluctantly
republican
resuscitate
resuscitating
resuscitation

-Romania / Roumania / Rumania

for Scots: ur & ir are on page 251

-or oo as in woodpecker

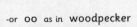

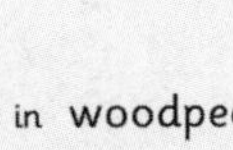

In these words you can hear the sound u as in duck

S

*

scrub bed
scruff
scrum
***scull** ed row / oar
sculpt
scum

-**shook**
-**should**
shove d
shrub
shrug ged
shrunk
shunt
shush es
shushed
shut
[shut]

***skull** bone of the head
skunk

sludge
slug
slum med
slump ed
slunk
slush

smudge d
smug
smut

snuff ed
snug

***some** a certain number or amount
***son** male child
-**soot**

sponge d
sprung
spun

* *

scrubbing
scuffle d
scuffling
sculptor
sculptress es
sculpture
scumbling
scurry -ies
scurried
scuttle d
scuttling

-**secure** d

-**shouldn't**
shovel led
shrugging
shudder ed
shuffle d
shuffling
shutdown
shutter ed
shutting
shuttle d
shuttling

sluggish
slumber ed
slumming
slurry

smother ed
smudging
smuggle d
smuggler
smuggling

snuffing
snuffle d
snuffling
snuggle d
snuggling

somehow
someone
something
sometime
sometimes
somewhat
somewhere
***sonny** laddie
southern

* * *

scullery -ies

seduction
seductive

shrubbery -ies
shuttlecock

slovenly

somebody
somersault
son-in-law

-**spurious**

structural ly
structuring
studying

subdivide
submarine
subsection
subsequent
subsidence
subsidise d
ze
subsidy -ies
substantive
substitute
subtitle d
subtitling
subtlety -ies
subtrahend
suddenly
sufferer
suffering
suffocate
sulphuric
sultana
summarise d
ze
***summary** -ies brief account
summertime
***summery** like summer
sumptuous
sunflower
supplement
suppleness

* * * * *

circumference

-**security** -ies

structurally

subcommittee
subdividing
subjectivity
subsequently
subsidising
zing
substituting
substitution
subterranean
subtropical
suffocating
summarising
zing
supplementary -ies

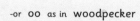

for Scots: ur & ir are on page 252

-or oo as in woodpecker

In these words you can hear the sound u as in duck

*

-stood
struck
strum med
strung
strut ted
stub bed
stuck
stud ded
stuff ed
stump ed
stun ned
stung
stunk
stunt

such
suck ed
suds
sulk ed
***sum** med total / exercise with numbers
***sun** source of sunlight
sung
sunk
sunned
-sure

swung

* *

splutter ed
sponging
spongy -ier, -iest
-sputnik

stomach ed
structure d
struggle d
struggling
strumming
strutting
stubbing
stubble
stubborn
stubby -ier, -iest
studding
study -ies
studied
stuffing
stuffy -ier, -iest
stumble d
stumbling
stunning
stutter ed

subject
subset
subsoil
substance
subtle
subtly
suburb
subway
***succour** help
***sucker** person or thing that sucks / shoot from stem or root / person who is easily tricked
suckle d
suckling
suction
sudden
suffer ed
suffix es
suffrage
-sugar ed
sulky -ier, -iest
sullen
sully -ies
sullied
sulphate
sulphur
sultan
☛

for Scots: ur & ir are on page 252 ▶

-or oo as in woodpecker 

* *

summer
summing
summit
summon ed
summons
sumptuous
sunbathe d
sunburn ed
[sunburnt]
***sundae** sweet dish
***Sunday** day
sundry -ies
sunflower
sunken
sunlight
sunlit
sunning
***sunny** -ier, -iest light and pleasant
sunrise
sunset
sunshade
sunshine
sunstroke
suntan ned
supper
supple
-**surely**
suspect

for Scots: ur & ir are on page 252

In these words the first letter 'u' is a neutral vowel. It sounds like the 'u' in 'suspicious'.

S*U*CCESSFUL WORDS

subdue d
subduing
subject ed
subjection
subjective
submerge d
submerging
submission
submissive
submit ted
submitting
subordinate
subscribe d
subscribing
subscription
subside
subsidiary -ies
subsiding
subsist
subsistence
substantial ly
subtend
subtract
subtracting
subtraction
suburban
succeed
success es
successful ly
succession
successive
successor
succinct ly
sufficient ly
suggest ed
suggestible
suggesting
suggestion
suggestive
supplied
supplier
supply -ies
support ed
supporter
supporting
suppose d
supposedly
supposing
suppress es
suppressed
suppression
surrender ed
surround ed
surrounding
surroundings
susceptibility -ies
susceptible
suspect ed
suspend
suspense
suspension
suspicion
suspicious ly
sustain ed
sustainable

-or oo as in woodpecker

In these words you can hear the sound u as in duck

T

SHORT VOWEL **u** SHORT VOWEL **oo**

*

thrush es
thrust
[thrust]
thud ded
thug
thumb ed
thump ed
thus

***ton** measure of weight
tongue d
***tonne** 1000 kilos
-**took**
touch es
touched
tough
-**tour** ed

truck
trudge d
trunk
truss es
***trussed** tied up firmly
***trust** faith

tub
tuck ed
tuft
tug ged
***tun** large barrel
tusk

* *

thorough
thudded
thudding
thumbnail
thunder ed

tongue-tied
touchdown
touching
touchline
touchy -ier, -iest
toughen ed
tougher
toughest
-**tourist**

trouble d
troubling
trudging
trumpet ed
truncheon
trundle d
trundling
trussing
trustee

tubby -ier, -iest
tugging
tumble d
tumbling
tummy -ies
tundra
tungsten
tunnel led
turret
tussle d
tussling

* * *

thoroughbred
thoroughfare
thoroughly
thunderbolt
thunderclap
thundercloud
thunderous
thunderstorm
thunderstruck

-**tournament**

troublesome
trumpeted
trumpeting
trustworthy

tunnelling

* * * *

thoroughgoing

for Scots: ur & ir are on page 253

-or **oo** as in woodpecker

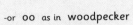

In these words you can hear the sound **u** as in duck

U

SHORT VOWEL **u** SHORT VOWEL **oo**

*

up ped

us

* *

onion

other

oven

udder

ugly -ier, -iest

ulcer
Ulster

umpire d

unarmed
unbend
[unbent]
unbind
[unbound]
unblock ed
unbolt
unborn
unchanged
uncle
unclean
unclear
under
*__undo__ reverse an act
[undid]
[undone]
undress es
undressed
*__undue__ beyond normal limits
unearth ed
unfair
unfit ted
unfold
unharmed
unheard
unhurt
unjust
unkind
unknown
unlatch es
unlatched
unless
unlike
unload
unlock ed
unpack ed
unpaid
*__unreal__ not actual
*__unreel__ unwind
unrest
unroll ed

* * *

otherwise

ugliest
ugliness

ultimate

umbrella
umpiring

unable
unabridged
unafraid
unaided
unaware
unbeaten
unbroken
unbutton ed
uncanny -ier, -iest
uncertain
unchallenged
uncommon
unconcerned
unconscious
uncontrolled
uncover ed
undamaged
undaunted
undefined
underclothes
underfoot
undergo
[underwent]
[undergone]
underground
undergrowth
underlie
[underlay]
[underlain]
underline d
undermine d
underneath
underscore d
undersell
[undersold]
understand
[understood]
undertake
[undertook]
[undertaken]
underwear
underworld
underwrite
[underwrote]
[underwritten]
undisturbed
undoing

* * * * * *

ultimately
ultimatum
ultrasonic ally
ultraviolet

unabated
unacceptable
unaccountably
unaffected
unambiguous ly
unattractive
unavailable
unavoidable
unbearable
unbelievable
unbreakable
uncannier
uncanniest
uncertainty -ies
uncomfortable
uncomfortably
uncompromising
unconditional ly
unconsciously
uncontrollable
unconventional ly
uncooperative
undecided
undeniable
undercover
undercurrent
underdeveloped
underestimate d
underestimating
undergraduate
underlining
underlying
undermining
understandable
understandably
understanding
understudy -ies
understudied
undertaken
undertaker
undertaking
underwater
underwriting
underwritten
undesirable
undoubtedly

for H . . . see page 123

for Scots: ur & ir are on page 254

-or oo as in woodpecker

In these words you can hear the sound u as in duck

* *

unsafe
unscathed
unscrew ed
unseen
unskilled
unsolved
unsure
untie d
until
unto
untold
untouched
untrained
untrue
unused
unveil ed
unwell
unwind
[unwound]
unwise
unwrap ped

update
upgrade
uphill
uphold
[upheld]
upkeep
upland
uplift
upload
upper
upright
uproar
uproot
upset
[upset]
upside
upstairs
upstream
upsurge
uptake
upturn ed
upward
upwards

usher ed

utmost
utter ed

* * *

unduly
uneasy -ier, -iest
unemployed
unending
unequal led
uneven
unexplored
unfasten ed
unfinished
unfriendly -ier, -iest
unfurnished
ungrateful ly
unguarded
unhappy -ier, -iest
unhealthy -ier, -iest
unhelpful
uninjured
uninstal led /
uninstall ed
unlawful ly
unlikely
unlucky -ier, -iest
unmarried
unnatural
unnoticed
unpleasant
unravel led
unravelling
unreal
unscramble d
unscrambling
unselfish
unsettled
unstable
unsteady
untangle d
untangling
untidy -ier, -iest
untying
unusual ly
unwanted
unwelcome
unwilling
unworthy
unwrapping

upbringing
upheaval
upholster ed
uprising
upsetting
upside down
up-to-date

* * * * * * *

uneasily
unemotional ly
unemployment
unequivocal ly
unexpected ly
unfamiliar
unfavourable
unforgettable
unfortunate ly
ungratefully
unhappily
unhappiness
unidentified
unimportant
uninhabitable
uninhabited
uninstalling
unjustified
unlawfully
unlimited
unmistakable
unnecessarily
unnecessary
unoccupied
unofficial ly
unorthodox
unpopular
unprecedented
unpredictable
unprotected
unqualified
unquestionably
unravelling
unrealistic ally
unreasonable
unrelated
unreliable
unsanitary
unsatisfactory
unscrupulous ly
unsociable
unspecified
unsuccessful ly
unsuitable
unthinkable
unusually
unwillingness
unwittingly

upholstery

Here the 'u' has a neutral sound.

upon

for Scots: ur & ir are on page 254

-Uranus

-or oo as in woodpecker

utterance
utterly

for H . . . see page 123

In these words you can hear the sound u as in duck

V

*****

******

vulgar
vulture

****

vulnerable

****** ****

vulgarity -ies
vulnerability
vulnerable

for Scots: ur & ir are on page 254

W

*****

once
*one 1

*rung step of ladder / sounded

-wolf wolves
-wolfed
***won** gained
*-**wood** timber / area with many trees
*-**woof!** bark of dog
*-**woof** weft
-wool
*-**would** was willing to / used to / was going to

***wrung** twisted

******

oneself

-woman [women]

wonder ed
wondrous
-wooden
-woodland
-woodwind
-woodwork
-woollen
-woolly
worry -ies
worried
-worsted
-would-be
-wouldn't

****

-womanhood
wonderful ly
wondering
-woodcutter
-woodpecker
worrying

****

wonderfully

for Scots: ur & ir are on page 255

Y

*****

young
*-**your** belonging to you
*-**you're** you are
-yours

******

younger
youngest
youngster
-yourself
-yourselves

yummy -ier, -iest

****

****

-or oo as in woodpecker

In these words you can hear the sound u as in duck

A

LONG VOWEL **ae**

*

ace d
ache d

age d

***aid** help
***aide** helper
***aids** sources of help / does help
***Aids / AIDS** acquired immune deficiency syndrome
***ail** ed grow weak
aim ed
ain't

***ale** beer

ape d

***ate** did eat

eh

*eight 8
eighth

for H . . .
see page 144

* *

abate
ablaze
able
ably
abstain

acclaim ed
aching
acorn
acquaint
acre

afraid

again
against
aged
ageing / aging
agent

ailment

amaze d
amen

ancient
angel
anus es

apex
appraise d
April
apron

arrange d
array ed

ashamed
Asia
Asian
assail ed
astray

attain ed

avail ed

await
awake d
[awoke]
[awoken]
away

éclair

eighteen th
eighty -ies

élite

* * *

abating
abeyance
abrasive

acquaintance
acreage

adjacent

agency -ies

alien

amazement
amazing
amiable

aorta s / -ae

appraisal
appraising
apricot

aqueous

arrangement
arranging

asexual
assailant

atheist
attainment

availing

awaken ed
awaking

eightieth
eisteddfod

élitist

* * * * * *

Albania
alienation

amiable

Arabia

asymmetric al
asymmetry -ies

atheism

Australia

availability
available
aviation
aviator

awakening

élitism

for Scots: ae -r
is on page 236

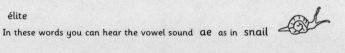

In these words you can hear the vowel sound ae as in snail

B

*

babe
*bail bar on cricket stumps / payment for release / bail out
bailed
bait
*baize cloth
bake d
*bale bundle / bale out
baled
*base foot / central establishment / worthless
*based established
*bass low sound
*baste cover with melted fat / tack together
bathe d
bay ed
*bays more than one bay

beige

blade
blame d
blaze d

brace d
*brae hillside
*braes more than one brae
*braid plait / edging cloth
braille
brain ed
*braise d gently cook in liquid
*braise / braize fish
*brake means of slowing or stopping
brave d
*bray hee-haw
*brayed did bray
*braze d join with hard solder
*break smash in pieces / interrupt / suddenly change [broke] [broken]

* *

babied
baby -ies
bacon
bailey
bailiff
baker
baking
baling
basal
baseball
baseline
basement
basic ally
basin
basing
basis
basting
bathing

became
behave d
betray ed

blaming
blatant
blazer
blazing

bracelet
braces
bracing
braising / braizing
braking
bravely
braving
brazen
brazier
brazing
breakage
breakdown
breakers
breaking
breakthrough
break-up
brigade
brocade

* * *

babysit / baby-sit
bakery -ies
basically
bayonet ed / ted

behaving
behaviour
belated
betrayal

blatantly

bravery
brazier
breakable
breakaway
breakwater

* * * *

babysitter
babysitting
basically
bayoneted / bayonetted

behavioural
belatedly

for Scots: ae -r is on page 236

In these words you can hear the vowel sound ae as in snail

C

LONG VOWEL **ae**

*

cage d
cake d
came
cane d
cape
case d
cave d

chafe d
chain ed
change d
chase
***chased** did chase
***chaste** pure

claim ed
clay

crane d
crate
crave d
craze
crêche
crêpe / crepe

for Qu . . .
see page 148

* *

cable d
cabling
caking
caging
canine
caning
casing
cater ed
caving

chafing
chamber
changing
chaos
chasing

claimant

complain ed
complaint
constrain ed
constraint
contain ed
convey ed

cradle d
cradling
craning
crater ed
craving
crayon ed
crazy -ier, -iest
create
cremate

* * *

capable
catering
causation

changeable
chaotic ally

complacent
contagious
container
conveyor / conveyer
courageous

crayoning
craziest
crazily
created
creating
creation
creative
creator
cremating
cremation
Croatia
crustacean

* * * * *

Canadian
capability -ies

chaotically

complacency

for Scots: ae -r
is on page 236

D

*

dale
dame
***Dane** citizen of Denmark
date
day
***days** more than one day
***daze** state of not thinking clearly
dazed

***deign** pretend to lower oneself socially

drain ed
drake
drape d

* *

dahlia
daily
dainty -ier, -iest
daisy -ies
danger
Danish
data
dated
dating
daybreak
daydream ed
daylight
daytime

debate
debris
début / debut
***decade** ten years
decay ed
***decayed** did decay
décor
defame d
deflate
deist
delay ed
derail ed
detain ed
détente

dictate
disdain ed
disgrace d
dismay ed
displace d
display ed

domain
donate

drainage
draper
draping

* * *

dahlia
daintily
dangerous
database

debating
defaming
deflated
deflating
deflation
deism
deity -ies
derailment

dictating
dictation
dictator
disable d
disabling
disgraceful ly
disgracing
displacement
displacing

donated
donating
donation

drapery -ies

* * * *

dangerously

disablement
disdainfully
disgracefully
distastefully

for Scots: ae -r is on page 237

In these words you can hear the vowel sound ae as in snail 

E

*

*ate did eat

eh

***eight** 8
eighth

for H . . . see page 144

for I . . . see page 144

* *

éclair

eighteen th
eighty -ies

élite

embrace d

encase d
engage d
engrave d
enrage d
enslave d
entail ed

equate

erase d

escape d
estate
estranged

evade

exchange d
exclaim ed
exhale d
explain ed

* * *

eightieth
eisteddfod

elated
elation
élitist

embracing

enable d
enabling
encasing
endanger ed
engagement
engaging
engraving
enraging
enslaving

equating
equation
equator

eraser
erasing

escaping

evading
evasion
evasive

exchanging
exhaling
explaining

* * * *

élitism

extraneous

for Scots: ae -r is on page 237

F

LONG VOWEL **ae**

*

faced
fade
failed
***faint** weak
faith
faked
famed
***fate** destiny
***fay** fairy
***fays** more than one fairy
***faze**d unnerved

feigned
***feint** mock attack
***fete** festival
***fey** strange and otherworldly

flaked
flamed

frail
framed
frayed
***frays** noisy fights / wears away at edges
freight

*phased staged
*phrase meaningful sequence of words, notes or movements in dance
phrased

for th . . .
see page 151

* *

fabled
facecloth
facial
facing
faded
fading
failing
failure
faintly
faithfully
***faker** fraud
faking
***fakir** begging holy man (Muslim or Hindu)
famous
fatally
favoured
favourite

flagrant
flaking
flaming
flavoured

forgave
forsake
[forsook]
[forsaken]

fragrance
fragrant
framework
framing
freighter
Fresnel
frustrate

phasing
phrasing

* * *

faithfully
fallacious
fatally
favourable
favourite

filtration
fixation

flavouring
flotation

formation
forsaken
forsaking

frustrating
frustration

* * * * *

favourable
favourably
favouritism

phraseology

for Scots: ae -r
is on page 238

G

*

Gael Celt
gain ed
gait way of walking
gala
gale strong wind
game
gaol / jail
gaoled / jailed
gape d
gate entrance
gauge d
gave
gay
gays homosexuals
gaze d stare d

glaze d

grace d
grade standard
grain ed
grape
grate grid / rub hard
grave
gray / grey
graze d eat growing grass / scrape the skin
great big / important
grey / gray
greyed turned grey
greys / grays neutral colours between white and black

* *

gable
Gaelic
gaily
gaining
gaming
gaoler / jailer
gaping
gaseous
gatecrash es
gatecrashed
gateway
gauging
gazing

glacial
glazing

graceful ly
gracing
gracious
graded
gradient
grading
grapefruit
grapevine
grateful ly
grater gadget for grating
grating
gratis
graveyard
gravy -ies
grazing
greater more great
greatest
greatly
greatness
grenade
greyhound
grimace d

* * *

gaiety -ies

glacier mass of slow-moving ice
glazier worker who fits glass in windows

gracefully
gradation
gradient
gratefully
grimacing

* * * *

geranium

gymnasium

for Scots: ae -r is on page 238

H

*	* *	* * *	* * * *
***hail** hard frozen	**Haiti**	**halfpenny** -ies	
rain / call name	**halo** ed	**hastily**	
or greetings /	**hasten** ed		
come from	**hasty** -ier, -iest	**herbaceous**	
hailed	**hated**		
***hale** very healthy	**hateful** ly	**hiatus**	
haste	**hating**		
hate	**hatred**		
***hay** dried grass	**haven**		
haze	**haystack**		
	hazel		
***hey!** ho!	**hazy** -ier,-iest		
	heinous		
	heyday		
	humane		
	hurray!		

for Scots: ae -r is on page 238

I

*	* *	* * *	* * * * *
	inflame d	**impatience**	**impatiently**
	inflate	**impatient**	
	inhale d		**incapable**
	innate	**inflaming**	**inflationary**
	insane	**inflating**	**insatiable**
	invade	**inflation**	
		inhaler	**Iranian**
		inhaling	
		invaded	
		invader	
		invading	
		invasion	

for E . . . see page 141

for Scots: ae -r is on page 239

In these words you can hear the vowel sound ae as in snail

J

*

jade
jail / gaol
jailed / gaoled
jay

**

jaded
jailer / gaoler
jailhouse

***

Jamaica
Jamaican

****

geranium
gymnasium

for dr . . .
see page 140

K

*

***knave** rascal

*nave part of church

for C . . .
see page 139

for Qu . . .
see page 148

L

*

laced
laid
***lain** rested
lake
lamed
***lane** narrow road
late
lathe
lay
[laid]
***lays** does lay / poems
***laze** take it easy

**

labelled
laboured
lacing
laden
ladies
ladled
ladling
lady-ies
Laos
***laser** apparatus making light beams that can cut
lately
latent
later
latest
latex
lay-by
layer
laying
layman [laymen]
layout
lazing
lazy-ier, -iest

***

labelling
labourer
ladybird
***lazier** more lazy
laziest
lazily
laziness

liaison

location

lumbago

****

for Scots: ae -r
is on page 239

M

*

mace
***made** formed
***maid** girl
***mail** post / armour
mailed
maim ed
***main** chief / strength
***maize** corn
make
[made]
***male** masculine
***mane** hair, as on neck of horse or lion
mate
may
***maze** puzzle with many paths

* *

maelstrom
maiden
mailbox es
mailer
mainframe
mainland
mainly
mainsail
mainstream
maintain ed
major
maker
makeshift
make-up
making
manger
mangy -ier, -iest
mania
maple
mason
matrix es [matrices]
matron
maybe
maypole

mislay
[mislaid]
mistake
[mistook]
[mistaken]

moraine

mundane

* * *

maintenance
majorette
Malaya
Malaysia
mammalian
mania
maniac
masonry
matriarch
mayonnaise

mistaken
mistaking

* * * *

Malaysia
matriarchal
matriarchy -ies

for Scots: ae -r is on page 239

N

*

*knave rascal

nail ed
name d
***nave** part of church
***nay** no

***née** born with the name...
***neigh** noise made by horses
neighed

* *

naked
namely
naming
narrate
nasal ly
nation
native
nature
***naval** concerning warships
***navel** tummy-button
navy -ies

negate
neighbour

* * *

narration
narrating
narrator
nasally
nationwide

negation
neighbourhood
neighbouring
neighbourly

* * * *

In these words you can hear the vowel sound ae as in snail

O

* * *

obey ed
obtain ed

* * * *

occasion

oration

outrageous

* * * * *

Australia

obtainable

occasional ly

P

*

***faze** d unnerve d
***fays** more than one fairy

***frays** noisy fights / wears away at edges

pace
***paced** did pace
page d
paid
***pail** bucket
***pain** suffering
paint
***pale** whitish
***pane** sheet of glass
***paste** mixture of powder and liquid
pave d
pay
[paid]

***phase** d stage d
***phrase** meaningful sequence of words, notes or movements in dance
phrased

***place** d position
plague d
***plaice** fish
***plain** area of level land / simple
***plane** aeroplane / flat surface / smoothing tool / tree
plate
play ed

***praise** d glorify / high approval
***pray** ask for help
***prays** asks for help
***prey** victim
***preys** hunts to feed

* *

pagan
painful ly
painted
painter
painting
papal
paper ed
parade
pastry -ies
patent
***patience** ability to wait for results
patient
***patients** people under medical treatment
patron
pavement
paving
paying
payment
payroll

persuade
pervade

phrasing

placement
placing
plainly
***plaintiff** person who takes legal action
***plaintive** sad-sounding
player
playful ly
playground
playgroup
playing
playmate
playtime
playwright

portray ed

prevail ed
proclaim ed
profane

* * *

pacemaker
painfully
painstaking
palatial ly
papacy -ies
paperback
paperboy
paperclip
papergirl
paperwork
parading
patiently
patriarch
patriot
payable

persuading
persuasion
persuasive
pervading

playfully
plagiarist

potato es

prevailing
probation

* * * * * *

palaeontologist /
paleontologist
palatially
papier-mâché
patriarchal
patriarchy -ies
patriotic ally
patriotism

phraseology

plagiarism

for Scots: ae -r is on page 239

Q

*

quail ed
quaint
quake d

* *

quailing
Quaker
quaking
quasar
quaver ed

* * *

quotation

* * * *

R

*

race d
rage d
raid
rail ed
***rain** water falling from clouds
rained
***raise** d lift up
rake d
range d
rape d
rate
rave d
ray
***rays** beams
***raze** d tear down

***reign** rule
***rein** strap to control an animal

* *

rabies
racecourse
racehorse
racial ly
racing
racist
***radar** radio detection
raging
***raider** person who raids
railing
railway
rainbow
raincoat
raindrop
rainfall
raining
rainy -ier, -iest
raises
raisin
raising
raking
rapist
rating
raven
raving
rayon
razor

reclaim ed
refrain ed
regain ed
regime / régime
reindeer
relate
remain ed
renege d
repay [repaid]
replace d
restrain ed
restraint
retain ed

* * *

racially
racism
radial ly
radiant
radiate
radio s
radioed
radium
radius [radii]
rainforest
rainier
rainiest
rapier
rateable
ratio s

reagent
related
relating
relation
remainder
remaining
Renaissance
reneging
replacement
replacing
restraining

rotation

* * * * * * *

radially
radiation
radiator
radioactive
radioactivity
radiographer
radiography
radiologist
radiology

relationship

Romania / Roumania / Rumania

for Scots: ae -r is on page 240

S

LONG VOWEL **ae**

*

safe
sage
***sail** travel by boat / sheet fixed to mast
sailed
saint
sake
***sale** selling
same
***sane** of sound mind
save d
say
[said]

scale d
scrape d

***seine** weighted fishnet
***Seine** French river

shade
***shake** move quickly in different directions
[shook]
[shaken]
shale
shame d
shape d
shave d
***sheikh / sheik** Arab ruler

skate
skein

slain
slate
slave d
***slay** kill
[slew]
[slain]
***sleigh** sledge

snail
snake d

space d
***spade** tool
Spain
spate
***spayed** operated on to remove ovaries
sprain ed
spray ed
☛

* *

sable
sabre
sacred
sadist
safeguard
safely
safer
safest
safety
sago
sailing
sailor
salesgirl
salesman [salesmen]
saline
Satan
***saver** person or thing that saves
saving
savings
***saviour** rescuer
***savour** enjoy a taste or smell
saying

***scalar** measurable on a scale
scalene
***scaler** pulse counter
scaling
scaly
scapegoat
scathing
scraper
scraping

séance

shaded
shading
shady -ier, -iest
shaker
shaking
shaky -ier, -iest
shameful ly
shaming
shaver
shaving

skateboard
skater
skating

slater
slaving

snaking
☛

* * *

sadism
salesperson
saleswoman
[saleswomen]
salient
savoury -ies

shakily
shamefully

slavery

spacewoman
[spacewomen]
spatially / spacially

stabilise d
ze
stadium
***stationary** still
***stationery** writing materials
straightaway
straightforward
stratosphere

surveillance
surveying
surveyor

* * * *

stabiliser
zer
stabilising
zing
***stationary** still
***stationery** writing materials

sustainable

for Scots: ae -r is on page 240

S

*

stage d
***staid** serious and dull
stain ed
***stake** stick / bet / prize
staked
stale
state
stave d [stove]
stay
***stayed** did stay
***steak** meat
***straight** without curves
strain ed
***strait** channel
straits
strange
stray ed

***suede** soft undressed leather

sway
***swayed** did sway

* *

spacecraft
spaceman [spacemen]
spaceship
spacesuit
spacing
spacious
spatial / spacial

stable d
stabling
stagecoach
staging
stainless
staking
stalemate
stamen
staple d
stapling
stated
stately
statement
statesman [statesmen]
station ed
status
staving
staying
straighten ed
strangely
stranger
stratus [strati]

survey ed
sustain ed

for Scots: ae -r is on page 240

In these words you can hear the vowel sound ae as in snail

T

*

***tail** part at the back
tailed
taint
take
[took]
[taken]
***tale** story
tame d
tape d
taste

they
they'd
they'll
they've

trace d
trade
trail ed
train ed
***trait** characteristic
***tray** board with raised edges, for carrying things

* *

table d
tabling
tailor ed
taken
takeoff
taking
takings
taming
***taper** ed become thinner towards one end / waxed spill or wick
taping
***tapir** animal
tasted
tasteful ly
tasting
tasty -ier, -iest

terrain

today

tracing
traded
trademark
trader
trading
trailer
trainee
trainer
trainers
training
traitor

* * *

tablecloth
tablespoon
takeaway
takeover
tastefully

tenacious

* * * *

titanium

for Scots: ae -r is on page 241

U

*

* *

* * *

Uranus

* * * *

V

*

vague
***vain** conceited
***vale** valley
***vane** blade
vaned

***veil** ed cover
***vein** blood vessel / mood / streak

* *

vacant
vacate
vaguely
valence
vapour

* * *

vacancy -ies
vacating
***vacation** holiday / process of leaving
valency -ies

vivacious

***vocation** calling / occupation

* * * * *

vocational ly

for Scots: ae -r is on page 241

W

*

*wade walk in water
wage d
waif
*wail ed cry
*wain old farm wagon
*waist narrow part of body
*wait stay
*waive no longer enforce
wake d
[woke]
[woken]
*Wales country
*wane d grow smaller
*waste rubbish
*wave hand signal / surge
waved
*way path

*weigh find the weight of
*weighed found the weight of
*weight heaviness / value

*whale sea-mammal
*whales more than one whale
*whey watery part of sour milk

* *

wading
wader
wafer
wager ed
*wailer loud-crying mourner
waistcoat
*waited did wait
waiter
waiting
waitress es
*waiver releasing statement
*waiving no longer enforcing
waken ed
waking
waning
wastage
wasted
wasteful ly
wasteland
wasting
wavelength
*waver ed hesitate d
*waving using the hand to signal
wavy -ier, -iest
waylay
[waylaid]
wayside

weighbridge
weighing
*weighted having added weight
weightless
weighty -ier, -iest

*whaler ship for whale-hunting
whaling

* * *

wastefully

weightlessness

* * * *

for Scots: ae -r is on page 241

Y

*

yea

* *

* * *

* * * *

A

LONG VOWEL *ee*

*

* *

achieve d

adhere d

agree d

anneal ed
antique

appeal ed
appear ed
appease d

asleep

austere

* * *

achievement
achieving

adhering
adhesive

Aegean
aesthetic ally

agreement

allegiance

amino
amoeba

anaemic / anemic

appearance
appeasement
appeasing

arena

* * * * *

abbreviation

aesthetically

agreeable

amenable
amenity -ies

anaemia / anemia
anaesthetist /
anesthetist

appreciable
appreciate
appreciating
appreciation
appreciative

B

LONG VOWEL ee

*

***be** to be / exist
***beach** es shore
beached
bead
beak ed
beam ed
***bean** vegetable
beard
beast
***beat** batter / defeat
[beat]
[beaten]
***bee** insect
***beech** tree
beef ed
***been** from 'to be'
***beer** drink
***beet** plant with sweet root

***bier** frame to bear coffin

bleach es
bleached
bleak
bleat
bleed
[bled]
bleep ed

***breach** es gap / break
breached
bream
breathe d
***breech** es bottom part of gun
breed
[bred]
breeze d
brief ed

* *

batik

beacon
beagle
beagling
beaker
beanbag
beanstalk
beaten
***beater** person or thing that beats
beating
beaver ed
beehive
beeswax
***beetle** insect
beetroot
being
belief
believe d
beneath
bereave d
[bereft]
beseech es
beseeched
[besought]
besiege d
***beta** Greek letter b
***betel** leaves and nut
between

bleeding

***breaches** gaps / does breach
breathing
***breeches** trousers for riding / bottom parts of guns
breeder
breeding
breezing
briefcase
briefly

* * *

beefburger
beefeater
believer
believing
bereavement
besieging

bikini

* * * *

believable

Here the first letter 'e' has a short 'i' sound.

BEHAVING WORDS

beatitude
became
because
become
[became]
[become]
becoming
befall
[befell]
[befallen]
before
beforehand
befriend
begin
[began]
[begun]
beginner
beginning
behalf
behave d
behaving
behaviour
behavioural
behead
beheld
behind
behold
[beheld]
belated ly
belong ed
belonging s
beloved
below
bemuse d
bemusing
benevolent
benign
bereft
beset
[beset]
besetting
beside
besides
besotted
besought
bestow ed
betray ed
betrayal
betwixt
beware
bewilder ed
bewilderment
bewitch es
bewitched
beyond

In these words you can hear the vowel sound ee as in eagle

C

*

cease d
***cede** give up

***cheap** at low cost
cheat
cheek ed
***cheep** chirp
cheeped
cheer ed
cheese d
chic
chief

clean ed
clear ed
cleat
cleave d
[cleft]
[clove]
[cloven]
clique

***creak** make a high-pitched noise
creaked
cream ed
crease d
creed
***creek** inlet / stream
creep
[crept]

keeled
keen
keep
[kept]
*key lever for lock or other mechanism / important / musical scale
keyed

*quay wharf

*seed part of a plant from which a new one can grow / selected player in a tournament draw

for Qu . . .
see page 167

* *

career ed

ceasefire
ceasing
***cedar** tree
***ceiling** inner roof of room

cheaper
cheapest
cheaply
***cheater** deceiver
cheating
cheeky -ier, -iest
cheerful ly
***cheetah** animal
chiefly
chieftain

cleaner
cleaning
clearance
clearer
clearest
clearing
clearly
cleavage
cleaving
cliché

compete
complete
conceal ed
concede
conceit
conceive d

creasing
creature
creeper
critique

cuisine

keeper
keeping
Kenya
keyboard
keyhole
keynote

kilo
kiosk
kiwi

*sealing fastening
*seeder device for sowing or removing seeds

* * *

casino s
cathedral

***cereal** food from grain / plant producing grain

cheerfully
cheeseburger

clientele

coeliac
competing
completely
completing
completion
conceited
conceiving
concerto s

creosote
critiquing

Korea
Korean

*serial parts in order

* * * * *

chameleon
chemotherapy

comedian
comedienne
congenial ly
convenience
convenient ly

creativity
creosoting

Here the first letter 'e' has a short 'i' sound.

CR*E*ATIVE WORDS

celestial
cement
create d
creating
creation
creative
creator
credential
cremate
cremating
cremation
crescendo s
crevasse

In these words you can hear the vowel sound ee as in eagle

D

LONG VOWEL **ee**

*

deal
[dealt]
***dean** presiding officer
***dear** beloved / expensive
deed
deem ed
deep
***deer** [deer] animal
***dene** small valley

dream ed
[dreamt]

* *

dealer
decease d
deceit
deceive d
decent
decode
decrease d
decree d
deepen ed
deeper
deepest
deeply
defeat
defect
deflate
defrost
degree
deist
delete
demean ed
demon
detail ed
detour

diesel
***discreet** careful not to embarrass
***discrete** separate
disease d
displease d

dreary -ier, -iest

* * *

deceitful ly
deceiving
decency -ies
decoding
decompose d
decreasing
defeated
deflated
deflating
deflation
defragment
deism
deity -ies
deleting
deletion
demeanour
detainee
devalue d
deviance
deviant
deviate
devious

* * * * * * *

deceitfully
decelerate
decelerating
deceleration
decentralisation
zation
decomposer
decomposing
decomposition
decompression
deformation
denitrify -ies
denitrified
deodorant
departmental
deposition
depreciate
depreciating
depreciation
deregulation
deteriorate
deteriorating
deterioration
devaluation
devaluing
deviating
deviation
devolution

In these words the first letter 'e' is pronounced like the short 'i' in 'pig'.

D***E***LIGHTFUL WORDS

debate
debating
decamp ed
decay ed
December
deception
deceptive
decide
deciding
deciduous
decipher ed
decision
decisive
declare d
declaring
decline d
declining
decry -ies
decried
deduce d
deducing
deduct ion
deductive
defect or
defective
defence

defend ant
defender
defensive
defer red
deferring
defiance
defiant
deficiency -ies
deficient
define d
defining
deflect ion
deform ed
defy -ies
defied
delay ed
deliberate ly
deliberating
delicious
delight ed
delightful ly
delirious
deliver ed
deliverance
delivery -ies
delusion

demand ed
demanding
demise
demob bed
democracy -ies
demolish es
demolished
demonstrative
denial
denomination
denominator
denote
denoting
denounce d
denouncing
denunciation
deny -ies
denied
depart ure
department
depend ed
dependable
dependant s
dependence
dependency -ies
dependent

depending
deploy ed
deployment
deport
deposit ed
depositing
depress es
depressed
depression
depressive
deprive d
derail ed
derailment
derivative
derive d
deriving
derogatory
descend ed
descendant
descendent
descent
describe d
describing
description
descriptive
desert ed

deserter
deserve d
deserving
design ed
designer
desirable
desire d
desiring
despair ed
despatch es
despatched
despise d
despising
despite
despondency
despondent
dessert
destroy ed
destroyer
destruction
destructive
detach es
detached
detain ed
detect ion
detective

detector
detention
deter red
detergent
determination
determine d
determining
deterrence
deterrent
deterring
detest
detract
develop ed
developer
developing
development
developmental
device
devise d
devising
devoid
devote d
devoting
devotion
devour ed
devout

In these words you can hear the vowel sound *ee* as in *eagle*

E

LONG VOWEL **ee**

*****

each
ear
ease d
east
eat
[ate]
[eaten]
eaves
eel
eke d
eve

*** ***

eager
eagle
earache
eardrum
earmark ed
earring
easel
Easter
eastern
eastward
easy -ier, -iest
eaten
eating

***eerie / eery** weird

ego
Egypt

***either** one or the other

élite

email / e-mail
emu

endear ed

equal led

era

***ether** solvent
ethos

even
evening
evil ly

exceed
excrete
extreme

***eyrie / eyry** -ies nest of bird of prey

*** * ***

aesthetic ally

eagerly
eagerness
easier
easiest
easily

egoist / egotist

élitist

endearment

equalise d
ze
equalling
equally

evening
evenly

exceeding
excreting
excretion
extremely
extremist

Oedipal
Oedipus
oestrogen

See also E on page 65

See also I on page 72

for H . . . see page 160

for I . . . see page 161

*** * * * * * ***

aesthetically

easygoing

ecclesiastical ly
ecological ly
economic
economical ly
economics
economy -ies
ecosystem
ecumenical ly

egoism / egotism
egoistic / egotistic

élitism
elongation

equalising
zing
equatorial ly
equiangular
equidistant
equilateral
equilibrium

esophagus / oesophagus
[esophagi]

Ethiopia

evangelical
evangelist
evolution
evolutionary

exceedingly
expediency
expedient
experience d
experiencing
exterior

First sound = 'i'.

***E*FFECTIVE WORDS**

eclipse d
eclipsing
ecologist
ecology
economist
edition
effect ive ly
effectiveness
efficient ly
Egyptian
eject or
elaborate
elaboration
elastic ally
elasticity
elated
elation
elect ion
elector
electoral ly
electorate
electric al ly
electrician
electricity
electrocute
electrode
electrolysis
electrolyte
electrolytic ally
electromagnetic ally
electron
electronic ally
electronics
eleven th
elicit ed
eliciting
eliminate
eliminating
elimination
Elizabethan
ellipse
elliptical ly
elope d
eloping
elucidate
elude
eluding
elusive
emancipate d
emancipating

emancipation
emerge d
emergence
emergency -ies
emerging
emission
emit ted
emitting
emotion al ly
emotive
emulsion ed
enable d
enabling
enact
enamel led

enamelling
enamour ed
enormous ly
enough
enumerate
epitome
equality
equate
equation
equator
equip ped
equipment
equipping
equivalence
equivalent

erase d
eraser
erasing
erect ion
erode
eroding
erosion
erotic ally
erratic ally
erroneous ly
erupt ed
eruption
escape d
escaping
escarpment

especially
essential ly
establish es
established
establishment
estate
estrange d
etcetera
eternal ly
eternity
evacuate
evacuation
evacuee
evade
evading

evaluate
evaluating
evaluation
evaporate
evaporating
evaporation
evasion
evasive
event
eventual ly
evict
evoke d
evoking
evolve d
evolving

F

LONG VOWEL ee

*

fear ed
feast
*__feat__ act
fee
feed
[fed]
feel
[felt]
*__feet__ more than one foot

field
fiend
fierce
fiord / fjord

*__flea__ insect
*__flee__ run away
[fled]
fleece d
fleet

freak ed
free d
*__frees__ releases
*__freeze__ chill /change from liquid to solid / hold steady
[froze]
[frozen]
*__frieze__ decorated band / type of cloth

for th . . .
see page 172

* *

faeces
fatigue d

fearful ly
fearless
fearsome
feature d
feeble
feedback
feeding
feeler
feeling
female
fever ed

fielder
fiercely
Fiji
fiord / fjord

fleecing
fleecy -ier, -iest

foetal / fetal
foetus es **/ fetus** es
foresee
[foresaw]
[foreseen]

freebie
freedom
freehand
freehold
freelance d
freely
freeman [freemen]
freer
freestyle
freeware
freezer
freezing
frequent

phenyl

* * *

facetious

fearfully
feasible
featuring
feverish

fiasco s
fiesta

freelancing
frequency -ies
frequently

* * * * *

feasibility

Here the first letter 'e' has a short 'i' sound.

ferocious ferocity frenetic ally

G

LONG VOWEL **ee**

*

gear ed
gee
geek
geese
gene
***genes** more than one gene

ghee

gleam ed
glee

***grease** oily substance
greased
***greave** armour to protect the lower leg
***Greece** country
greed
Greek
green
greet
grief
***grieve** d feel sadness

*jeans trousers
jeep
jeer ed

* *

gearbox es
gee-gee
geekish
geeky
genie
genome
geyser

greasing
greasy -ier, -iest
greedy -ier, -iest
greenbelt
greengage
greenhouse
Greenland
greeted
greeting
grievance
grieving
grievous

Jesus

* * *

galena

genial ly
genius es
genotype

graffiti
greedily
greenery
Greenlander

* * * * *

genealogy -ies
genially
geographic al ly
geological ly
geometric al ly

Here the first letter 'e' has a short 'i' sound.

genetic ally
geography -ies
geology
geometry -ies
geranium
gregarious

H

*

he
***heal** ed cure / get better
heap ed
***hear** receive by ear
[heard]
***hears** does hear
heat
heath
heave d
[hove]
heaved
***he'd** he had / he would
***heed** notice / take seriously
***heel** part of foot / shoe
heeled
***he'll** he will
***here** in this place
***here's** here is
he's

* *

healer
hearing
hearsay
heated
heater
heathen
heating
heatwave
heaving
Hebrew
heedless
heinous
helix es [helices]
hereby
hero es

* * *

haematite / hematite

helium
hereafter
heretofore

* * * *

hysteria

Here the first letter 'e' has a short 'i' sound.

heroic ally

for E . . .
see page 157

See also E
on page 65

See also I
on page 72

*	* *	* * *	* * * * * *
	idea	**idea**	**idealise** d
	ideal ly	**ideal** ly	**ze**
		idealise d	**idealising**
	impede	**ze**	**zing**
			idealism
	increase d	**illegal** ly	**ideally**
	indeed		
	intrigue d	**immediate**	**illegally**
		impeachment	
		impeding	**immediate**
			immediately
		increasing	**imperial** ly
		indecent	**imperialism**
		infrequent	**imperious**
		ingenious	
		intriguing	**increasingly**
			inferior
			inferiority
			ingenious
			ingredient
			interior

J

LONG VOWEL **ee**

*

gee
gene
*genes more than one gene

jeans trousers
jeep
jeer ed

* *

gee-gee
genie
genome

Jesus

* * *

genial ly
genius es
genotype

* * * * *

geneology -ies
genially

for dr . . .
see page 156

K

*

keel ed
keen
keep
[kept]
***key** lever for lock or other mechanism / important / musical scale
keyed

***knead** press with hands
knee
***kneed** hit with the knee
kneel ed
[knelt]

*need require

*quay wharf

* *

keenly
keeper
keeping
Kenya
keyboard
keyhole
keynote
keypad
keyword

kilo
kiosk
kiwi

kneeler

* * *

Korea
Korean

* * * *

for C . . .
see page 155

for Qu . . .
see page 167

In these words you can hear the vowel sound **ee** as in **eagle**

L

LONG VOWEL **ee**

*

***lea** meadow
***leach** es cause a liquid to pass through
***lead** show the way by going first / leash [led]
leaf [leaves]
league
***leak** unwanted escape
leaked
lean ed [leant]
leap ed [leapt]
lease
***leased** rented
leash es leashed
***least** smallest amount
leave [left]
leaves
***lee** shelter / sheltered side
***leech** es bloodsucker
***leek** vegetable
leer ed

***lied** German song

* *

leaching
***leader** leading person or thing
leading
leaflet
leafy -ier, -iest
leaning
leapfrog ged
leasehold
leasing
***leaver** person who leaves
leaving
leeward
legal ly
legion
lesion
lethal ly
***lever** tool
levered

***lieder** German songs
litre

* * *

leadership
leafier
leafiest
legalise d
ze
legally
lenient
leotard
leverage

liaison
Lima-bean

* * * * *

legalisation
zation
legalising
zing

Liberia

Here the first letter 'e' has a short 'i' sound.

legality -ies
legato
legitimacy -ies
legitimate
lethargic

M

*

*me myself
mead
meal
*mean intend / miserly / poor [meant]
means
*meat flesh of animal
meek
*meet be in contact / encounter [met]
mere
*mete deal

*mi third note in a musical scale
*mien bearing / look of person

* *

machine d
marine

meagre
mealtime
meaning
meantime
meanwhile
measles
meaty -ier, -iest
meeting
merely
*meter measuring machine
metered
methane
*metre unit of length / verse rhythm

misdeal [misdealt]
mislead [misled]

mystique

* * *

machining
machinist
Madeira
marina

meaningful ly
meaningless
*meatier more substantial
media
median
mediate
medium
*meteor shooting star
meteorite

misleading

* * * * * * * *

machinery
material ly
materialism
materialist
materialistic

meaningfully
mediation
mediator
mediocre
meteorite
meteorological ly
meteorology

mysterious ly

Here the first letter 'e' has a short 'i' sound.

meander ed
mechanic ally
medicinal ly
melodic ally
melodious
memento es / s
memorial
meniscus es/-i
meridian
methodical ly
meticulous
metropolis es
mnemonic

N

LONG VOWEL ee

*

*knead press with hands
knee
*kneed hit with the knee
kneel ed
[knelt]

near ed
neat
***need** require

niche
niece

* *

kneeler

nearby
nearer
nearest
nearing
nearly
neatly
needed
needle d
needless
needling
needy -ier, -iest
negro es
neither
neon

* * *

needlessly

* * * * *

Neapolitan
neolithic

Here the first letter 'e' has a short 'i' sound.

necessity -ies
negate
negation
neglect
neglectful ly
negotiable
negotiate
negotiating
negotiation
negotiator

O

*

* *

oblique
obscene

* * *

Oedipal
Oedipus
oestrogen

* * * *

obedience
obedient

oesophagus / esophagus
[oesophagi]

P

LONG VOWEL *ee*

*

***pea** vegetable
***peace** period without war
peach es
***peak** highest point
***peaked** reached a maximum / pinched
***peal** ringing
***pealed** rang
peat
***pee** urinate
***peek** peep
***peel** rind / skin
***peeled** removed the rind or skin
peen ed
peep ed
***peer** ed look hard / person of equal rank / lord

***piece** part
***pieced** correctly fitted
***pier** upright support / structure extending into the sea
pierce d
***pique** hurt pride
***piqued** annoyed
***piste** ski run

plea
plead
***pleas** requests
***please** used when asking / give pleasure
pleased
pleat

police d

***pre-** prefix meaning 'before'
preach es
preached
preen ed
priest
***prix** French for 'prize'

* *

peaceful ly
peacetime
peacock
peahen
peanut
peevish
penal
penis es
people d
perceive d

phenyl
phoenix

pianist
piano s
piecing
pierrot

pleasing

police d
policeman [policemen]
policing

preacher
precede
precinct
prefect
prefix es
prefixed
pre-school / preschool
pretext
preview
pre-war
priestess es
priesthood
proceed

* * *

paedophile
paprika

peaceable
peacefully
penalise d
ze
period

pianist
piano s
pierrot

placebo s

policeman [policemen]
policewoman [policewomen]
policing

preceded
preceding
premature
premium
premolar
presuppose d
previous
procedure
proceeding
proceedings

* * * * * *

paediatric
paediatrician
paedophilia

penalising
zing
periodic
periodical
periodically

pianoforte

policewoman [policewomen]

predecessor
prefabricate
prehistoric ally
presupposing
previously
proscenium

In these words the first letter 'e' is pronounced like the 'i' in 'pig'.
PH*E*NOMENAL WORDS

peculiar	[phenomena]	preliminary -ies	presiding
peculiarity -ies	precaution	prepare d	presumably
pedestrian	precipitate	preparing	presume d
peninsula	precipitating	prescribe d	presuming
peninsular	precipitation	prescribing	presumptuous
perimeter	precise ly	prescription	pretence
peripheral ly	precision	present ed	pretend ed
periphery -ies	precocious	presentable	pretentious
peroxide	predict able	presenting	prevail ed
petition ed	prediction	preservative	prevailing
petroleum	predominant ly	preserve d	prevent
phenomenal ly	prefer red	preserving	prevention
phenomenon	preferring	preside	preventive

Q

*

*key lever for lock or other mechanism / important / musical scale

*quay wharf
queen ed
queer
quiche

* *

quayside
queasy -ier, -iest
query -ies
quinine

* * *

* * * *

R

*

reach es
reached
*read look at and understand
[read]
*real genuine
ream ed
reap ed
rear ed
*reed plant / vibrating strip
reef ed
*reek ed stink
*reel ed spool / wind / stagger

*wreak ed bring about
wreath ed

* *

ravine

reaches
reaching
react
reader
reading
realise d
ze
really
reamer
rearm ed
reason ed
rebate
rebound
rebuild
[rebuilt]
recede s
receipt
receive d
recent
recess es
recessed
reclaim ed
recoil ed
recount
redeem
redo
[redid]
[redone]
refill ed
reflex es
refuel led
refund
regain ed
regent
regime / régime
region
regroup ed
reject
☛

* * *

reaction
reactor
readable
readjust
reagent
realising
zing
realism
realistic ally
reappear ed
rearrange d
reasoning
reassure d
recapture d
receding
receiver
receiving
recently
reconstruct
recycle d
recycling
refuel led
refuelling
regional ly
reinforce d
releasing
relieving
renaming
repayment
repeated
repeating
replacement
replacing
reproduce d
researcher
retailer
retrieval
retrieving
reunion
rewiring
rewritten
rewriting

rheostat

* * * * * *

reactionary -ies
realistically
reality -ies
rearranging
reasonable
reasonably
reassemble
reassurance
reassuring
recapturing
rechargeable
reconstitute
reconstruction
redevelopment
refuelling
regionally
rehabilitation
reincarnation
reinforcement
reinforcing
reiteration
relaxation
remedial
reorganisation
zation
reorganise d
ze
reorganising
zing
repatriate
repatriating
repatriation
repercussion
reproducing
reproduction
reproductive
restructuring
reunification
reunion

In these words you can hear the vowel sound ee as in eagle

* *

*__relaid__ laid again
relapse
relay
[relaid]
*__relayed__ sent on as received
release d
relief
relieve d
remake
[remade]
remit
renal
rename d
repay
[repaid]
repeal ed
repeat
repent
replace d
replay
reprieve d
research es
researched
reset
[reset]
retail ed
retell
[retold]
retread
retreat
retrieve d
reveal ed
rewire d
rewrite
[rewrote]
[rewritten]

routine

Here the first letter 'e' has a short 'i' sound.

R*E*FRESHING WORDS

rebel led
rebelling
rebellion
rebellious
rebound
rebuke d
rebuking
recall ed
receptacle
reception ist
receptive
receptor
recession
recessive
recipient
reciprocal ly
reciprocate
recital
recite
reciting
reclaim ed
recline d
reclining
recoil ed
record ed
recorder
recording
recount
recourse
recover ed
recovery -ies
recruit
recuperate
recur red
recurrence
recurrent
recurring
redemption
reduce d
reducing
reduction
redundancy -ies
redundant
refer red
referral
referring
refine d
refinery -ies
refining
reflect ed
reflection
reflector
reflexive
reform ed
refract ion
refractive
refrain ed
refresh es
refreshed
refreshment
refrigerator
refund
refusal
refuse d
refusing
refute
refuting
regain ed
regard ed
regardless
regatta
regret ted
regretful ly
regretting
rehearsal
rehearse d
rehearsing
reject ion
rejoice d
rejoicing
rejoin ed
relate d
relating
relation ship
relax es
relaxed
relent less
reliability
reliable
reliance
religion
religious
relinquish es
relinquished
reluctance
reluctant ly
rely -ies
relied
remain ed
remainder
remaining
remark ed
remarkable
remember ed
remembering
remembrance
remind ed
reminder
remote
removable /
removeable
removal
remove d
removing
Renaissance
renege d
reneging
renew ed
renewal
renown ed
repair ed
repel led
repellent
repelling
repentance
repetitive
reply -ies
replied
report er
repose d
reposing
repress ed
repression
repressive
reprisal
reproach es
reproached
republic an
repudiate
repudiating
repulsive
repute
request
require d
requirement
requiring
resemblance
resemble d
resembling
resent ful ly
resentment
reserve d
reserving
reside
residing
resign ed
resist ance
resistor
resolve d
resolving
resort
resource d
resources
resourcing
respect able
respectful ly
respective ly
respire d
respiring
respond
response
responsibility -ies
responsible
responsive
restore d
restoring
restrain ed
restraint
restrict ion
restrictive
result ed
resultant
resulting
resume d
resuming
resuscitate
resuscitating
resuscitation
retain ed
retard ed
retire d
retirement
retiring
retort
return ed
returnable
returning
revenge d
revenging
reverberate
reverberating
reversal
reverse d
reversible
reversing
review ed
revise d
revising
revision
revival
revive d
reviving
revolt
revolve d
revolver
revolving
revue
revulsion
reward

In these words you can hear the vowel sound ee as in eagle

*

cease d
*cede give up

***scene** part of play / display / place / view
scheme d
scream ed
screech es
screeched
screen ed

***sea** very large area of water / part of an ocean
seal ed
***seam** ed join
***sear** burn the surface with sudden heat
***seas** very large areas of water / parts of oceans
seat
***see** register by eye / understand
[saw]
[seen]
***seed** part of a plant from which a new one can grow / selected player in a tournament draw
***seek** look for
[sought]
***seem** ed appear
***seen** registered by eye / understood
seep ed
***seer** prophet
***sees** does see
seethe d
***seize** grab
seized
***sere** withered
☛

* *

*cedar tree
*ceiling inner roof of room

scenic ally
schema s [schemata]
scheming
screening
screenshot

seafood
seafront
seagull
***sealing** fastening
sealskin
***seaman** sailor
***seamen** sailors
seaport
seashore
seasick
seaside
season ed
seated
seaweed
***secret** kept hidden
***secrete** produce liquid in body / hide
***seeder** device for sowing or removing seeds
seedling
seeing
seeking
seesaw
seething
seizing
seizure
***semen** sperm-carrying liquid
sepal
sequel
sequence
sequin ned
serene
series
serum
settee
severe

shearer
sheepdog
sheepish
sheepskin

***signor** Italian for 'Mr.'
sincere
☛

* * *

*cereal food from grain / plant producing grain

coeliac

scenery
scenically
sclerosis
screensaver

seafarer
seasickness
seasonal
seasoning
secrecy
secreting
secretion
secretive
secretly
seemingly
***senior** older / more important
sequencing
***serial** ly parts in order
serious
severely

signora
Sikhism
sincerely

sleepier
sleepiest
sleepily

speedily

strategic ally

* * * * * *

scenically

seniority -ies
serially
seriously
seriousness

signorina

Slovenia

speedometer

stereotype
strategically

superior
superiority

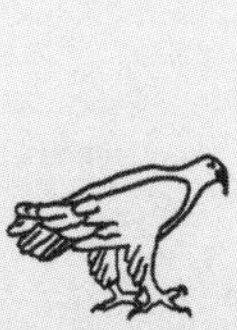

*

she
sheaf [sheaves]
***shear** ed cut off wool or hair [shorn]
shears
sheath ed
she'd
sheen
sheep [sheep]
***sheer** pure / very steep / very thin / go off at an angle
sheered
sheet
she'll
she's
shield
shriek ed

siege
***Sikh** member of an Indian religious group

ski ed

sleek
sleep [slept]
sleet
sleeve d

smear ed

sneak ed
sneer ed
sneeze d

speak [spoke] [spoken]
spear ed
speech es
speed [sped]
sphere
spree

squeak ed
squeal ed
squeeze d

**

skier
skiing

sleeper
sleeping
sleepless
sleepy -ier, -iest
sleeving

sneezing

speaker
speaking
species
speechless
speeding
speedo s
speedy -ier, -iest

squeegee
squeezing

stealing
steamer
steeple
steering
steroid
streaky -ier, -iest
streamer
streaming
streamlined

succeed

Sweden
Swedish
sweeper
sweeping
sweetheart
sweetly
sweetness

*

***steal** thieve / move quietly
[stole]
[stolen]
steam ed
steed
***steel** metal
steeled
steep
steer ed
streak ed
stream ed
street

***suite** pieces that go together

***Swede** Swedish person
***swede** type of turnip
sweep
[swept]
***sweet** of sugary taste / nice

Here the first letter 'e' has a short 'i' sound.

S*E*LECTED WORDS

scenario s
secession
seclude d
secure d
security -ies
seduce d
seducing
seduction
seductive
select ed
selecting
selection
selective ly
selector
semantic ally
semantics
sequential ly
sequoia
serenity
severity -ies
specific ally

T

LONG VOWEL **ee**

*

*tea drink / meal
teach es
[taught]
teak
*team working group / playing side
*teamed made a team
*tear sign of distress
*teas drinks / meals
*tease d mock in fun / comb
teat
*tee support for golf ball
*teem swarm
*teemed swarmed
teens
*tees more than one tee
teeth

thee
theme d
these
thief [thieves]
three

*tier one of a number of levels
tiered

treat
tree

tweed
tweet

* *

T-shirt / teeshirt

teacher
teaching
team-mate
teamwork
teapot
tearful ly
teasing
teaspoon
teatime
teeming
teenage
teepee / tepee
teeshirt / T-shirt
teething

theatre
theorem
theorist
theory -ies
thesis -es

trapeze
treacle
treason
treating
treatment
treaty -ies
treetops
trio

tweezers

* * *

tearfully
teaspoonful
tedious
tedium
teenager

three-quarters

trachea

* * * * * *

theatrical ly
theodolite
theologian
theological ly
theology -ies
theoretical ly

trapezium

Here the first letter 'e' has a short 'i' sound.

TERRIFIC WORDS

telegraphy
telephonist
terrestrial ly
terrific ally
thematic ally
thesaurus es / -i
tremendous ly

In these words you can hear the vowel sound ee as in eagle

V

LONG VOWEL **ee**

*	* *	* * *	* * * *
veal	**vehement**	**vehement**ly	**vehemently**
	vehicle	**vehicle**	
via	**veneer**ed	**Venetian**	
	***venous** concerned with veins	**vetoing**	
	***Venus** planet / goddess of love	**viola**	
	vetoes vetoed		
	via		
	visa		

In these words the first 'e' is a neutral vowel.

velocity -ies | veranda / verandah

W

LONG VOWEL **ee**

*

*reek ed stink

***we** people speaking
***weak** feeble
***weal** mark left on skin by whip
***weald** open or wooded country
***weave** interlace threads [wove] [woven]
***we'd** we had / we would
***wee** small / pass water
***weed** passed water
***weed** unwanted wild plant
***week** seven days
weep [wept]
***weir** dam across river
weird
***we'll** we will
***we're** we are
***we've** we have

wheat
***wheel** round rotating frame or disc
***wheeled** did wheel
wheeze d

***wield** have and use

***wreak** ed bring about
wreath ed

* *

weaken ed
weaker
weakest
weakling
***weakly** feebly
weakness es
weary -ier, -iest
weasel
weaver
weaving
weekday
weekend
***weekly** every week / a weekly magazine
weeping
weevil
werewolf [werewolves]

wheelchair
wheeler
wheelie s
wheezing

* * *

wearily
weariness

wheelbarrow

* * * *

In these words you can hear the vowel sound ee as in eagle

Y

*	* *	* * *	* * * *
ye	**year-old**		
year	**yearly**		
yeast			
	yielding		
yield			

Z

*	* *	* * *	* * * *
zeal	**Zaire**		
	zebra		
	zero es / s		

A

*

*aisle part of church / gangway

*aye yes

*eye visual organ

*I the person speaking
*I'll I will

for H . . .
see page 182

* *

abide

acquire d

admire d
advice
advise d

alight
align ed
alike
alive
ally -ies
allied

apply -ies
applied

arise
[arose]
[arisen]
arrive d

ascribe d
aside
aspire d
assign ed

awhile
awry

* * *

abided
abiding

acquiring

admirer
admiring
adviser
advising

alignment
alliance
almighty

appliance
applying

arising
arrival
arriving

ascribing
aspiring
assignment
asylum

* * * * *

advisable
advisory

annihilate
annihilating
annihilation

In these words you can hear the vowel sound ie as in lion

B

LONG VOWEL **ie**

*

bide d
[bode]
***bight** broad bay / loop
bike d
bile
bind
[bound]
***bite** tear with teeth
[bit]
[bitten]

blight
blind

bribe d
bride
bright
brine

***buy** purchase
[bought]
***buyer** purchaser

***by** beside / not after / past / through / on
***bye** goodbye / pay-off for not playing
***byre** cow-house
***byte** unit of information

* *

behind
benign
beside
besides

bias ed / sed
***Bible** holy book for Christians
***bible** copy of Bible / best reference book
biceps
biking
binder
binding
biped
biro
bisect
bison
biting

blimey!
blindfold
blindly
blindness

bribing
***bridal** of the bride
bridegroom
bridesmaid
***bridle** headgear for controlling a horse
bridled
bridling
brighten ed
brighter
brightest
brightly
brightness

***buyer** purchaser
buying

bye-bye
bygone
bypass ed
byway

* * *

biasing / biassing
bicycle d
bicycling
bifocal
bilingual
binary
biofuel
biopsy -ies
bisector

bribery

by-product

* * * * * *

biennial ly
bifurcated
bilateral ly
binomial
biochemical
biochemist
biochemistry
biodiesel
biographer
biographical ly
biography -ies
biological ly
biologist
biology
biotechnology

by-election

In these words you can hear the vowel sound ie as in lion

C

*

child
chime d
*__choir__ singing group / part of church
Christ

*__cite__ give as an example / quote

*__climb__ ed go up / upward slope
*__clime__ climate

cried
cries
crime
cry -ies
cried

kind
kite

*quire 24 sheets of writing paper

*sight vision
*site place

for Qu . . .
see page 189

* *

childbirth
childhood
childish
chiming
china
China
Chinese

cider
*__citing__ quoting

client
climate
climax es
climaxed
climber
climbing

collide
combine d
compile d
comply -ies
complied
comprise d
concise
confide
confine d
conspire d

crisis [crises]
crying

cycle d
cycling
cyclist
cyclone
*__cypress__ es tree
*__Cyprus__ island

kayak

kindly
kindness

psychic ally

*sighting act of spotting
*siting placing

* * *

climatic
clitoris

colliding
combining
compiling
comprising
confiding
confinement
confining
conspiring

cybershop
cyberspace

kinetic ally

psychical ly
psychosis [psychoses]
psychotic ally

* * * * * *

climatology

criterion [criteria]

cybercafé
cyclorama
cytoplasm

kaleidoscope

kinetically

psychiatric ally
psychiatrist
psychiatry
psychically
psychoanalyse d
psychoanalysis
psychoanalyst
psychological ly
psychologist
psychology
psychotherapist
psychotherapy
psychotically

D

*

dial led
dice d

* *

decide
decline d
decry -ies
decried

* * *

decided
deciding
decipher ed
decisive
declining

* * * *

delightfully
desirable

In these words you can hear the vowel sound ie as in lion

D

LONG VOWEL ie

*

***die** cease living / small cube / tool for stamping or shaping
died
dike / dyke
***dine** have dinner
dined
***dire** desperate
dive d

dried
drive
[drove]
[driven]
dry -ies
dried

***dye** d stain
***dyer** person using dyes
dyke / dike
***dyne** unit of force

* *

define d
defy -ies
defied
delight
demise
deny -ies
denied
deprive d
derive d
describe d
design ed
desire d
despise d
despite
***device** gadget / plan
***devise** d invent / work out

dial led
dialling
diamond
diary -ies
dicey
dicing
diecast
diet
digest
dilute
dining
direct
disguise d
dislike d
dissect
diver
diverge d
diverse
divert
divide
divine d
diving

***drier** more dry / machine that dries
driest
drily / dryly
driver
driveway
driving
***dryer / drier** person, substance or machine that dries
drying
dryly / drily

***dyeing** using dye
***dying** ceasing to live

* * *

defiance
defiant
defining
defying
delighted
delightful ly
denial
depriving
deriving
describing
designer
desiring
despising
devising

diagnose d
diagram
dialect
dialling
dialogue
diamond
diaphragm
diarrhoea
diatom
dicier
diciest
didactic
dietary
digestion
dilemma
diluted
diluting
dilution
dimension
dining-room
dinosaur
dioxide
directed
direction
directive
directly
director
disciple
disguising
disliking
divergent
diverging
diversion
diverted
divided
dividers
dividing
divining
divisor

dynamic ally
dynamite
dynamo s

* * * * * * *

diabetes
diabetic
diabolical ly
diagnosing
diagnosis -es
diagnostic ally
diagonal ly
diagrammatic ally
dialectic al ly
diameter
diarrhoea
dichotomy -ies
dietary
digestible
dimensional
directory -ies
diversification
diversify -ies
diversified
diversity

dynamically
dynamometer

In these words you can hear the vowel sound ie as in lion

E

LONG VOWEL **ie**

*

*aye yes

*__eye__ visual organ
*__eyed__ looked at with interest

*I the person speaking
*I'd I would / I had

*for H . . .
see page 182*

*for I . . .
see page 183*

* *

eider
either

enquire / inquire d
entire

esquire

excite
expire d

eyeball
eyebrow
eyeing / eying
eyelash es
*__eyelet__ small hole
eyelid
eyesight

*islet small island

* * *

eisteddfod

enlighten ed
enquiring / inquiring
enquiry / inquiry -ies
entirely
entitle d
entitling

excited
excitement
exciting
expiring

eyewitness es

* * * * * * *

encyclopedia
entitlement
environment
environmental ly
environmentalism
environmentalist

excitable
excitedly

In these words you can hear the vowel sound ie as in lion

F

*

fight
[fought]
***file** tool / information system / line of people
filed
***find** discover
[found]
fine
***fined** made to pay a fine
fire d
five

flier / flyer
flies
flight
fly -ies
[flew]
[flown]

***friar** religious man who lived by begging
fried
***frier / fryer** person or equipment that fries
fright
fry -ies
fried
***fryer / frier** person or equipment that fries

*phial small vessel or bottle

for th . . .
see page 192

* *

fibre
fibrous
fiery
fighter
fighting
filename
filing
final
finance d
finding
finely
finer
finest
fining
finite
firearm
firefly -ies
firelight
fireman [firemen]
fireplace
fireproof
fireside
firewall
firewood
firework
firing
fiver

flier / flyer
flying
flywheel

***friar** religious man who lived by begging
Friday
***frier / fryer** person or equipment that fries
frighten ed
frightening
frightful ly
***fryer / frier** person or equipment that fries

*phial small vessel or bottle
phylum [phyla]

* * *

fibreglass
fibrosis
finalise d
ze
finalist
finally
financial ly
financing
fire-engine
firefighter
firewoman [firewomen]

frightening

* * * *

finalising
zing
finality
financially
financier

forsythia s

In these words you can hear the vowel sound ie as in lion

G

*

*gibe / jibe taunt

glide

*gneiss rock

grime
grind
[ground]

*guide show the way
*guise appearance
guy
*guyed ridiculed
*guys more than one guy / does guy

*gybe / gibe / jibe alter course by swinging sail

jive d

*nice pleasant

* *

Geiger

giant
*gibing / jibing taunting

glider
gliding

goodbye
goodnight

grimy -ier, -iest
grinder

guidance
guideline
guiding

*gybing / gibing / jibing altering course by swinging sail
gyrate

jiving

* * *

gigantic
ginormous

Guyana

gyrating
gyroscope

* * * * ***

gynaecological ly
gynaecologist
gynaecology
gyroscopic

H

*

height

*hi greeting
hide
[hid]
[hidden]
*high tall / great
*higher taller / greater
hike d
hind
*hire d grant or obtain use if a payment is made / employ
hive d

hype d

* *

haiku

heighten ed

hiding
hi-fi
*higher taller / greater
highest
highlands
highlight
highly
Highness
highrise
highroad
highway
hijack ed
hiker
hiking
hindsight
hiring
hiving
*hiya greeting

hybrid
hygiene
hyphen

* * *

Hawaii
Hawaiian

hiatus es
hibernate
highwayman

horizon

hyacinth
hydraulic ally
hydrofoil
hydrogen
hydroxide
hygienic ally
hyperlink
hypertext
hyphenate

* * * * ***

hibernating
hibernation
hierarchical
hierarchy -ies
hieroglyphics

hydraulically
hydrocarbon
hydrochloric
hydroelectric ally
hydrometer
hygienically
*hyperbola form of curve
*hyperbole exaggeration
hyphenated
hypochondria
hypochondriac
hypotenuse
hypothesis [hypotheses]
hypothetical ly

In these words you can hear the vowel sound ie as in lion

I

LONG VOWEL ie

*

*aisle part of church / gangway

*aye yes

*eye visual organ
*eyed looked at with interest

*I the person speaking

ice d

I'd I would / I had

I'll I will

I'm

ion charged particle

iron metal
ironed

isle island

I've

for E . . .
see page 180

* *

eider
either

*eyelet small hole

iceberg
ice-cream
ice-floe
Iceland
icing
icon / ikon
icy -ier, -iest

idea
ideal ly
idle lazy
idly
idol image for worship

ignite

ikon / icon

imply -ies
implied

incite urge
incline d
indict
inquire / enquire d
inscribe d
inside
insight understanding
inspire d
invite

ion charged particle

irate
Ireland
iris es
Irish
iron metal
ironed
ironing

island
islet small island

item

ivy

* * *

eisteddfod

icicle

idea
ideal ly
idealise d
ze
idolise d
ze

ignited
igniting

incisive
incisor
incited
inciting
inclining
indictment
inquiring / enquiring
inquiry / enquiry -ies
inscribing
insider
inspiring
invited
inviting

iodine
iota

Irishman
ironic ally
ironing
irony -ies
ironmonger

islander
isolate
isotope

itemise d
ze

ivory -ies

* * * * * * *

idealism
idealistic ally
idealise d
ze
idealising
zing
ideally
identical ly
identifiable
identification
identified
identifier
identify -ies
identified
identity -ies
ideological ly
ideology -ies
idolising
zing

ironical ly
ironmonger

isolated
isolation
isometric ally
isomorphic
isosceles
isotopic

itinerant
itinerary -ies

In these words you can hear the vowel sound ie as in lion

J

*

*gybe / gibe / jibe alter course by swinging sail

***jibe / gibe** taunt
jive d

* *

giant

*gybing / gibing / jibing altering course by swinging sail
gyrate

***jibing / gibing** taunting
jiving

* * *

gigantic
ginormous

gyrating
gyroscope

* * * *

gyroscopic

for dr . . .
see page 179

K

*

kind
kite

knife [knives]
knifed
***knight** Sir — / chess piece

*night hours of darkness

* *

kayak

kindly
kindness

knifing

* * *

kinetic ally

* * * * *

kaleidoscope

kinetically

for C . . .
see page 178

for Qu . . .
see page 189

In these words you can hear the vowel sound ie as in lion

*

*liar **person who tells lies
lice
*lie**d tell untruth
*lie** place oneself in a horizontal position
[lay]
[lain]
life [lives]
light
[lit]
liked
limed
lined
lion
lithe

*lye** caustic solution
*lyre** musical instrument

* *

*liar** person who tells lies
*libel** harmful statement
*licence** official permission
*license**d give official permission
*lichen** plant
lidos
lifeboat
lifeless
lifelike
lifelong
lifespan
lifestyle
lifetime
lighted
lighter
lightest
lighthouse
lighting
lightly
*lightning** electric flash in the sky
lightweight
likely
*liken**ed point out similarities
likenesses
likewise
liking
lilac
limeade
limelight
limestone
liner
linesman [linesmen]
lining
linos
lion
lively -ier, -iest
livestock

lying
*lyre** musical instrument

* * *

*liable** likely / under obligation
library -ies
licensing
*lightening** making lighter
likelihood
livelihood
liveliness

* * * * *

liability -ies
Liberia
librarian
librarianship

In these words you can hear the vowel sound ie as in lion

M

*

mice
***might** would perhaps / power
mild
mile
mimed
***mind** system of thought and feeling / look after / watch / object
mine
***mined** did mine
mired
***mite** tiny thing

my

* *

maestros

mica
micros
microbe
mighty
migrant
migrate
mildly
mileage
milestone
miming
mindfully
mindless
***miner** worker in mine
mining
***minor** less important
minus
minute
miser
mitred
mitring

myself

* * *

Messiah

microchip
microphone
microscope
microwave
mightily
migrating
migration
migratory
mindfully

* * * * *

microcomputer
micrometer
microprocessor
microscopic
minority -ies
mitochondria

In these words you can hear the vowel sound ie as in lion

N

*

*gneiss rock

knife [knives]
knifed
*knight Sir — / chess piece

*nice pleasant
nigh
*night hours of darkness
nine
ninth

* *

knifing

naive

neither

nicely
nicer
nicest
nightclub
nightdress
nightfall
nightie
nightmare
night-time
nineteen th
ninety -ies
nitrate
nitric

nylon

* * *

nightingale
ninetieth
nitrify -ies
nitrified
nitrogen

* * * * *

Nigeria
nitrification
nitrifying

O

*

* *

alright

oblige d

* * *

almighty

obliging

* * * *

P

*

*file tool / information system / line of people

*phial small vessel or bottle

*pi 3·142 / Greek letter
*pie meat or fruit baked in pastry
pied
pike
pile d
pine d
pint
pipe d

pliers
plight
ply -ies
plied

price d
*pride high opinion of oneself
*pried did pry
*pries does pry or prise
prime d
prior
*prise / prize lever with a metal bar
*prised did prise
*prize reward / hold dear / prise
*prized did prize
pry -ies
pried

pyre

* *

perspire d

*phial small vessel or bottle
phylum [phyla]

piling
pilot
pining
pious
pipeline
piper
piping
pirate

pliers
plywood

polite

precise
prescribe d
preside
priceless
pricing
priding
primal
primate
priming
prior
priory -ies
*prising levering with a metal bar
private
*prizing holding dear / prising
provide

psyche
psychic ally

pylon
python

* * *

papyrus

perspiring

piety
pineapple
pioneer
pirated
pirating

politely

precisely
prescribing
presiding
primacy
primary -ies
primeval
priory -ies
privacy
privately
privatise d
ze
provided
provider
providing

psychical ly
psychosis [psychoses]
psychotic ally

pyrites

* * * * * * * *

primarily
priority -ies
privatisation
zation
proprietor

psychiatric ally
psychiatrist
psychiatry
psychically
psychoanalyse d
psychoanalysis
psychoanalyst
psychoanalytic ally
psychological ly
psychologist
psychology
psychotherapist
psychotherapy
psychotically

pyrotechnic

In these words you can hear the vowel sound ie as in lion

Q

*

*choir singing group / part of church

quiet
***quire** 24 sheets of writing paper
quite

* *

quiet

* * *

quietly

* * * *

R

*

Reich

***rhyme / rime** to end with the same sound
rhymed

rice
ride
[rode]
[ridden]
***right** correct / direction
rile d
***rime** hoar-frost
rind
ripe
rise
[rose]
[risen]
***rite** ceremony

***rye** grain

*write set down on paper
[wrote]
[written]
writhe d
*wry twisted

* *

recite
recline d
refine d
rely -ies
relied
remind
reply -ies
replied
require d
reside
resign ed
respire d
retire d
revise d
revive d
rewrite
[rewrote]
[rewritten]

rhyming

ribald
rider
riding
rifle d
rifling
righteous
rightful ly
right-hand
rightly
right-wing
riling
riot ed
ripen ed
rising
rival led

writer
writing
wryly

* * *

recital
reciting
reclining
refining
reliance
relying
reminded
reminder
replying
reprisal
requirement
requiring
residing
respiring
retirement
retiring
revising
revival
reviving
rewriting

rifling
rightfully
rioted
rioting
riotous
rivalling
rivalry -ies

* * * * * *

refinery -ies
reliability
reliable

rhinoceros es / -i

riboflavin

S

LONG VOWEL **ie**

*

*cite give as an example / quote

scribe
scythe d

shine
[shone]
***shire** county
shrine
shy -ies
shied
***shyer** more shy

***side** edge / surface / aspect / team
sigh
***sighed** did sigh
***sighs** more than one sigh
***sight** vision
***sign** ed mark with a meaning
***sine** function of an angle
sire d
***site** place
***size** spatial extent / a weak glue
sized

sky -ies

***sleight** quickness
slice d
slide
[slid]
***slight** small / thin and delicate / treat without respect
slime
sly

smile d
smite
[smote]
[smitten]

snide
snipe d

* *

cider
cipher ed
*citing quoting

cycle d
cycling
cyclist
*cypress es tree
*Cyprus island

psychic ally

science
scientist
scriber
scribing
scything

seismic

shining
shiny -ier, -iest
***shyer** more shy
shyly / shily
shyness

Siam
sideboard
sidelight
sideline d
sidetrack ed
sideways
siding
***sighting** act of spotting
signing
signpost
silage
silence d
silent
silo s
siphon
siren
siring
sisal
***siting** placing
sizing

skylark
skyline

slicing
sliding
slightest
slightly
slimy -ier, -iest
slyly / slily

* * *

psychically
psychosis [psychoses]
psychotic ally

saliva

scientist

seismograph

Siamese
sidelining
silencer
silencing
silently
sizable / sizeable

skydiving
skyscraper

society -ies

spiralling
spirally
spitefully

stylistic ally

subscribing
subsidence
subsiding
sufficing
supplier
supplying
surprising
survival
surviving
survivor

* * * * * *

cybercafé
cytoplasm

psychiatric ally
psychiatrist
psychiatry
psychically
psychoanalyse d
psychoanalysis
psychoanalyst
psychoanalytic ally
psychological ly
psychologist
psychology
psychotherapist
psychotherapy
psychotically

salivary

scientific ally

seismology

Siberia

society -ies

stylistically

surprisingly

In these words you can hear the vowel sound ie as in lion

S

*

spice d
spike d
spine
spire
spite
splice d
spline d
spy -ies
spied

squire

***stile** barrier
with steps
stride
[strode]
[stridden]
strife
strike
[struck]
[stricken]
stripe d
strive
[strove]
[striven]
***sty** -ies pen for pigs /
eye infection
***stye** s eye infection
***style** manner
styled

swine
swipe d

* *

smiley
smiling
smitten
smiting

sniper
sniping

spicing
spicy -ier, -iest
spider
spiking
spiky -ier, -iest
spinal
spiral led
spiral ly
spiteful ly
splicing
sprightly -ier, -iest
spying
spyware

stifle d
stifling
stipend
strident
striding
striker
striking
striving
styling
stylish
stylist
stylus es / -i

sublime
subscribe d
subside
suffice d
supply -ies
supplied
surprise d
survive d

swiping

T

LONG VOWEL **ie**

*

***Thai** citizen of Thailand
***thigh** upper part of leg
thine
thrice
thrive d
[throve]
[thriven]
***thy** your
***thyme** herb

***tide** ebb and flow
***tie** fasten with knot
***tied** fastened with knot
tight
tights
tile d
***time** period
timed
***tire** make weary / ring fitted to wheel
tired

trial led
tribe
tripe
try -ies
tried

twice
twine d

type d
***tyre** ring fitted to wheel

* *

Taiwan

Thailand
thriving
thyroid

tidal
tiding
tidings
tidy -ies
tidied
tiger
tighten ed
tightly
tiling
timeless
timely -ier, -iest
timer
timescale
timing
tiny -ier, -iest
tiresome
tiring
title d

tonight

triad
trial led
trialling
tribal ly
tribesman
triceps
trifle d
tripod
triumph ed
trying

twilight

tycoon
tying
typhoon
typing
typist
tyrant

* * *

thiamine

tidier
tidiest
tidily
tidying
timetable d
timetabling
tinier
tiniest

trialling
triangle
tribunal
tricycle
tripartite
triumphal ly
triumphant

typewriter

* * * *

titanium

triangular
triangulation
triceratops
triumphally
triumphantly

In these words you can hear the vowel sound ie as in lion

V

*

via
***vial** small bottle
vibe s
vice
vie d
***vile** disgusting
vine
***viol** stringed instrument

* *

via
***vial** small bottle
vibrant
vibrate
Viking
vinyl
***viol** stringed instrument
violence
violent
violet
viper
viral
virus es
viscount
visor
vital ly

vying

* * *

vagina
vaginal

viable
viaduct
vibrating
vibration
violate
violence
violent ly
violet
violin
vitally
vitamin

* * * * *

variety -ies

viability
vicarious ly
vice-president
vice-versa
vicissitude
violating
violation
violently
vitality
vivarium

W

*

*right correct / direction
*rite ceremony

*rye grain

***while** time / during the time that
***whiled** did while
whilst
***whine** d complain
white
why
***whys** causes / reasons

wide
wife -ves
***wild** untamed
***wile** trick
***wind** move by turning [wound]
***wine** drink
***wined** supplied with wine
wipe d
wire d
***wise** very sensible

***write** set down on paper [wrote] [written]
writhe d
***wry** twisted

* *

whiling
whining
Whitehall
whitewash es
whitewashed
whiting
whitish

widely
widen ed
wider
widespread
wi-fi
wildlife
wildly
wily -ier, -iest
winding
wining
wiper
wiping
wireless es
wiring
wiry -ier, -iest
wisely
wiser
wisest

writer
writhing
writing
wryly

* * *

* * * *

X

*	* *	* * *	* * * *
		xylophone	

Z

*	* *	* * *	* * * *
	Zaire	xylophone	

In these words you can hear the vowel sound ie as in lion

A

*

* *

abode

afloat

ago

alone
although

approach es
approached

arose

atone d

awoke

* * *

aerobic

approaching

aroma

atonement
atoning
atrocious

awoken

* * * * *

ammonia
ammonium

appropriate ly

associate d
associating
association
associative

for Scots: oe -r
is on page 256

B

*

***beau** dandy

bloke
blow
[blew]
[blown]

boast
boat
***bode** did bide
***bold** brave
***bole** tree-trunk
***boll** seed capsule
bolt
bone d
both
***bow** wood and string / knot / bend
***bowed** curved like a bow
***bowl** container / send a ball
***bowled** rolled / bowled out
bowls

***broach** es open up
broached
broke
***brooch** es ornament

* *

behold
[beheld]
below
bestow ed

blokey
blower
blowing
blowlamp
***blowup / blow-up** enlargement / big row
***blow-up** inflatable
***blow up** enlarge / inflate / destroy by explosion

boatman [boatmen]
***bogey / bogie / bogy** evil spirit
***bogey** one stroke over par / dried snot
***bogie** trolley
bogus
bolster ed
boning
bonus es
bony -ier, iest
boulder
bouquet
bowler
bowling

brocade
brochure
broken
broker

* * *

* * * *

In these words the first letter 'o' is a neutral vowel. It sounds like the 'o' in 'policeman'.

Bolivia bonanza botanical

for Scots: oe -r
is on page 257

C

*

choke d
chose
chrome d

cloak ed
clone d
close
closed
***clothe** d provide with clothes
***clothes** garments
***clove** spice / did cleave
***cloves** spice

coach es
coached
coal
coast
coat
***coax** es gently persuade
coaxed
code
coke d
***Cokes** more than one Coca Cola
cold
colt
comb ed
cone
cope d
cove

croak ed
crow ed
[crew]
[crown]

for Qu . . . see page 206

* *

chauffeur ed
choking
-**choral**
-**chorus** es
-**chorused**
chosen
chroming

cloakroom
closely
closing
closure
clothesline
clothing
clover

coastal
coastline
coating
cobalt
cobra
cocoa
coding
coerce d
colder
coldness
coleslaw
cologne
colon
coma
compose d
console d
control led
coping
corrode
cosine
cosy / cozy -ier, -iest

crochet ed
crocus es / -i
croquet
crowbar

kosher

* * *

chauvinist
chromatic
chromium
chromosome

cirrhosis

coconut
coercing
coherent
coincide
commotion
component
***composer** writer of music
composing
***composure** calmness
conifer
consoling
controller
controlling
corroding
corrosion
corrosive
cotangent

Croatia

kimono s

koala

* * * * * *

chauvinism
chauvinistic

coagulate
coagulating
coalition
coefficient
coincidence
collinear
colloquial ly
colonial ly
colonialism
coniferous
cooperate
cooperating
cooperation
cooperative
coordinate
coordinating
coordination
coordinator

custodial

for Scots: oe -r is on page 258

In these words the first letter 'o' is a neutral vowel. It sounds like the 'o' in 'policeman'.

COMMUNICATING WORDS

cholesterol	collection	comedian	commencing	committing	communion
chorale	collective ly	comedienne	commercial ly	communal ly	community -ies
cocoon ed	collector	command er	commission ed	commune d	commutative
collapse d	collide	commandment	commissioner	communicate	commute
collapsible	colliding	commemorate	commit ted	communicating	commuter
collapsing	collision	commemoration	commitment	communication	commuting
collect ing	colossal ly	commence d	committee	communing	corrupt ion

D

*

*__doe__ female deer
*__does__ more than one female deer
*__doh__ keynote
*__doh!__ how stupid!
dole d
dome d
don't
dope d
dose d
*__dough__ flour and water
*__doze__ d snooze d

droll
drone d
drove

* *

decode
denote
devote

disclose d
disown ed
dispose d

docile
doling
domain
donate
donor
dosing
doughnut
dozing

droning

* * *

decoding
denoting
devoted
devoting
devotion

diploma
disclosing
disclosure
disposal
disposing

domestic ally
donated
donation

* * * * *

deodorant

diplomacy
disposable

domestically
domesticate

for Scots: oe -r is on page 259

E

*

for H . . . see page 200

for I . . . see page 200

* *

elope d

enclose d
encroach es
encroached
enfold
engross es
engrossed
enrol led

erode

evoke d

explode
expose d

* * *

eloping

emotion
emotive

enclosing
enclosure
enrolling
enrolment

eroding
erosion

evoking

exploding
explosion
explosive
exponent
exposing
exposure

* * * * *

eau-de-cologne

emotional ly

erroneous ly

for Scots: oe -r is on page 259

F

*

float
***floe** floating ice-sheet
***flow** ed run

foal
***foaled** given birth to a foal
foam ed
foe
***fold** bend double / crease / sheep enclosure
folk

fro
froze

phone d

for th . . .
see page 208

* *

floated
floating
flowchart
flowing

foamy -ier, -iest
focal
focus es / ses / -i
focused / focussed
folded
folder
folding
folklore
foretold
forgo / forego
[forwent / forewent]
[forgone / foregone]

frozen

phobic
phoneme
phoning
photo s

* * *

ferocious

fibrosis

flotation

focusing / focussing
foliage
folio
fovea
foveal

phobia
photograph ed

* * * * * *

photocopier
photocopy -ies
photocopied
photoelectric
photofinish
photographic ally
photosynthesis

for Scots: oe -r
is on page 260

In these words you can hear the vowel sound oe as in goat

G

*

ghost

gloat
globe
glow ed

gnome

go
[went]
[gone]
goad
goal
goat
goes
gold

*__groan__ deep moan
groaned
grope d
gross ed
grove
grow
[grew]
*[grown] developed
growth

* *

ghostly -ier, -iest

global ly
glowing
glow-worm

goalie
goalpost
goatskin
gobo
going
golden
goldfish
goldsmith
gopher

*__grocer__ shopkeeper selling food and other goods
groping
*__grosser__ fatter / more disgusting
grossly
grotesque
grower
growing
grown-up

* * *

globally

goalkeeper

grocery -ies

* * * *

for Scots: oe -r is on page 261

In these words you can hear the vowel sound oe as in goat

H

*

hoax es
hoaxed
hoe d
***hoes** more than one hoe
***hold** grip / support / continue [held]
***hole** opening
***holed** hit ball into hole
holt
home d
hope d
***hose** flexible water-pipe / stockings
hosed
host
hove

*whole total / complete

* *

hallo / hello / hullo

holder
holding
hold-up
***holey** full of holes
holing
holster
***holy** -ier, -iest sacred
homeland
homeless
homely -ier, -iest
homemade
homepage
homesick
homestead
homeward
homework
homing
hopeful ly
hopeless
hoping
hosepipe
hosing
hostess es
hotel

wholegrain
wholemeal
wholesale
wholesome
*wholly totally / completely

* * *

heroic ally

holiness
holistic ally
hologram
holograph
homelessness
hopefully
hopelessly
hopelessness
hosiery

hypnosis

* * * * * * *

heroically

holistically
homeopathic ally
homeopathy
homogeneous
homosexual ly
homosexuality
hotelier

for Scots: oe -r is on page 261

Here the first letter 'o' has a neutral sound.
holography horizon horrendous horrific ally

I

*

for E . . . see page 197

* *

impose d

invoke d

* * *

immobile
imposing

invoking

* * * *

for Scots: oe -r is on page 262

In these words you can hear the vowel sound oe as in goat

J

*

joke d

**

joker

***

jovial ly

****

jovially

for dr . . .
see page 197

K

*

knoll
***know** understand
[knew]
[known]
***knows** does know

*no not any
*nose part of face

**

know-how
knowing

kosher

***

kimono s

knowingly

koala

****

In these words the first letter 'o' is a neutral vowel. It sounds like the 'o' in 'policeman'.

Korea Korean

for C . . .
see page 196

for Qu . . .
see page 206

L

*

***lo** behold
***load** amount carried
loaf [loaves]
loafed
loam
***loan** ed lend / amount lent
***loath / loth** unwilling
***loathe** d hate
lobe
***lode** vein of metal ore / ditch
***lone** single
lope d
***low** not high / moo
***lowed** mooed

**

loaded
loathing
loathsome
local ly
locate
locus [loci]
locust
lodestone
logo s
lonely
lonesome
loping
lotion
lotus
low-cost
lower ed
lowest
lowland
lowlands
lowly

***

locally
located
location
loneliness

****

locality -ies
locomotion
locomotive
loganberry -ies

for Scots: oe -r
is on page 263

M

*

mauve

***mo** moment
***moan** ed complain
***moat** surrounding defensive ditch
***mode** way / fashion
mole
mope d
most
***mote** speck
mould
moult
***mow** cut with blades
*[mowed] cut
*[mown] cut

* *

mobile
mocha
modem
molar
molten
moment
moping
morose
Moses
mostly
motel
***motif / motive** theme / figure
motion ed
***motive** cause of action
motor ed
mouldy -ier, -iest
mower

* * *

mobilise d
ze
Mohammed
molasses
momentary
momentous
momentum
***mosaic** a design made up of small pieces
***Mosaic** Moses-related
motionless
motivate
motorbike
motorist
motorway

* * * * *

melodious

mobilisation
zation
mobility
molecular
momentarily
momentary
motivation
motorcycle

for Scots: oe -r is on page 263

In these words the first letter 'o' is a neutral vowel. It sounds like the 'o' in 'policeman'.

moraine
morale
morality

N

*

gnome

knoll
*know understand
[knew]
[known]
*knows does know

***no** not any
node
***nose** part of face
nosed
note

* *

know-how
knowing

noble
Noel
nomad
no-one
nosebleed
nosing
nosy -ier, -iest
notebook
noted
notice d
notion
nova
nowhere

* * *

knowingly

neurosis -es

nobleman
[noblemen]
nobody
nomadic
notable
notably
notation
noteworthy
notify -ies
notified
November

* * * * *

negotiable
negotiate
negotiating
negotiation
negotiator

nobility
noticeable
noticeably
notification
notoriety
notorious

O

LONG VOWEL **oe**

*

oak
oath
oats

***ode** long poem

***oh!** exclamation

old

***owe** must pay
***owed** did owe
own ed

* *

oatmeal

obese
obey ed
oblique
oboe

ocean
ochre

odour

ogre
ogress es

okay ed

older
oldest

omen
omit ted

only
onus es

opal
opaque
open ed
opening
oppose d
opus es [opera]

-oral ly

***ova** eggs
oval
***over** above
overt
ovum [ova]

owing
owner

ozone

for H . . .
see page 200

* * *

oasis [oases]

odious

old-fashioned
Olympic

omission
omitted
omitting

opening
openly
openness
opium
opponent
opposing

-orally

ovary -ies
ovation
overall
overalls
overarm
overboard
overcast
[overcast]
overcoat
overcome
[overcame]
[overcome]
overdo
[overdid]
[overdone]
overdose
overdraft
overdrive
overdue
overeat
[overate]
[overeaten]
overfeed
[overfed]
overflow ed
overgrow
[overgrew]
[overgrown]
overhang
[overhung]
overhaul ed
overhead
overhear
[overheard]
overjoyed
overlap ped
overload
overlook ed

* * * * *

eau-de-cologne

obedience
obedient
obesity
obituary -ies

oceanic
oceanography

overcoming
overlapping
overlooking
overwhelming ly

for Scots: oe -r
is on page 264

In these words you can hear the vowel sound oe as in goat

O

In these words the first letter 'o' sounds like the neutral 'o' sound in 'policeman'.

*O*BLIGING WORDS

obligatory
oblige d
obliging
obliterate
obliterating
oblivion
oblivious
occasion
occasional ly
occur red
occurrence
occurring
o'clock
offence
offend
offender
offensive
official ly
opinion
opossum
oppression
oppressive
oppressor
original ly
originality
originate
originating

for H . . .
see page 200

* * *

overnight
overpower ed
override
[overrode]
[overridden]
overrun
[overran]
[overrun]
overseas
oversee
[oversaw]
[overseen]
overshoot
[overshot]
oversize
oversleep
[overslept]
overspill
overtake
[overtook]
[overtaken]
overthrow
[overthrew]
[overthrown]
overtime
overtone
overture
overturn ed
overview
overweight
overwhelm ed
overwork ed

ownership

for Scots: oe -r
is on page 264

P

*

phone d

poach es
poached
poke d
***pole** long rod
***poll** number of voters / head / cut off top
polled
pope
pose d
post
☛

* *

patrol led

phobic
phoneme
phoning
photo s
☛

* * *

pagoda
patrolling

phobia
photograph ed

poetic ally
poetry
polarise d
ze
polio
postmaster
postponing
potency
☛

* * * * * *

petroleum

photocopier
photocopy -ies
photocopied
photoelectric
photofinish
photographic ally
photosynthesis
☛

for Scots: oe -r
is on page 265

P

*

pro s
probe d
prone
***pros** points in favour / professionals
***prose** text that is not poetry

* *

poacher
poem
poet
poetry
poker
poking
Poland
polar
pole-vault
Polish
polo
pony -ies
posing
postage
postal
postcard
postcode
poster
posting
postman [postmen]
postpone d
postscript
post-war
posy -ies
potent
potion
poultry

probing
proceeds
process es
processed
profile d
***program** instructions for computer
***programme** plan of performance / broadcast
programmed
progress es
progressed
project
prologue
promote
pronoun
propos
propose d
protein
protest
proton
proven
provoke d

* * *

precocious
processor
profiling
programmer
programming
promoter
promoting
promotion
proposal
proposing
prosaic ally
protocol
prototype
provoking

* * * * *

pneumonia

poetically
polarising
zing
polarity -ies
postgraduate

prohibition
proletariat
proscenium
protoplasm
protozoa

In these words the first letter 'o' is a neutral vowel. It sounds like the 'o' in 'policeman'.

PR*O*GRESSIVE WORDS

phonetic ally
photographer
photography
police
policeman
[policemen]
policewoman
[policewomen]
policing
polite
politely
political ly
pollutant
pollute
polluting
pollution
polyphony
position ed
possess es
possessed
possession
possessive
potato es
potential ly
probation
procedure
proceed ing
proceedings
procession
proclaim ed
procure d
procuring
prodigious
produce d
producer
producing
production
productive
profane
profess es
professed
profession al ly
professionalism
professor
proficiency -ies
proficient
profound
profuse
profusion
progression
progressive ly
prohibit ed
prohibiting
prohibitive
projectile
projection
projector
proliferate
proliferation
proliferating
prolific ally
prolong ed
pronounce d
pronouncement
pronouncing
pronunciation
propel led
propeller
propelling
propensity -ies
proportional ly
proportionate ly
proprietor
propulsion
prospect ive
prospector
prospectus es
protect ed
protection
protective
protector
protractor
protrude
protruding
provide d
provider
providing
provincial
provision s
provisional ly
provocative

for Scots: oe -r is on page 265

In these words you can hear the vowel sound oe as in goat

Q

*

quote
quoth

* *

quota
quotient

* * *

quotation

* * * *

R

*

roach [roach]
***road** track
***roam** ed wander
roan
roast
robe d
***rode** travelled on / by
***roe** fish eggs or sperm / small deer
***roes** more than one roe
rogue
***role** actor's part
***roll** ed turn over and over
***Rome** city
rope d
***rose** flower / did rise
***rote** repetition
rove
***row** line / move with oars
***rowed** moved with oars
***rows** lines / moves with oars

*wrote set down on paper

* *

remote
repose d
reproach es
reproached
revolt
rewrote

roadblock
roadside
roadworks
robing
robot
robust
rodent
role-play
roller
rolling
Roman
romance d
roping
rosebud
rosette
rosewood
rosy -ier, -iest
***rota** system of taking turns to perform tasks
rotate
***rotor** rotating shaft and attachment
roving

* * *

reposing

rococo
rodeo
rolling-pin
romancing
romantic ally
rotary
rotating
rotation

* * * * *

rhododendron

romantically

for Scots: oe -r is on page 266

S

LONG VOWEL **oe**

*

scold
scone
scope
scroll ed

*__sew__ ed stitch
[sewn]

shoal
show ed
[shown]

*__sloe__ blackthorn fruit or bush
slope d
sloth
*__slow__ at a low speed
slowed

smoke d
smote

snow ed

*__so__ therefore / to such a degree / in that way
soak ed
soap ed
*__sold__ given for money
*__sole__ only / part of foot and shoe / fish
*__soled__ fitted with new sole
*__soul__ spirit
*__sow__ ed plant
[sown]

spoke

stoat
stoke d
stole
stone d
stove
stow ed
strobe
strode
stroke d
stroll ed
strove

* *

chauffeur

sauté

scrolling

sewing

shoulder ed

slogan
sloping
Slovak
slower
slowly

smoking
smoky -ier, -iest
smoulder ed

snowball ed
snowdrop
snowfall
snowflake
snowman [snowmen]
snowstorm
snowy -ier, -iest

sober ed
so-called
social ly
soda
sofa
solar
*__solder__ ed join metal
*__soldier__ ed serve in an army / army person
solely
solo s
sonar

spoken
spokesman [spokesmen]

stoking
stolen
stoma s [stomata]
stoneware
stony -ier, -iest
*-__storey__ floor
*-__story__ -ies tale
stowing
stroking
strolling

suppose d

swollen

* * *

chauvinist

samosa

sclerosis

showjumper
showjumping

sociable
socialise d
ze
socialist
socially
sodium
*__soldering__ joining metal
*__soldiering__ acting as an army person
soloist
soviet

spokesperson
spokeswoman
[spokeswomen]

stomata
stowaway

supposing

* * * * * * * * *

chauvinism
chauvinistic

Slovakia

socialisation
zation
socialism
socioeconomic ally
sociological ly
sociologist
sociology
Somalia

supposedly

symposium [symposia]

In these words the first letter 'o' is a neutral vowel. It sounds like the 'o' in 'policeman'.

society -ies
solicitor
solidify -ies
solidified
solidity
soliloquy -ies
solution
sophisticated
sophistication
soprano s
sporadic ally

for Scots: oe -r is on page 267

T

*

those
though
throat
***throe** sharp pain
***throne** state chair
throned
throve
***throw** hurl
[threw]
*[thrown] hurled

***toad** animal
toast
***toe** part of foot
***toed** placed toes against / fitted with a toe
***told** did tell
toll
***tolled** did toll
tone d
tote
***tow** pull behind
***towed** pulled behind

troll

* *

throwing

toadstool
toasted
toastie
tofu
token
tonal ly
toning
topaz
-**Tory** -ies
total led
totem

***trojan** harmful computer program
***Trojan** native of ancient Troy
trophy -ies

* * *

tonally
totalling
totally

* * * *

totality

In these words the first letter 'o' is a neutral vowel. It sounds like the 'o' in 'policeman'.

tobacco s
tobacconist
tomato es
topography
topology
torrential ly

for Scots: oe -r is on page 268

V

*

*-**vault** gymnastic leap / underground room / arched roof

vogue
vole
***volt** unit of electrical force
vote

* *

vocal ly
vocals
voltage
voted
voter
voting

* * *

viola

vocalist
vocally
voltmeter

* * * *

In these words the first letter 'o' is a neutral vowel. It sounds like the 'o' in 'policeman'.

vocabulary -ies
vocation
vocational ly

W

*	**	***	****
*hole opening *rote repetition ***whoa!** stop! ***whole** total / complete ***woe** distress **woke** **won't** **wove** ***wrote** set down on paper	*holey full of holes *holy sacred **wholegrain** **wholemeal** **wholesale** **wholesome** ***wholly** totally / completely **woeful**ly **woken** **woven**	**wholehearted**ly **woefully**	**wholeheartedly**

for Scots: oe -r is on page 269

Y

*	**	***	****
***yoke** neck-piece **yoked** ***yolk** yellow part of egg	**yeoman** [yeomen] **yodel**led / ed **yoga** **yoghourt /** **yoghurt / yogurt** **yogi** **yokel**	**yodelling / yodeling**	

for Scots: oe -r is on page 269

Z

*	**	***	***** **
zoned		**zodiac**	**zoological**ly **zoology**

A

*

for H . . .
see page 215

* *

-**about**
abuse d

accrue d
accuse d
acute

***adieu** goodbye
***ado** confused activity

-**afoot**

***allude** refer
aloof

amuse d

anew

approve d

assume d
-**assure** d

*elude avoid

* * *

abusing

accruing
accusing
acoustic

***allusion** reference

amusement
amusing

approval
approving

assuming
-**assurance**
-**assuring**

*illusion false belief or appearance

* * * * *

accumulate
accumulating
accumulation
accumulator
accusative
acoustical ly

adjudicate
adjudicating
adjudication
adjudicator

alluvial
alluvium

In these words you can hear oo as in smooth or ue as in newt

*

balloon ed

***blew** puffed
bloom ed
***blue** colour

boo ed
-**book** ed
boom ed
-**boor**
***boos** disapproving cries
boost
boot
booth
***booze** d consume alcohol / strong drink

brew
***brewed** fermented
***brews** does brew
***brood** offspring
-**brook** ed
broom
***bruise** injury
bruised
***bruit** spread rumours
***brute** beast

-**bull**
-**bush** es
-**bushed**

* *

baboon
balloon ed
bassoon

***beauty** -ies pleasing example / loveliness
bemuse d

bluebell
blueprint
bluetit

booby -ies
booing
-**bookcase**
-**booklet**
-**bookshelf** [bookshelves]
booster
***bootee** baby's woollen boot
***booty** stolen goods
boozer
boozing
-**bosom**
bouquet
-**bourgeois**
boutique

brewer
bruiser
bruising
brunette
brutal ly

-**Buddha**
-**Buddhist**
bugle
-**bulldog**
-**bullet**
-**bullfrog**
-**bullock**
-**bully** -ies
-bullied
-**bureau**
-**bushel**
-**butcher** ed

* * *

bazooka

beautiful ly
bemusing
Bermuda

blueberry -ies

boulevard
-**bourgeoisie**

brewery -ies
brutalise d
ze
brutally

-**Buddhism**
-**bulldozer** ed
-**bulletin**

* * * * * *

beautifully

brutality

-**bureaucracy** -ies
-**bureaucratic** ally

C

LONG VOWEL ue LONG VOWEL oo

*

chew ed
*chews does chew
*choose select
[chose]
[chosen]
*chute slope for
things to slide down

clue d

*coo ed speak softly /
sound made by pigeon
-cook ed
cool ed
coop
-could
*coup stroke /
successful action
-course d
-court

crew
*crewed acted as a
crew member
*crewel tapestry yarn
*crews more than
one crew
-crook
croon ed
*crude untreated /
done without skill
*cruel ly vicious
*cruise voyage
cruised

cube d
*cue rod / signal
*cued did cue
-cure d
cute

*queue waiting line
*queued did queue

*shoot fire / hit with
bullet / move very fast /
new growth from plant

for Qu . . .
see page 219

* *

canoe d
cashew

chewing
choosing

clueing

cocoon ed
commune d
commute
compute
conclude
confuse d
consume d
-cooker
-cooking
coolant
cooler
coolly
-couldn't
coupé
coupon
-coursing

*crewel tapestry yarn
-crooked
crucial ly
*cruel ly vicious ly
cruelty -ies
cruet
cruiser
cruising
crusade

Cuba
cubic
cuboid
-cuckoo
*cueing / cuing
prompting
culottes
-curate
-curing
-cushion ed

Kuwait

*queueing / queuing
waiting in a line

* * *

canoeing

communal ly
communing
communion
commuter
commuting
computer
computing
concluding
conclusion
conclusive
conducive
confusing
confusion
consumer
consuming
-courier

crucially
crucible
crucifix es
cruciform
crucify -ies
crucified
cruelly
cruelty -ies
crusading

*cubical cube-shaped
*cubicle small room
cubism
cucumber
cumulus
-curating
-curator
-curio s
-curious

* * * * *

circuitous

communally
communicate
communicating
communication
communicative
communion
community -ies
commutative
computerise d
ze

crucifixion

cumulative
-curiosity -ies
-curiously

In these words you can hear oo as in smooth or ue as in newt

D

*

deuce
***dew** moisture

do
[did]
[done]
***doer** active person
doom ed
***dour** unsmiling

drew
droop ed

***dual** double
***due** owing
***duel** led fight
duke
dune

* *

deduce d
dewdrop

diffuse d
disprove d
dispute
disused

doer
doing
doodle d
doodling

***dual** double
ducal
***duel** led fight
duelling
duet
duly
duo s
-**during**
duty -ies
duvet

* * *

deducing
delusion

diffusing
diffusion
disproven
disproving
disputing

dubious
duelling
duplicate
-**durable**
-**duration**
dutiful ly

* * * * *

disunity

duodenal
duplicating
duplication
-**durability**
dutifully

E

*

***ewe** female sheep
***ewes** more than one ewe

*use employ

*yew tree
*yews yew trees

*you person / people

* *

*allude refer

***elude** avoid

-**endure** d
*-**ensure** d make certain

-**euro** s
-**Europe**

exclude
excuse d
extrude

*insure d protect against loss

* * *

eluding
***elusive** hard to find

-**endurance**
-**enduring**
*-**ensuring** making certain

eucharist
-**eureka!**
Eustachian

excluding
exclusion
exclusive
excusing
extruding
extrusion
extrusive

*illusive deceptive

*insuring protecting against loss

* * * * * * *

elucidate

enthusiasm
enthusiast
enthusiastic ally
enumerate
enumerating

eucalyptus es
euphemism
euphonium
-**European**
Eustachian
euthanasia

exclusively
excruciating
exuberance
exuberant

for H . . .
see page 215

for I . . .
see page 215

F

LONG VOWEL **ue** LONG VOWEL **oo**

*

feud
***few** not many

***flew** passed in flight
***flu** influenza
***flue** pipe
fluke
flute

food
fool ed
-**foot**
-**fourth**

fruit

fuel led
fugue
-**full**
fume d
fumes
fuse d

*phew / whew relief!

for th . . .
see page 222

* *

feudal ly
fewer

fluent
fluid
-**fluoride**
-**fluorine**

foodstuff
foolish
foolproof
-**football**
-**foothill**
-**foothold**
-**footpath**
-**footstep**
-**forsook**

frugal
fruitful ly
fruitless

fuchsia
fuel led
fuelling
-**fulcrum**
-**fulfil** led
-**fully**
fuming
-**fury** -ies
fusing
fusion
futile
future

* * *

feudally

fluency
flugelhorn
-**fluorescence**
-**fluorescent**

foolhardy

fruiterer
fruitfully
fruition

fuelling
fugitive
-**fulfilling**
fumigate
funeral
-**furious**
fuselage

* * * * * * *

feudalism

-**fluorescence**
-**fluorescent**
-**fluoridation /**
fluoridisation
zation

foolhardiness
fortuitous ly

frugality

fumigating
-**furiously**
futility

G

*

gloom
glue d

***gnu** horned animal

-**good**
-**goods**
goose [geese]
gourd

grew
groom ed
groove d
group ed

*knew understood

*new unused

* *

gloomy -ier, -iest
glucose
gluten

-**goodbye**
-**goodness**
-**goodnight**
google d
googling
googly -ies
-**gooseberry** -ies
gourmet

grouping
gruelling
gruesome

-**guru** s

* * *

gloomily

-**gooseberry** -ies

gruelling

* * * *

gratuitous

In these words you can hear oo as in smooth or ue as in newt

H

*

***hew** ed cut down
[hewn]

-**hood**
hoof [hooves]
hoofed
-**hook** ed
***hoop** large ring or band
hoop ed
hoot
hooves
-**house**

***hue** colour
huge

*who which person or people
who'd
who'll
whom
*whoop ed shout joyfully
*who's who is
*whose belonging to whom or what

* *

hoover ed
*-**hoummos / hommus / hummous / hummus / houmous / humus** chickpea spread

hugely
hula
***human** person
***humane** showing concern for others
humid
humour ed
***humous** containing humus
***humus** organic matter in soil
-**hurrah!**
-**hurray!**

* * *

hooligan

humanist
***humerus** bone in upper arm
humorist
***humorous** funny

whoever
whooping-cough

* * * * * *

hallucination

humanism
humanitarian
humanities
humanity
humidity
humiliate
humiliating
humiliation
humility

I

*

* *

*-ensure d make certain

immune
improve d
-**impure**

include
induce d
*-**insure** d protect against loss
intrude

* * *

*allusion reference

*elusive hard to find
*-ensuring making certain

***illusion** false belief or appearance
***illusive** deceptive

improvement
improving

included
including
inclusion
inclusive
inducement
inducing
inhuman
-**insurance**
*-**insuring** protecting against loss
intruder
intrusion
intrusive

* * * * *

illuminate
illuminating
illumination
illusory

immovable
immunity
impunity
-**impurity** -ies

-**incurable**
-**infuriate**
-**infuriating**
-**injurious**
innumerable
inscrutable
insuperable
intuitive

*for E . . .
see page 213*

In these words you can hear oo as in smooth or ue as in newt

J

*

*deuce tennis score / devil
*dew moisture

drew

*dual double
*due owing
*duelled fight
duke
*dune hill of sand

***Jew** Jewish person
***jewel** gem

***joule** unit of energy

***juice** liquid from fruit, meat and vegetables
***June** month

for dr . . .
see page 213

* *

*dual double
ducal
*duelled fight
duelling
duet
duly
during
duty -ies
duvet

***jewel**led gem
jeweller
jewellery / jewelry
Jewess es
Jewish
***Jewry** all Jews

judo
juicy -ier, -iest
jukebox es
July
-**juror**
*-**jury** -ies judging panel

* * *

duelling
duplicate
durable
duration
dutifully

Jacuzzi s

jeweller
jewellery / jewelry

jubilant
jubilee
judicial ly
judicious
juicier
juiciest
jujitsu
junior
Jupiter
juvenile

* * * * *

durability
dutifully

jubilation
Judaism
judicially
judiciary -ies
-**jurisdiction**
-**jurisprudence**

K

*

*gnu horned animal

***knew** understood

*new unused

* *

Kuwait

for C . . .
see page 212

* * *

for Qu . . .
see page 219

* * * *

L

*

***lieu** place

***loo** toilet
-**look** ed
loom
loop ed
***loos** toilets
loose d
***loot** stolen goods
***lose** have no longer / fail to win
[lost]

-**lure** d
***lute** musical instrument

* *

lagoon
lasso s / es

-**lookout**
loophole
loosely
loosen ed
loser
losing
louvre

lucid
ludo
lukewarm
lunar
lupin
-**luring**

* * *

lubricant
lubricate
lucrative
ludicrous
luminous

* * * *

leukaemia / leukemia

lubricating
lubrication

In these words you can hear oo as in smooth or ue as in newt

M

*

mew ed
*__mewl__ ed mew
*__mews__ houses converted from stables

moo
*__mood__ state of feeling
*__mooed__ went 'moo'
moon ed
-**moor** ed
*__moose__ animal
-**mourn** ed
*-**mouse** animal
*__mousse__ sweet dish
move d

*__mule__ animal
*__muse__ think deeply
mute

* *

-**manure** d
maroon ed
-**mature** d

-**mistook**
misuse d

moody -ier, -iest
moonlight
moonlit
-**mooring**
-**moorland**
-**Moslem / Muslim**
-**mournful**
-**mourning**
movement
mover
movie
moving

*__mucous__ of / covered with mucus
*__mucus__ slimy liquid
muesli
-**mural**
music ally
musing
-**Muslim / Moslem**
mutant
mutual ly

* * *

manoeuvre d

movable / moveable

museum
musical ly
musician
mutation
mutilate
mutineer
mutiny -ies
mutinied
mutually

* * * * *

-**maturity**

mercurial

municipal ly
musically
mutilating
mutilation

N

LONG VOWEL **ue** LONG VOWEL **oo**

*

*gnu horned animal
*knew understood
***new** unused
***news** reported information
newt
-nook
noon
***noose** loop that can be tightened
-now
nude

* *

-neural
-neuron / neurone
neutral ly
neutron
newborn
newer
newest
newly
newscast
newton
noodle
nougat
nuance
nudist
nuisance

* * *

-neurosis -es
-neurotic ally
neutralise d
ze
neutrally
newcomer
newsagent
newsgroup
newsletter
newspaper
New Zealand
nuclear
nucleus [nuclei]
nudism
nudity
numeral
numeric al
numerous
nutrient
nutrition
nutritious
nutritive
pneumatic

* * * * * *

-neurological ly
-neurologist
-neurology
-neurotically
neutralising
zing
neutrality
numeration
numerator
numerical ly
nutritional
nutritionist
pneumonia

O

*

ooh
oops
ooze d
-out

* *

-obscure d
obtuse
oozes
oozing

* * *

-obscuring

* * * *

-obscurity -ies

for H . . . see page 215

In these words you can hear oo as in smooth or ue as in newt

P

*

*few not many

pew

***phew / whew** relief!

plume d

pool ed
***poor** badly off
***-pour** ed flow out

proof
prove d
[proven]
prune d

-pull ed
***-pure** unmixed
-push es
-pushed
-puss es
-put
-[put]

* *

perfume d
Peru
pewter

platoon
plumage
-plural ly
Pluto

pollute
poodle
-poorer
-poorest
-poorly
-pouring

presume d
-procure d
produce d
profuse
proofread
protrude
proven
prudence
prudent
pruning

-pudding
-pulley
-pulpit
puma
puny -ier, -iest
pupa [pupae]
pupil
-purée
-purely
pursue d
pursuit
-pushchair
-pussy -ies
putrid
-putting

* * *

peculiar
perfuming

-pluralist
-plurally

pneumatic

pollutant
polluting
pollution

presuming
-procuring
producer
producing
profusion
protruding

puberty
pubescent
-pullover
punitive
-purify -ies
-purified
-puritan / Puritan
-purity
pursuant
pursuer
pursuing
putrify -ies
putrified

* * * * * *

peculiar ly
peculiarity -ies

-pluralism

pneumonia

presumably

pugilistic ally
-purification
-puritanical
-puritanism

Q

*

*cue rod / signal
cued

***queue** waiting line
queued

* *

*cueing / cuing prompting

***queueing / queuing**
waiting in a line

* * *

quintuplet

* * * *

*

*rood crucifix / an acre
roof ed
-rook
room ed
roost
*root part of plant / origin
rouge
*route way

ruche d
*rude impolite
rue d
*rued regretted
*rues does regret
rule d
rune
*ruse trick

* *

raccoon / racoon

rebuke d
recoup ed
recruit
reduce d
refuse d
refute
remove d
renew ed
repute
-resource d
resume d
*review survey
reviewed
*revue theatrical entertainment

rhubarb

rooftops
roommate
rooster
rouble / ruble
roulette
routine

ruby -ies
ruin ed
ruler
ruling
rumour ed
rupee
-rural ly
ruthless

* * *

rebuking
recruitment
reducing
refusal
refusing
refuting
removal
removing
renewal
renewing
-resourceful
-resources
-resourcing
resuming
reunion

rheumatic

-rookery -ies
routinely

rubella
ruinous
-rurally
ruthlessly

* * * * *

recuperate
removable / removeable
repudiate
repudiating
reunion

rheumatism

-Romania / Roumania / Rumania

rudimentary -ies

In these words you can hear oo as in smooth or ue as in newt

*

*chute slope for things to slide down

school ed
scoop ed
scoot
screw ed

*__shoe__ footwear [shod]
*__shoo__ ed scare away
-**shook**
*__shoot__ fire / hit with bullet / move very fast / new growth from plant [shot]
-**should**
shrewd

skew ed

sleuth ed
slew
sluice

smooth ed

snoop ed
snooze d

soon
-**soot**
soothe d
*__sou__ coin of low value
soup

spook
spool ed
spoon ed
spruce

stew ed
-**stood**
stool
*__stoop__ ed bend down
*__stoup__ basin for holy water
strew ed [strewn]

*__sue__ d take legal action / plead
suit
-**sure**

swoop ed

* *

saloon
salute

schoolboy
schoolgirl
schooling
schooner
scooter
scuba

seclude
-**secure** d
seduce d
sewage
*__sewer__ big waste pipe

shoeing
shooting
-**shouldn't**

skewer ed

smoothie
smoothly

snooker ed
snoozing

sooner
soothing
soufflé
soupçon

spoonful
-**sputnik**

steward
strudel
Stuart
student
stupid
stupor

subdue d
Sudan
*__suer__ person who seeks justice or marriage
sueing / suing
suet
-**sugar** ed
suitcase
suited
suitor
super
superb
supreme
-**surely**
sushi

* * *

saluting

schoolchildren
schoolmaster
schoolmistress es
schoolteacher
screwdriver
scrutinise d
ze
scrutiny

secluded
secluding
-**securing**
seducing

solution
souvenir

spurious

stewardess es
studio s
studious
stupefy -ies
stupefied
stupendous

subduing
Sudanese
suicide
suitable
suitably
superbly
supersede
superstar
supervise d

* * * * * *

scrutinising
zing

-**security** -ies

stupidity -ies

suicidal ly
suitability
superannuation
superconductor
superego
superficial ly
superfluous
superhuman
superimpose d
superimposing
superintendent
superior
superlative
supermarket
supermini
supermodel
supernatural ly
superpower
superseding
supersonic ally
superstition
superstitious
supervising
supervision
supervisor
supervisory
supremacy

T

LONG VOWEL **ue** LONG VOWEL **oo**

*

***threw** hurled
***through** by way of / because of

***to** towards
tomb
***too** also
-**took**
tool ed
toot
tooth ed
-**tour** ed

***troop** ed move as a group
***troupe** group of entertainers
truce
true d
truth

tube d
tune d

***two** 2

* *

taboo ed
tattoo ed

throughout

today
to-do
tombstone
tonight
toolbar
toolbox es
toolkit
toothbrush es
toothcomb
toothpaste
toothpick
toucan
toupee
-**tourist**
toward
towards

trousseau
truant
truly
truthful ly

***tuba** wind instrument
***tuber** underground stem or root
tubing
Tudor
Tuesday
tulip
tumour
tumult
***tuna** fish
***tuner** person who tunes
tunic
tuning
tutor ed
tutu

twofold
two-thirds

* * *

together
tomorrow
-**tourism**
-**tournament**

truancy
truthfully

tubular
tuition

* * * * *

tubercular
tuberculin
tuberculosis
tumultuous
Tunisia
tutorial

In these words you can hear oo as in smooth or ue as in newt

U

LONG VOWEL **ue** LONG VOWEL **oo**

*

*ewe female sheep
*ewes more than one ewe

***use** employ
used

*yew tree
*yews yew trees

*you person / people

* *

-euro s
-Europe

Ukraine

union
unique
unit
unite

-urine

usage
useful ly
useless
user
using
usual ly
usurp ed

* * *

eucharist
-eureka!
Eustachian

Uganda

unicorn
uniform ed
unify -ies
unified
union
unionist
unison
unitary
united
unity
universe

-Uranus
-urethane
-urinary
-urinate
-Uruguay

usable
usefully
usefulness
usually

utensil
uterus es / -i
utile
utilise d
ze

* * * * *

eucalyptus
euphemism
euphonium
-European
Eustachian
euthanasia

ubiquitous

ukelele
Ukrainian

unanimity
unanimous ly
unicellular
unicycle
unification
uniformity
unilateral ly
unionist
unitary
universal ly
university -ies

-uranium
-urinary

utilisation
zation
utilising
zing
utility -ies
utopia

for H . . .
see page 215

for Y . . .
see page 224

V

*

view ed

* *

viewer
viewpoint

* * *

* * * *

voluminous

W

*

*few not many

*hew ed cut down

*hoop large ring or band

*hue colour

***whew / phew** relief!

* *

-woman
-wooden
-woodland
-woodwork
-woollen
-woolly
-wouldn't
wounded

* * *

whoever
whooping-cough

-woodcutter
-woodpecker

* * * *

In these words you can hear oo as in smooth or ue as in newt

W

*

*who which person or people
who'd
who'll
whom
*whoop ed shout joyfully
*who's who is
*whose belonging to whom or what

-wolf [wolves]
-wolfed
womb
*-wood timber / area with many trees
*woof weft
*-woof! bark of dog
-wool
*-would was willing to / used to / was going to
wound

Y

*

*ewe female sheep
*ewes more than one ewe

*yew tree
*yews yew trees

*you person / people
you'd
*you'll you will
*-your belonging to you
*-you're you are
-yours
youth
you've

*yule Christmas time

* *

-euro s
-Europe

-yourself
-yourselves
youthful ly

for U . . .
see page 223

* * *

eucharist
-eureka!
Eustachian

youthfully
youthfulness

* * * * *

eucalyptus
euphonium
-European
Eustachian
euthanasia

Yugoslavia

Z

*

zoo
zoom ed

* *

* * *

* * * * * *

zoological ly
zoology

*

aft
ah
*alms gifts to the poor
*arc curve
arch es
arched
are
*aren't are not
*ark (Noah's)
arm ed
*arms more than one arm / weapons of war
art
ask ed
*aunt relative

for H . . .
see page 230

* *

aardvark
advance d
afar
after
aghast
ajar
alarm ed
almond
amen
answer ed
apart
*arbor shaft
*arbour garden or part shaded by trees
arcade
archer
archive
arctic
ardent
ardour
argon
argue d
armchair
armful
armour ed
armpit
army -ies
arson
artist
artwork
asking
Auntie / Aunty

* * *

advancement
advancing
advantage
advantaged
aftermath
afternoon
afterwards
answering
apartheid
apartment
arbitrate
arbutus
archaic
archbishop
archery
architect
arduous
arguing
argument
armada
armament
armature
armistice
armoury -ies
arsenal
arsenic
artefact / artifact
artery -ies
artesian
arthritis
arthropod
artichoke
article
artifact / artefact
artisan
artistic ally
artistry

* * * * * *

adagio
advantaging
arbitrarily
arbitrary
arbitrating
arbitration
arbitrator
archaeological / archeological
archaeologist / archeologist
archaeology / archeology
archipelago
architecture
Argentina
arguable
arguably
argumentative
armadillo s
arterial
artesian
articulate
articulating
articulation
artificial ly
artillery
artistically

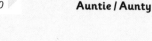

B

*

***baa** lamb's cry
***balm** ointment
***bar**red prevent / barrier / rod
barbed
***bard** poet
barged
***bark**ed sound like that of a dog / outer covering of a tree
***barm** yeasty froth
barn
***barque** boat
***barred** prevented / fixed with bars
***bask**ed enjoy
***Basque** person living near the Pyrenees
bathed

blah
blast

bra
branches branched
brasses

* *

***balmy** -ier, -iest sweet-smelling / mad
banal
barbel
barber
bargained
barging
barking
barley
barman [barmen]
***barmy / balmy** mad
barndoor
barney
barring
bartered
basket
basking
bastard
bathroom
***bazaar** Eastern market

behalf

***bizarre** peculiar

bombard

branches
brassy -ier, -iest

* * *

Bahamas
banana
Barbados
barbecued
barnacle
barwoman [barwomen]
basketball

bombardment
Botswana

brassier
bravado

* * * *

barbarian
barbecuing

In these words you can hear the vowel sound ar as in shark

C

*

calf [calves]
calm ed
***calve** d produce a calf
can't
car
card
carp ed
cart
***carve** d cut
cask
***cast** throw / mould / decide parts in a play / squint [cast]
***caste** social class

***chance** lucky event / risk
chanced
chant
***chants** does chant / more than one chant
char red
charge d
charm ed
chart

clasp ed
class es
classed
clerk

craft

czar / tsar

* *

calmly
carafe
carbon
carcass es
cardboard
cargo es
carmine
carpet
carton
cartoon
cartridge
cartwheel
carving
***caster / castor** powdered sugar / swivelling wheel
casting
castle
castling
***castor** oil
catarrh

chancing
chandler
charade
charcoal
charging
charming
charring
charter ed
***chorale** hymn tune

cigar

classmate
classroom
classy -ier, -iest

command
contrast
***corral** enclosure for cattle and horses

craftsman [craftsmen]
crafty -ier, -iest

khaki

Koran / Qur'an

* * *

cacao
carbonate
cardiac
cardigan
cardinal
carnation
carnival
carnivore
carpenter
carpentry
cartilage
cartoonist
castaway

chancellor
chapati
chargeable

commander
commandment
compartment

craftier
craftiest

karate

koala

* * * * *

carbohydrate
carbonation
carboniferous
carburetter / carburettor
carcinogenic
carcinoma
carnivorous

D

*

daft
dal / dhal
dance d
dark
darn ed
dart

*__draft__ rough plan / selected group
*__draught__ current of air / depth of ship in water / piece in game
draughts

* *

dancer
dancing
darker
darken ed
darkness
darling
data

demand
depart

disarm ed
discard
discharge d

drama
drastic ally
draughty -ier,-iest

* * *

demanded
demanding
department
departure

disaster
disastrous
discharging
dishearten ed

drastically

* * * *

disarmament

drastically

E

*

for H . . .
see page 230

for I . . .
see page 230

* *

embark ed

enchant
enhance d
enlarge d
entrance d

* * *

embargo es
embargoed

enchanting
enhancing
enlarging
entrancing

escarpment

example

* * * *

F

*

far
farce
farm ed
fast

flask

France

* *

facade / façade
far-fetched
farmer
farmhouse
farming
farmland
farmyard
*__farther__ greater distance
farthest
fasten ed
faster
fastest
*__father__ male parent
fathered

* * *

faraway
farcical
fastener

*__fiancé__ man engaged to be married
*__fiancée__ woman engaged to be married
finale

pharmacist
pharmacy -ies

* * * * *

father-in-law

pharmaceutical

G

*

gasp ed

glance d
glass es

gnarled

gouache

*__graft__ cause to grow together / hard work
grant
graph ed
*__graphed__ made a graph
grasp ed
grass es
grassed

guard

* *

gala
garage d
garbage
garden ed
gardener
gardening
gargle d
gargling
garish
garland
garlic
garment
garnet
garter ed

Ghana
ghastly -ier, -iest

giraffe

glancing
glasses
glassy -ier, -iest

gouache

granted
grasping
grassland
grassy -ier, -iest

gratis

guitar

* * *

garaging
gardener
gardening

Ghanaian

grasshopper

guardian
guitarist

gymkhana

* * * *

Guatemala

H

*

half [halves]
halve d
hard
hark ed
harm ed
harp ed
harsh
***hart** male deer

***heart** organ that pumps blood / centre / inmost feelings
hearth

* *

halal
half-time
halfway
halving
harbour ed
hardboard
hard-boiled
harden ed
harder
hardest
hardly
hardship
hardware
hardwood
hardy -ier,-iest
harem
harmful ly
harmless
harness es
harnessed
harpoon ed
harvest

heartbeat
heartbreak
heartburn
hearty -ier,-iest

hijab

hurrah!

* * *

harlequin
harmfully
harmonic ally
harmonise d
ze
harmony -ies
harpsichord
harvester
Hawaii
Hawaiian

* * * * *

harmonica
harmonically
harmonious
harmonisation
zation
harmonising
zing
harmonium

I

*

for E . . .
see page 228

* *

impart
impasse

Iran
Iraq

Islam

* * *

impartial ly

incarnate

Iraqi

* * * *

impartially
impassable

J

*

jar red

for dr . . .
see page 228

* *

giraffe

jargon
jarring

jihad

* * *

gymkhana

* * * *

K

*

* *

khaki

Koran / Qur'an

* * *

karate

koala

* * * *

for C . . .
see page 227

L

*

lance d
larch es
lard
large
lark ed
last
laugh ed

* *

lager
lancing
larder
largely
larger
large-scale
largest
largo
larkspur
***larva** [larvae] insect grub
lasted
lather ed
latte
laughter
***lava** melted rock from volcano

llama

* * *

lasagne

legato
lethargic

* * * *

M

*

***ma** mother
ma'am
***mar** spoil
marred
March
march es
marched
mark ed
***mars** spoils
***Mars** planet
marsh es
mask ed
mass es
mast

* *

macho
madame
mama
marble d
marbling
marching
margin
marker
market ed
marking
***marquee** very big tent
***marquess** British nobleman
***marquis** nobleman
marring
***marshal** officer / arrange in order
marshalled
***marten** animal
***martial** warlike
***martin** bird
martyr ed
marvel led
Marxist
massage d
master ed

mirage

morale
moustache d

* * *

macabre
mafia
Malawi
Mardi Gras
margarine
marginal ly
markedly
marketed
marketing
marketplace
marmalade
marmoset
marshalling
marshmallow
martini
marvelling
marvellous
Marxism
marzipan
massaging
masterpiece
mastery

* * * *

marginally
marsupial

N

*

gnarled

nan / naan

* *

nasty -ier, -iest
Nazi

* * *

narcissus es / -i
narcotic
nastier
nastiest
Nazism

* * * *

P

*

*__pa__ father
*__pah__ scornful exclamation
palm ed
*__par__ what is normal
parch es
parched
park ed
part
pass es
*__passed__ went by
*__past__ time that has passed / beyond
path

plant

prance d

psalm

* *

papa
parcel led
parchment
pardon ed
parka
parking
parlour
parsley
parsnip
parson
partake
[partook]
[partaken]
partial led
partly
partner ed
partridge
part-time
party -ies
passing
passport
password
pasta
pastime
pasture d
pathway

pianist
piano s

planted
planter
planting
plaster ed

prancing

* * *

Pakistan
parcelling
Parkinson's
parliament
partaken
partaking
partialling
partially
particle
partisan
partition ed
partnership
passers-by
Passover
pasteurise d
ze
pastoral ly
pasturing

pharmacist
pharmacy -ies

pianist
piano s
piranha

plantation

ptarmigan

pyjamas

* * * * *

Pakistani
parliamentary
participant
participate
participating
participation
participle
pasteurising
zing
pastorally

pharmaceutical

pianoforte
pistachio s

In this word the 'ar' is neutral.
particular ly

Q

*

* *

Qur'an / Koran

* * *

* * * *

R

*

raft
ranch es
rasp ed

* *

rafter
rascal ly
raspberry
rather

regard
remark ed
retard

* * *

rascally
raspberry -ies

regarded
regarding
regardless
retarded

* * * *

rechargeable
remarkable
remarkably

In these words you can hear the vowel sound ar as in shark

S

VOWEL SOUND **ar**

*

psalm

scar red
scarf -ves
schwa

shaft
shark
sharp

slant

smart

snarl ed

*__spa__ resort with mineral spring
*__spar__ pole / practise boxing
spark ed
sparred
sparse

staff ed
stance
star red
starch es
starched
stark
start
starve d

suave

* *

charade

cigar

saga
salmon
sample d
sampler
sampling
sardine
sari

scarlet
scarring

sergeant

sharpen ed
sharpening
sharply
sharpness

slalom

smartly

sparkle d
sparkler
sparkling
sparring
spartan

starboard
starchy -ier, -iest
stardom
starfish
starlight
starling
starring
starry
started
starter
starters
starting
startle d
startling
startup / start-up
starving
stratum [strata]

surpass es
surpassed

* * *

safari
Sahara
salami
sarcasm
sarcastic ally
sardonic

sharpening
sharpshooter

soprano s

staccato
starvation

sultana
surpassing

* * * * *

sarcastically
sardonically

scenario s

Somalia

In these words you can hear the vowel sound ar as in shark

T

*	* *	* * *	* * * *
tar red	**target** ed	ptarmigan	
tart	**tarmac**		
task	**tarnish** es	**targeted**	
	tarnished	**targeting**	
trance	**tarring**	**tarpaulin**	
	tartan		
tsar / czar		**tiara**	
		tomato es	
		tripartite	

V

*	* *	* * *	* * * *
vase	**vantage**	**vibrato**	
vast	**varnish** es		
	varnished		

Y

*	* *	* * *	* * * *
yard	**yardage**		
yarn ed	**yardstick**		

Z

*	* *	* * *	* * * *
czar / tsar		**Zimbabwe**	

VOWEL SOUND **air**

A

*

*__air__ atmosphere / manner / feeling / tune
aired

*-err ed make a mistake

*heir next owner

for H . . .
see page 238

* *

affair

aircraft
airfield
airline
airmail
airport
airtight
airway
airy -ier, -iest

aware

Eire

heiress es
heirloom

* * *

aerial
aerobic
aerodrome
aerofoil
aeroplane
aerosol
aerospace

*__airier__ more airy
airliner

*__area__ field / space

awareness

* * * * * * *

aerobatic
aerobatics
aerodynamic ally
aerodynamics
aeronautic
aeronautical
aeronautics

aquarium

B

*

*__bare__ uncover (ed)
*__bared__ uncovered

*__bear__ animal
*__bear__ carry
[bore]
[born / borne]

*-__bird__ feathered animal

*__blare__ d sound loudly
*-__blur__ red go fuzzy

*-__bur__ bur oak
*-__burr / bur__ prickly seedcase / rough edge
*-__burred__ prickly / rough

* *

barefoot
barely
*__baring__ uncovering

bearer
*__bearing__ carrying
beware

*__blaring__ sounding loudly
*-__blurring__ going fuzzy

*-__burring__ removing the burrs

* * *

barium

bewaring

* * * *

Bulgaria

C

*

cairn
*__care__ attention / worry / look after
*__cared__ looked after

chair ed

*-__cur__ worthless dog
*-__curd__ soft, fatty substance

*-Kurd Kurdish person

* *

carefree
careful ly
careless
carer
caring

chairlift
chairman [chairmen]

compare d

* * *

canary -ies
carefully
carelessly
caretaker

chairperson
chairwoman
[chairwomen]

comparing
contrary

-Kurdistan

* * * *

In these words you can hear the vowel sound air as in bear

D

*	**	***	****
dare d	**dairy** -ies **daring** **declare** d **despair** ed	**declaring**	

E

*	**	***	**** ***
*air atmosphere / manner / feeling / tune aired ***-err** ed make a mistake *heir next owner	aircraft airfield airline airmail airport airtight airway airy -ier, -iest **éclair** **Eire** heiress es heirloom	aerial aerobic aerodrome aerofoil aeroplane aerosol aerospace *airier more airy airliner *area field / space	aerobatic aerobatics aerodynamic ally aerodynamics aeronautic aeronautical aeronautics

for H . . .
see page 238

for I . . .
see page 239

F

*

*fair just / funfair / market / fine weather / light in colour
*fairs more than one fair
*fare charge for ride / food / get on
*fared did fare
*fares more than one fare / gets on

*flair natural skill
*flare burst into flame / get wider at the bottom
flared

*-fur coat of animal
*-furred coated with fur
*-furs coats of animals
*-furze gorse

* *

*faerie/faery fairy / fairyland
fairground
fairly
fairness
*fairy -ies magical tiny person
farewell
faring

flaring

forbear [forbore] [forborne]

*-furry -ier, -iest feeling like fur

pharoah

* * *

* * * *

G

*

glare d

* *

glaring

* * *

* * * *

gregarious

H

*

*hair thread-like growth
*haired having hair
*hare animal
*hared ran like a hare

*heir next owner
*-her she / belonging to her
*Herr [Herren] German for 'Mr'

* *

hairbrush es
haircut
hairdo
hairpin
hairspray
hairstyle
hairy -ier, -iest
haring

heiress es
heirloom
*-heron large bird
*Herren title for German men

* * *

haircutting
hairdresser
hair-drier
hairstyling

* * * *

hilarious

Hungarian

In these words you can hear the vowel sound air as in bear

I

*	* *	* * *	* * * * *
	impair ed		**invariably**

for E . . .
see page 237

L

*	* *	* * *	* * * *
lair			

M

*	* *	* * *	* * * *
***mare** female horse ***mayor** head of town or city ***-myrrh** fragrant oil or gum	**mayoress** es		**malaria**

P

*	* *	* * *	* * * *
***pair** set of two / get or put together in twos **paired** ***pare** d trim / peel ***pear** fruit ***-per** for each **prayer** ***-purr** ed sound of happy cat	***pairing** making pairs **parent** ***paring** trimming / peeling **pharaoh** **pierrot** **prairie** **prepare** d ***-purring** sounding like a happy cat	**parenthood** **pierrot** **preparing**	

In these words you can hear the vowel sound air as in bear

R

*	**	***	****
rare	**rarely**	**rarity** -ies	
	repair ed	**repairing**	

S

*	**	***	****
scarce	**scarcely**	**scarcity**	
scare d	**scarecrow**		
	scaring	**shareholder**	
share d	**scary** -ier, -iest		
		sparingly	
snare d	**shareware**		
	sharing		
***spare** extra / give / keep from giving	**snaring**		
***spared** did spare			
***-spur** projecting part / urge on	**sparing**		
***-spurred** urged on	**squaring**		
square d	**staircase**		
	staring		
***stair** step or steps			
***stare** d look fixedly			
***-stir** red move around			
swear [swore] [sworn]			

In these words you can hear the vowel sound air as in bear

T

*

***tare** weed / weight or empty vehicle or container

***tear** rip
[tore]
[torn]

***their** belonging to them
***theirs** something belonging to them
***there** to/in that place / also used with 'is', 'are', 'was', 'were' and other forms of 'to be'
there'd
there'll
***there's** there is / there has
***they're** they are

* *

tearing

thereby
therefore
therein
thereof
therewith

* * *

thereafter
thereupon

* * * *

V

*

* *

vary -ies
varied

* * *

variant
various
varying

* * * * * *

variability
variable
variation

vicarious ly

W

*

***ware** products for sale / pottery

***wear** carry on body / get worse with use
[wore]
[worn]
*-**were** form of verb 'to be'

***where** to/in which place

* *

warehouse
wary -ier,-iest

wearing
werewolf
[werewolves]

whereas
whereby
wherefore
wherein

* * *

whereabouts
whereupon
wherever

* * * *

A

VOWEL SOUND **er**

*

***-air** atmosphere / manner / feeling / tune
-aired

*err ed make a mistake

*-heir next owner

for H . . . see page 247

* *

absurd

adjourn ed

-affair
affirm ed

-aircraft
-airfield
-airline
-airmail
-airport
-airtight
-airway
-airy -ier, -iest

alert

assert
astern

avert

-aware

-Eire

-heiress es
-heirloom

* * *

-aerial
-aerobic
-aerodrome
-aerofoil
-aeroplane
-aerosol
-aerospace

***-airier** more airy
-airliner

allergic
alternate

***-area** field / space

assertion
assertive

attorney

-awareness

* * * * * * *

adverbial ly
adversity -ies
advertisement

-aerobatic
-aerobatics
-aerodynamic ally
-aerodynamics
-aeronautic
-aeronautical
-aeronautics

affirmative ly

alternative ly

-aquarium

assertiveness

In these words you can hear the vowel sound **er** as in **bird**

B

*

*-**bare** uncover(ed)
*-**bared** uncovered

*-**bear** animal
*-**bear** carry
[bore]
[born / borne]
***berth** bunk / place for ship at quay
berthed

birch es
birched
***bird** feathered animal
***birth** delivery of child / origin

*-**blare** d sound loudly
***blur** red go fuzzy
blurt

***bur** bur oak
burn ed
[burnt]
***burr / bur** prickly seedcase / rough edge
***burred** prickly / rough
burst
[burst]

* *

-**barefoot**
-**barely**
*-**baring** uncovering

-**bearer**
*-**bearing** carrying
-**beware**

birdie
birdseed
birthday
birthplace

*-**blaring** sounding loudly
***blurring** going fuzzy
blurry -ier, -iest

burden ed
***burger** sandwich
***burgher** citizen
burglar
burka / burqa
burlap
burly -ier, -iest
Burma
burner
burning
***burring** removing the burrs
bursar

* * *

-**barium**

-**bewaring**

burglary -ies
burgundy -ies
bursary -ies

* * * *

-**Bulgaria**

Here 'er' is neutral, like the 'er' in 'perhaps'.
Bermuda

C

VOWEL SOUND **er**

*

-**cairn**
*-**care** attention / worry / look after
*-**cared** looked after

-**chair** ed
chirp ed
church es
churn ed

cirque

***cur** worthless dog
***curb** ed restrain
***curd** soft, fatty substance
curl ed
curse d
curt
curve d

*kerb edge of pavement

kirk

*Kurd Kurdish person

for Qu . . .
see page 251

* *

-**carefree**
-**careful** ly
-**careless**
-**carer**
-**caring**

certain

-**chairlift**
-**chairman** [chairmen]
churchyard

circle d
circling
circuit
circus

clergy

***colonel** army officer
-**compare** d
concern ed
confer red
confirm ed
conserve d
converge d
converse d
convert
courteous

curdle d
curdling
curfew
curling
curly -ier, -iest
cursed
cursing
cursor
curtail ed
curtain ed
curtsey s / **curtsy** -ies
curtseyed / curtsied
curving
curvy -ier, -iest

*kernel seed in nut

* * *

-**canary** -ies
-**carefully**
-**carelessly**
-**caretaker**

certainly
certainty -ies
certify -ies
certified

-**chairperson**
-**chairwoman**
-[chairwomen]

circular
circulate
circumscribe d
circumstance

clergyman [clergymen]

commercial ly
-**comparing**
concerning
conferring
conserving
-**contrary**
convergent
converging
conversely
conversing
conversion
courteous
courtesy -ies

curlier
curliest
curvature

Kurdistan

* * * * *

circuitous
circulating
circulation
circulatory
circumcision
circumference
circumnavigate
circumscribing
circumstances
circumstantial

commercially
conservatism
conservative
conservatory -ies
convertible

Here the 'er' is neutral.
certificate

In these words you can hear the vowel sound er as in bird

D

*

-dare d

dearth

dirge
dirt

* *

-dairy -ies
-daring

-declare d
defer red
***desert** leave
deserve d
-despair ed
***dessert** sweet dish
deter red

dirty -ies
dirtied
dirty -ier, -iest
discern ed
disperse d
disturb ed
diverge d
diverse
divert

* * *

-declaring
deferring
deserted
deserter
deserving
detergent
determine d
deterring

dirtier
dirtiest
dispersing
dispersion
disservice
disturbance
diverging
diverted

* * * * * *

determination
determining

discernible
diversification
diversify -ies
diversified
diversity

E

*

*-air atmosphere / manner / feeling / tune
-aired

earl
***earn** ed get money by working
earth ed

***err** ed make a mistake

*-heir next owner

irk ed

urge d
*urn vase / vessel

for H . . . see page 247

for I . . . see page 247

* *

-aircraft
-airfield
-airline
-airmail
-airport
-airtight
-airway
-airy -ier, -iest

early -ier, -iest
earnest
earnings
earthquake
earthworm
earthy -ier, -iest

-éclair

-Eire

emerge d

exert

-heiress es
-heirloom

irksome

urban
urchin
urgent
urging

* * *

-aerial
-aerobic
-aerodrome
-aerofoil
-aeroplane
-aerosol
-aerospace

*-airier more airy
-airliner

*-area field / space

earlier
earliest
earnestness
earthenware

emergence
emerging

encircle d
encircling

eternal ly

excursion
exertion
external ly

urgency
urgently

* * * * * * *

-aerobatic
-aerobatics
-aerodynamic ally
-aerodynamics
-aeronautic
-aeronautical
-aeronautics

emergency -ies

ergonomics

eternally
eternity

exterminate
exterminating
extermination
externally

In these words you can hear the vowel sound er as in bird

F

*

***-fair** just / funfair / market / fine weather / light in colour
***-fairs** more than one fair
***-fare** charge for ride / food / get on
***-fared** did fare
***-fares** more than one fare / gets on

fern

***fir** tree
firm ed
***firs** more than one fir
first

***-flair** natural skill
***-flare** burst into flame / get wider at the bottom
-flared

***fur** coat of animal
furl ed
***furred** coated with fur
***furs** coats of animals
***furze** gorse

* *

***-faerie / faery** fairy / fairyland
-fairground
-fairly
-fairness
***-fairy** -ies magical tiny person
-farewell
-faring

ferment
fertile
fervour

firmly
firstly

-flaring

-forbear
[forbore]
[forborne]

furnace
furnish es
furnished
furring
***furry** -ier, -iest like fur
further ed
furtive

-pharaoh

* * *

fertilise d
ze

fleur-de-lis
flirtation

furniture
furthermore

for th . . .
see page 253

* * * * *

fermentation
fertilisation
zation
fertiliser
zer
fertilising
zing
fertility

fraternity -ies

G

*

germ

girl
girth

-glare d

jerk ed

* *

gerbil
German

gherkin

girder
girdle d
girlfriend
girlie / girly

-glaring

gurgle d
gurgling

jerkin
*jersey woollen jumper
*Jersey Channel Island

journal
journey ed

* * *

Germany
germicide
germinate

journalist

* * * * * *

germicidal
germinating
germination

-gregarious

journalism
journalistic ally

In these words you can hear the vowel sound er as in bird

H

*

*-**hair** thread-like growth
*-**haired** having hair
*-**hare** animal
*-**hared** ran like a hare

*__heard__ did hear
*__hearse__ funeral car
*-**heir** next owner
*__her__ she / belonging to her
herb
*__herd__ group of animals
*-**Herr** [Herren] German for 'Mr'
*__hers__ her property
*__hertz__ measure of frequency in cycles per second

hurl ed
hurt
[hurt]
*__hurts__ does hurt

* *

-**hairbrush** es
-**haircut**
-**hairdo**
-**hairpin**
-**hairspray**
-**hairstyle**
-**hairy** -ier, -iest
-**haring**

-**heiress** es
-**heirloom**
herdsman [herdsmen]
hermit
*-**heron** large bird
*-**Herren** title for German men

hurdle d
hurdling
hurtful ly
hurtle d
hurtling

* * *

-**haircutting**
-**hairdresser**
-**hair-drier**
-**hairstyling**

herbaceous
herbivore

hurtfully

Here 'er' is neutral, like the 'er' in 'perhaps'.
herself

* * * *

-**hilarious**

-**Hungarian**

I

*

irk ed

* *

immerse d
-**impair** ed

incur red
inert
infer red
infirm
insert
inter red
invert

irksome

* * *

immersion
imperfect

incurring
inertia
inferring
insertion
internal ly
interpret ed
interring
inversion

* * * * *

impermeable
impersonal
impersonate
impersonating
impersonation
impertinent
impervious

infirmary -ies
interminable
internally
interpolate
interpolating
interpretation
interpreted
interpreter
interpreting
-**invariably**

*for E . . .
see page 245*

J

*

germ

jerk ed

* *

gerbil
German

jerkin
***jersey** woollen jumper
***Jersey** Channel Island

journal
journey ed

* * *

Germany
germicide
germinate

journalist

* * * * * *

germicidal
germinating
germination

journalism
journalistic ally

K

*

*-cared looked after

*curd soft, fatty substance

kerb ed

kirk

knurl ed

***Kurd** Kurdish person

* *

*colonel army officer

***kernel** seed in nut

* * *

* * * *

for C . . . *see page 244*

for Qu . . . *see page 251*

L

*

-lair

learn ed
[learnt]

lurch es
lurched
lurk ed

* *

learned
learner
learning

* * *

* * * *

M

*

***-mare** female horse
***-mayor** head of town or city

merge d

mirth

***myrrh** fragrant oil or gum

* *

-mayoress es

merchant
mercy -ies
merger
merging

murder ed
murky -ier, -iest
murmur ed

* * *

maternal ly

mercenary -ies
merchandise
merciful ly
merciless
***mercury** liquid metal
***Mercury** planet

murderer
murderess es
murderous
murmuring

* * * *

-malaria
maternally
maternity

mercenary -ies
mercifully
mercurial

N

*

knurl ed

nerve

nurse d

* *

nervous
nervy -ier, -iest

nursing
nurture

* * *

nasturtium

nervously
nervousness

nursery -ies

* * * *

O

*

* *

observe d

occur red

* * *

alternate

observance
observant
observer
observing

occurring

* * * * *

alternative

observable
observatory -ies

P

*

*-**pair** set of two / get or put together in twos
-**paired**
*-**pare**d trim / peel

*-**pear** fruit
***pearl** jewel
***per** for each
perches
perched
permed
pert

-**prayer**

purged
***purl** knitting stitch
***purr**ed sound of happy cat
purse

* *

*-**pairing** making pairs
-**parent**
*-**paring** trimming / peeling

perfect
perfumed
perky-ier, -iest
permit
Persia
Persian
person
perspex
perverse
pervert

-**pharaoh**

-**pierrot**

-**prairie**
preferred
-**prepare**d
preserved

purchased
purple
purpose
***purring** sounding like a happy cat

* * *

-**parenthood**

percolate
perfectly
perforate
perfuming
permanent
permeable
permeate
pernicious
perpetrate
persecute
persevered
personally
personnel
pertinent
perversion

-**pierrot**

preferring
-**preparing**
preserving

purchaser
purchasing
purposefully

* * * * *

percolating
percolator
perforating
perforation
permanently
permeable
perpendicular
perpetuity
persecuting
persecution
persevering
personality-ies
personally
perspiration

preservative
proverbially

purposefully

In these words 'er' and 'ur' are pronounced as neutral sounds, like the 'er' in 'persist'.

P***ER***SISTENT WORDS

perceive d
percent
percentage
perceptible
perception
perceptive
perceptual ly
percussion
percussive
perfect ion
perfectionist
perform ed
performance
performer
performing
perhaps
perimeter
peripheral ly
periphery
permissible
permission
permit ted
permitting
peroxide
perpetual ly
perplex es
perplexed
perplexing
persist
persistence
persistent ly
personification
personify -ies
personified
perspective
perspire d
perspiring
persuade
persuasion
persuasive
purport
pursuant
pursue d
pursuer
pursuit

for pre . . .
see page 82

In these words you can hear the vowel sound er as in bird

Q

*

quirk

* *

quirky -ier, -iest

* * *

* * * *

R

*

-rare

* *

-rarely

recur red
refer red
rehearse d
-repair ed
research es
researched
reserve d
return ed
reverse d
revert

* * *

-rarity -ies

recurring
recursion
referral
referring
rehearsal
rehearsing
-repairing
researcher
reserving
returning
reversal
reversing

* * * * *

returnable
reverberate
reverberating
reversible

S

*

cirque

-scarce
-scare d
scourge d
scurf

search es
searched
*serf slave
*serge woollen cloth
serve d

-share d
shirk ed
shirt

Sir

skirt

slur red

smirk ed

-snare d

*-spare extra / give / keep from giving
*-spared did spare
sperm
*spur projecting part / urge on
spurn ed
*spurred urged on
spurs
spurt

-square d
squirm ed
squirt

*-stair step or steps
*-stare d look fixedly
stern
*stir red move around

surd
*surf foaming sea
surfed
*surge d rush forward

-swear
[swore]
[sworn]
swerve d
swirl ed

* *

certain

circle d
circling
circuit
circus

-scarcely
-scarecrow
-scaring
-scary -ier, -iest
scurvy

searching
searchlight
sermon
serpent
servant
server
service d
serviette
servile
serving

-shareware
-sharing
sherbet

sirloin

skirmish es
skirmished

-snaring

-sparing
spurring

-squaring

-staircase
-staring
sterling
stirring
sturdy -ier, -iest

submerge d
surface d
surfboard
surfer
surfing
surgeon
surging
surly -ier, -iest
surname
*surplice church gown
*surplus es excess
survey

* * *

certainly
certainty -ies
certify -ies
certified

circular
circulate
circumscribe d
circumstance

-scarcity

Serbia
servicing
serviette

-shareholder

-sparingly

submerging
suburban
surgery -ies
surgical ly

* * * * *

circuitous
circulating
circulation
circulatory
circumcision
circumference
circumnavigate
circumscribing
circumstances
circumstantial

serviceable

superfluous
surgically

Here 'er' is neutral, like the 'er' in 'perhaps'.

SURPRISING WORDS

surmount	surround
surpass es	surroundings
surpassed	surveillance
surpassing	surveying
surprise d	surveyor
surprising	survival
surprisingly	survive d
surrender ed	survivor

In these words you can hear the vowel sound er as in bird

T

VOWEL SOUND **er**

*

***-tare** weed / weight or empty vehicle or container

***-tear** rip
[tore]
[torn]
term ed
***tern** bird
terse

***-their** belonging to them
***-theirs** something belonging to them
***-there** to/in that place / also used with 'is', 'are', 'was', 'were' and other forms of 'to be'
-there'd
-there'll
***-there's** there is / there has
therm
***-they're** they are
third
thirst

turf ed
Turk
***turn** ed change direction

twirl ed

* *

-tearing

-thereby
-therefore
-therein
-thereof
-therewith
thermal ly
thermos
thirdly
thirsty -ier, -iest
thirteen th
thirty -ies
Thursday

***turban** head-covering
***turbine** engine
turbot
***Turkey** country
***turkey** bird
Turkish
turmoil
turner
turning
turnip
turnout
turnpike
turnstile
turquoise
turtle

* * *

terminal ly
terminate
terminus es / -i
ternary
tertiary

-thereafter
-thereupon
thermally
thermostat
thirtieth

turbojet
turbulence
turbulent
turmeric
turnover
turpentine

* * * * *

terminally
terminating
termination
terminology -ies

tubercular
tuberculin
tuberculosis

Here 'er' is neutral, like the 'er' in 'perhaps'.

thermometer

U

*	**	***	****
earl	early -ier, -iest	earlier	ergonomics
*earn ed get money by working	earnest	earliest	
earth ed	earnings	earnestness	
	earthquake	earthenware	
	earthworm		
err ed	earthy -ier, -iest	**urgency**	
		urgently	
irk ed	irksome		
urge d	**urban**		
***urn** vase / vessel	**urchin**		
	urgent		
	urging		

V

*	**	***	**** **
verb	**-vary** -ies	**-variant**	**-variability**
verge d	-varied	**-various**	**-variable**
verse d		**-varying**	**-variation**
verve	**verbal** ly		
	verdict	**verbally**	**versatility**
	verger	**vermilion**	**vertically**
	verging	**vernier**	
	vermin	**versatile**	**-vicarious** ly
	version	**vertebra** s / -ae	**virtually**
	versus	**vertebral**	**virtuosity**
	vertex [vertices]	**vertebrate**	**virtuoso** s
		vertical ly	
	virgin	**vertices**	
	virtual ly		
	virtue	**virginal**	
		virtually	
		virtuous	

In these words you can hear the vowel sound er as in bird

W

*

***-ware** products for sale / pottery

***-wear** carry on body / get worse with use
[wore]
[worn]
***were** form of verb 'to be'
weren't

***-where** to/in which place
***whirl** ed spin around
***whirr / whir** sound
***whirred** did whirr
***whorl** turn of spiral
***whorled** shaped in a spiral

***word** unit of meaning
work ed
***world** the earth
worm ed
worse
worst
worth

* *

-warehouse
-wary -ier, -iest

-wearing
werewolf [werewolves]

-whereas
-whereby
-wherefore
-wherein
whirlpool
whirlwind
whirring

workbench
workbook
worker
workforce
workhouse
wording
working
workload
workman [workmen]
workout
workplace
workroom
worksheet
workshop
worktop
worldly -ier, -iest
worldwide
worsen ed
worship ped
worthless
worthwhile
worthy -ies

* * *

-whereabouts
-whereupon
-wherever

workable
working-class
workmanlike
workmanship
workstation
workwoman
[workwomen]
worldlier
worldliest
worshipper
worshipping

* * * *

workaholic

Y

*

-year
yearn ed

* *

yearning

* * *

* * * *

*

***all** every one

***aught** anything at all

***awe** fear and wonder
***awed** made to feel awe
***awl** boring tool

*oar rowing blade

*-odd unusual

*or marks choice
*ore mineral

*ought should

* *

aboard
abroad
absorb ed

accord

adore d
adorn ed

afford

almost
alright
also
***altar** holy table
***alter** ed change
although
always

appal led
applaud
applause

ashore
assault
assure d

auburn
auction ed
audit
***auger** tool
***augur** suggest for the future
***August** month
***august** impressive
aura s / -ae
***aural** ly by the ear
austere
author
autumn

award
awesome / awsome
***awful** ly dreadful
awkward

*-offal less valuable meat

*oral ly by the mouth
orbit ed
orchard
orchid
ordeal
order ed
organ
orgy -ies
ornate
orphan ed

* * *

abortion
absorber
absorbing
absorption

accordance
according

adoring
adsorption

albeit
almighty
already
alternate

appalling

assorted
assortment
assurance
assuring

audible
audience
auditor
auditory
***aurally** by the ear
aurora
Austria
authentic ally
authorise d
ze
autograph ed

awfully

*orally by the mouth
oration
orbital
orbited
orbiting
orchestra
orchestral
orchestrate
ordeal
ordering
orderly -ies
ordinal
ordinary
organic ally
organise d
ze
organist
orgasm
orient
ornament
orthodox

* * * * * * * *

accordingly
accordion

adorable

affordable

alteration
alternating
alternative ly
alternator
altogether

auditorium
auditory
authentically
authorising
zing
authority -ies
autobiographical ly
autobiography -ies
autocracy -ies
autocratic ally
automatic ally
automation
automobile
autonomic
autonomous
auxiliary -ies

orchestrating
orchestration
ordinarily
ordinary
organically
organisation al
zation al
organiser
zer
organising
zing
organism
oriental
orientate
orientation
ornithologist
ornithology
orthographic ally
orthography -ies

for H . . .
see page 261

In these words you can hear the vowel sound or as in horse

*

***bald** lacking hair
balk / baulk ed
***ball** round object / dance
***balled** made into a ball
baulk / balk ed
***bawl** yell
***bawled** did yell

***boar** male pig
***board** plank / daily meals / committee
***boor** rough fellow
***bore** drill / drilled hole / carried / fail to interest / tide-wave
***bored** drilled / lacking an interest
***born** delivered at birth
***borne** carried
bought

brawl ed
brawn
broad
brought

* *

ballpoint
ballroom
balsa
balti
Baltic
basalt
bauxite

because
befall
[befell]
[befallen]
before
besought

***boarder** person who pays for food and bed
boarding
borax
***border** edge / frontier
bordered
boredom
boring
bourgeois

brawny -ier, -iest
broadcast
[broadcast]
broadly
broadside

* * *

befallen
beforehand

bourgeoisie

broadcaster
broadcasting

* * * *

borealis

C

*

call ed
***caught** got / trapped
***caulk** ed fill gaps with fibre and tar
***cause** bring about / reason
caused
***caw** harsh bird cry
***cawed** did caw
***caws** does caw

chalk ed
***chord** notes sounded together / string / term in geometry
chore

***clause** words in sentence / part of written agreement
claw ed
***claws** curved nails or limbs

***coarse** rough
***cord** string
***core** central part / take out the core from
***cored** did core
***cork** bark of cork tree
corked
corm
corn
corned
***corps** group
corpse
***course** track / direction / part of meal / of course
coursed
***court** enclosed area / friends of sovereign / seek favour

crawl ed

* *

callback
calling
cauldron
causal ly
causing
caustic ally
caution ed
cautious

chlorate
chloric
chloride
chlorine
***choral** for or by a choir
choroid
chortle d
chorus es
chorused

conform ed
cordial ly
corgi
corkscrew ed
corner ed
cornet
cornfield
cornflakes
cornflower
corporal
corporate
corpus [corpora / corpuses]
cortex [cortices / cortexes]
coursework
courting
courtroom
courtship
courtyard

crawling

*-coral substance formed from bones of sea creatures

* * *

causally
causation
caustically
cautiously

chlorinate
chloroplast

conformist
cordial ly
corduroy
cormorant
cornea
corneal
cornerstone
cornflower
corpora
corporal ly
corporate
courtier

* * * * *

caustically

chlorinating
chlorination

conformity
coordinate
coordinating
coordination
coordinator
cordially
corporally
corporation

for Qu . . .
see page 266

D

*

daub ed
dawn ed

door

***draw** pull / sketch
[drew]
[drawn]
***drawer** sliding container
drawl ed

dwarf ed

* *

daughter
dawdle d
dawdling

deform ed
deport

distort
distraught
divorce d

doorbell
doorknob
doorstep
doorway
dormant
dormouse [dormice]
dorsal

drawback
drawbridge
drawing

* * *

discordant
disorder ed
distortion
divorcee
divorcing

dormitory -ies

* * * *

daughter-in-law

deformity -ies
deplorable

disorganised
ze

dormitory -ies

E

*

* *

endorse d
enforce d
***ensure** d make certain

escort

exalt
exhaust
explore d
export

*inshore near the shore
*insure d protect against loss

* * *

endorsing
enforcement
enforcing
enormous
***ensuring** making certain

exalted
exhausted
exhaustion
explorer
exploring

*insuring protecting against loss

* * * * * * *

enormously

exorbitant
extraordinarily
extraordinary

for I . . .
see page 262

*

fall
[fell]
[fallen]
false
fault
***faun** goat-god
***fawn** young deer / colour / try to win favour
***fawned** did fawn

fiord / fjord

flaunt
***flaw** ed fault
***floor** ed levelled area

*-**fond** showing love
***for** in place of / to belong to / because
force d
ford
***fore** front / leading position
forge d
fork ed
form ed
***fort** fortress
***forth** forward
***fought** contested
***four** 4
***fourth** 4th

fraud
fraught

for th . . .
see page 268

* *

falcon
fallen
falling
fallout
falter ed
faulty -ier, -iest

fiord / fjord

flawless
flora
floral
fluoride
fluorine

***forbear** hold back
[forbore]
[forborne]
forceful ly
forceps
forearm
***forebear / forbear** ancestor
forecast
[forecast]
forefoot
foreground
forehand
foreleg
foreman [foremen]
foremost
forename
foresee
[foresaw]
[foreseen]
foresight
foreskin
forestall ed
foretell
[foretold]
forewarn ed
***foreword** preface
forfeit
forging
forgo / forego
[forwent / forewent]
[forgone / foregone]
forlorn
formal ly
format ted
former
forming
***forte** loud / strength
fortnight
fortress es
fortune
***forty** 40

* * *

fluorescence
fluorescent

forcefully
forecaster
forefather
forefinger
forensic
forever
forgery
formalise d
ze
***formally** officially
formation
formatted
formatting
***formerly** previously
formula s [formulae]
formulate
forthcoming
fortieth
fortify -ies
fortitude
fortunate

fraudulent

* * * * * *

fluorescence
fluorescent
fluoridation /
fluoridisation
zation

foreseeable
forget-me-not
formality -ies
formidable
formulating
formulation
forsythia s
fortification
fortuitous ly
fortunately

Here the 'or' is neutral, like 'or' in 'forget'.

F***OR***GOTTEN WORDS

forbid
[forbade / forbad]
[forbidden]
forbidding
forgave
forget ting
[forgot]
[forgotten]
forgetful ly
forget-me-not
forgive
[forgave]
[forgiven]
forgiveness
forgiving
forsake
[forsook]
[forsaken]
forsaking

F

for th . . .
see page 268

* *

forum
***forward**s onward
fourteenth

Fräulein

G

*

***gall** cheek / bitterness/ sore / swelling
***Gaul** ancient region of Europe
gaunt
gauze

***gnaw** keep biting
***gnawed** did gnaw

gored
gorged
gorse

jaunt
jawed

*-nodded move head down and up
*nor and not

* *

galling
galore
gaudy -ier, -iest
gauntlet

Georgian

glory -ies
gloried

gorgeous
gorging
goring

jaunty -ier, -iest
jawing

Jordan

* * *

Gibraltar

glorify -ies
glorified
glorious

* * * *

Jordanian

H

*

***hall** large room / passage
halt
***haul** drag / amount gained
hauled
haunches
haunt
hawked

***hoar** white
***hoard** store
***hoarse** rough and husky
***horde** gang / tribe
horned
***horse** animal

*whore prostitute
*whored used prostitutes

* *

halter
haughty -ier, -iest
haulage
haunches
haunted
hawthorn

hoarding
hormone
hornblende
hornet
horseback
horsehair
horseman [horsemen]
horsepower
horseshoe

whoring

* * *

haughtily

horsemanship
horsepower
horsewoman
[horsewomen]

* * * *

historian

horticultural
horticulture

I

*

**

*ensure d make certain

ignore d

implore d
import

indoors
indorse / endorse d
inform ed
***inshore** near the shore
instal led **/ install** ed
***insure** d protect against loss

***

*ensuring making certain

immortal ly
importance
important

indorsing / endorsing
informal ly
informant
informer
installing
instalment / installment
insurance
***insuring** protecting against loss

**** *

immortality
immortally

inaugural
inauguration
incorporate d
incorporation
informally
informative

for E . . . see page 259

J

*

jaunt
jaw ed

**

jaunty -ier, -iest
jawing

Jordan

***

****

Jordanian

for dr . . . see page 259

K

*

**

Koran / Qur'an

***

****

Here the 'or' is neutral, like 'or' in 'forget'.

Korea   Korean

for C . . . see page 258

for Qu . . . see page 266

L

*

launch es
launched
***law** rules enforced in a country
lawn

lord
***lore** traditions and facts

* *

launcher
launder ed
laundry -ies
laurel
lawful ly
lawyer

lordship

* * *

launderette
laureate
lawfully

* * * * *

laborious ly

M

*

***mall** public walk / walk lined with shops
malt
*-**maul** ed handle roughly / heavy mallet
mauve

*-**moll** gangster's girl
***moor** open land / fasten to land or to buoy
***more** additional / a larger amount
***morn** morning
Morse
***mourn** show sadness at loss or death
mourned

* *

Malta

moorland
***morning** before midday
morpheme
morphine
morsel
mortal ly
mortar
mortgage d
mortice d /
mortise d
mourner
mournful ly
***mourning** showing sadness at loss or death

* * *

Majorca
marauder
marauding

Minorca
misfortune

moreover
mortally
mortgaging
mournfully

* * * *

memorial

mortality -ies

N

*

*gnaw keep biting
*gnawed did gnaw

*-knot ted tied fastening / hard part of wood / sea mile (per hour)

***naught / nought** zero

*-**nod** ded move head down and up
***nor** and not
norm
north
*-**not** used in denial, negation, refusal
***nought / naught** zero

* *

*-knotty -ier, iest full of knots

***naughty** -ier, -iest badly behaved

normal ly
Norman
north-east
northern
northward
north-west
Norway

* * *

naughtier
naughtiest
naughtiness
nausea
nauseous
nautical ly

normally
northeaster
northerner
northernmost
northwester
Norwegian

* * * *

nautically

normality
notorious

O

*

*all every one
*aught anything at all
*awe fear and wonder
*awed made to feel awe
*awl boring tool

***oar** rowing blade
*-**odd** unusual
***or** marks choice
orb
***ore** mineral
***ought** should

for H . . .
see page 261

* *

almost
alright
also
*altar holy table
*alter ed change
although
always

auburn
auction ed
audit
*auger tool
*augur suggest for the future
*August month
*august impressive
aura s / -ae
*aural ly by the ear
austere
author
autumn

awesome / awsome
*awful ly dreadful
awkward

*-**offal** less vauable meat

***oral** ly by the mouth
orbit ed
orchard
orchid
ordeal
order ed
organ
orgy -ies
ornate
orphan ed

* * *

albeit
almighty
already
alternate

audible
audience
auditor
auditory
*aurally by the ear
aurora
Austria
authentic ally
authorise d
ze
autograph ed

awfully

***orally** by the mouth
oration
orbital
orbited
orbiting
orchestra
orchestral
orchestrate
ordeal
ordering
orderly -ies
ordinal
ordinary
organic ally
organise d
ze
organist
orgasm
orient
ornament al
orphanage
orthodox

* * * * * * * *

alteration
alternating
alternative ly
alternator
altogether

auditorium
auditory
authentically
authorising
zing
authority -ies
autobiographical ly
autobiography -ies
autocracy -ies
autocratic ally
automatic ally
automation
automobile
autonomic
autonomous
auxiliary -ies

orchestrating
orchestration
ordinarily
ordinary
organically
organisation al
zation al
organiser
zer
organising
zing
organism
oriental
orientate
orientation
ornamental
ornithologist
ornithology
orthodoxy -ies
orthographic ally
orthography -ies

In these words you can hear the vowel sound or as in horse

*

paunch es
***pause** brief gap / hesitate
paused
***paw** foot of animal
***pawed** examined by paw
pawn
***pawned** left in return for loan
***paws** feet of animal

*-**pod** ded form pods / casing
*-**pond** pool
***poor** badly off
porch es
***pore** tiny hole / study closely
***pored** studied closely
***pores** tiny holes
pork
port
***pour** flow out
***poured** did pour

prawn

* *

palfrey
palsy
pausing
pawpaw

perform ed

poorly
poring
porous
porpoise
portal
porter
porthole
portion
portrait
portray ed
pouring

purport

* * *

performance
performer
performing

plausible

porcelain
porcupine
portable
portcullis
portico
portrayal
Portugal
Portuguese

precaution
proportion

* * * * * * *

pictorial ly

pornographic ally
pornography
portfolio

proportional ly
proportionate ly

Q

*	**	***	****
quart	**quarter**	**quarterly**	**quartermaster**
***quarts** more than one quart	**quartet**		
***quartz** mineral	**quartile**		

R

*	**	***	**** **
***raw** untreated / sore / chilly	**recall** ed	**recorded**	**reorganisation**
	record	**recorder**	**zation**
	recourse	**recording**	**reorganise** d
***roar** loud noise	**reform** ed	**reformer**	**ze**
roared	**report**	**reported**	**reorganising**
	resort	**reporter**	**zing**
*-rot ted decay	**resource** d	**resourceful**	
	restore d	**resources**	
wrath	**retort**	**resourcing**	
*wrought made to fit	**reward**	**restoring**	
	roaring		

In these words you can hear the vowel sound or as in horse

S

*

salt
***sauce** tasty liquid / rude talk
***saw** looked at / cutting tool
***sawed** did saw [sawn]

scald
scorch es scorched
score d
scorn ed
scrawl ed

shawl
***shore** coast
shored
shorn
short
shorts

small

snore d

***soar** fly high
***soared** flew high
*-**sod** turf
***sore** painful
***sort** group
***sought** looked for
***source** origin

spawn ed
spore
sport
sprawl ed

squawk ed

***stalk** stem / hunt / walk stiffly
stalked
stall ed
staunch es staunched
*-**stock** ed supply
store d
***stork** bird
storm
straw

***sure** certain

swarm ed
***sword** weapon
swore
sworn

* *

salty -ier, -iest
saucepan
saucer
saucy -ier, -iest
sauna
saunter ed
sawdust

scorer
scoring
scornful ly
scorpion

shoring
shortage
shortening
shorter
shortest
shortfall
shorthand
shortly
short-term

signor [signori]

slaughter ed

smaller
smallest
smallpox
small-scale

snoring
snorkel

sportsman [sportsmen]

stalker
***stalking** hunting / walking stiffly
stalling
stalwart
*-**stocking** ed covering for legs and feet / providing
storage
storehouse
***storey** floor
storing
stormy -ier, -iest
***story** -ies tale
strawberry -ies

support
surely

swarthy -ier, -iest

* * *

saucily

scornfully
scorpion

shortcoming

signora
signori

sonorous

sorcerer
sorcery
sportswoman [sportswomen]

strawberry -ies

supported
supporter
supporting

* * * * *

subordinate
subordinating

T

*

***talk** speak
talked
tall
***taught** instructed
taunt
***taut** tight

thaw ed
thorn
thought
thwart

***tor** hill
torch es
torched
***tore** did tear
torn
***torque** turning force / necklace
***-tot** young child / small amount / add

* *

talking
taller
tallest
tawny -ier, -iest

thorax es / -ces
thoughtful ly

Torah
torment
torsion
torso s
tortoise
torture d
Tory -ies
toward
towards

transform ed
transport
trauma s [traumata]

* * *

talkative

thesaurus es / -i
thoughtfully

tornado es
torpedo es
tortilla
torturing

traumata
traumatic

* * * *

tutorial

V

*

vase
***vault** gymnastic leap / underground room / arched roof

***-volt** unit of electrical force

* *

* * *

* * * *

Victorian
victorious

W

VOWEL SOUND **or**

*

*hoar white
*hoard store
*horde gang / tribe

*-rot ted decay

***walk** ed go in steps
wall ed
waltz es
waltzed
***war** conflict
***ward** part of hospital / person under legal protection
warm ed
warmth
***warn** caution
warned
warp ed
***warred** waged war
wart

wharf [wharves]
***whore** prostitute
***whored** used prostitutes

*-**wok** cooking pan
***wore** was dressed in
***worn** carried on the body / worse for wear

wrath
***wrought** made to fit

* *

walker
walking
wallflower
walnut
walrus
warble d
warbler
warbling
warden
wardrobe
warfare
warhead
warlike
warmer
warmly
warning
warpath
warring
warship
wartime
water ed

whoring

withdraw
[withdrew]
withdrawal
withdrawn

* * *

wallflower
wallpaper ed
waterfall
waterfowl
waterproof ed
watershed
watertight
waterway
watery

withdrawal

* * * *

walkie-talkie
watercolour

Y

*

yawn ed

***yore** ancient times
***your** belonging to you
***you're** you are
yours

* *

Yorkshire
yourself
yourselves

* * *

* * * *

A

*	* *	* * *	* * * *
	ahoy!	**adjoining**	
	annoy ed	**annoyance**	
	anoint	**annoying**	
	appoint	**appointment**	
	avoid	**avoidance**	
		avoided	

B

*	* *	* * *	* * * *
boil ed	**boiler**	**boisterous**	
***boy** lad	**boiling**		
	boycott	**buoyancy**	
broil ed	**boyfriend**		
	boyhood		
***buoy** marker			
buoyed	**buoyant**		

C

*	* *	* * *	* * * *
choice	**cloister** ed		
coil ed	**coinage**		
***coin** money			
coined			
coy			
*quoin cornerstone			

for Qu . . .
see page 274

In these words you can hear the vowel sound oi as in oyster

D

*	* *	* * *	* * * *
	deploy ed	**deployment**	**disloyally**
	destroy ed	**destroyer**	**disloyalty**
	devoid		
		disloyally	
	disloyal ly	**disloyalty**	
	doily -ies / **doyley** s		

E

*	* *	* * *	* * * *
	embroil ed	**embroider** ed	**embroidery**
	employ ed	**employee**	
		employer	**enjoyable**
	enjoy ed	**employment**	
	exploit		
		enjoying	
		enjoyment	

F

*	* *	* * *	* * * *
foil ed	**foyer**	**Freudian**	
	Fraülein		

In these words you can hear the vowel sound oi as in oyster

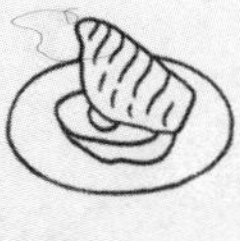

G

*	* *	* * *	* * * *
***groin** part where legs join body ***groyne** low structure built out into water			

H

*	* *	* * *	* * * *
hoist			

J

*	* *	* * *	* * * *
joined **joint** **joist** **joy**	**joiner** **joining** **joyful**ly **joyous**	**joinery** **joyfully**	

In these words you can hear the vowel sound oi as in oyster

L

*	* *	* * *	* * * *
loyal ly	**loyal** ly **loyalist** **loyalty** -ies	**loyalist** **loyally** **loyalty** -ies	

M

*	* *	* * *	* * * *
moist	**moisture**	**moisturise** d **ze**	**moisturiser** **zer** **moisturising** **zing**

N

*	* *	* * *	* * * *
noise	**noisy** -ier, -iest	**noisier** **noisiest** **noisily**	

O

*	* *	* * *	* * * *
oil ed	**oilstone** **oily** -ier, -iest **ointment** **oyster**		

for H . . .
see page 272

In these words you can hear the vowel sound oi as in oyster

P

*	**	***	****
ploy	**poignant**	**pointedly**	
	pointed	**poisoner**	
point	**pointer**	**poisonous**	
poise d	**pointing**		
	pointless		
	poison ed		

Q

*	**	***	****
*coin money			
***quoin** cornerstone			
quoit			

R

*	**	***	****
royal ly	**recoil** ed	**rejoicing**	
	rejoice d		
	rejoin ed	**royally**	
		royalty -ies	
	royal ly		
	royalty -ies		

In these words you can hear the vowel sound oi as in oyster

S

*	* *	* * *	* * * *
soil ed	**Savoy**	**sequoia**	
spoil ed [spoilt]	**soya**		

T

*	* *	* * *	* * * *
toil ed	**toilet**		
toy ed			

V

*	* *	* * *	* * * *
voice d	**voicing**	**voice-over**	
void	**voyage** d	**voyaging**	

A

*

* *

abound
about

account

allow
***allowed** permitted
***aloud** loud enough to be heard

amount

announce d

around
arouse d

astound

* * *

accountant
allowance

announcement
announcer
announcing

arousal
arousing

astounded
astounding

* * * *   * *

accountability
accountable
accountancy

allowable

B

*

blouse

***bough** branch
bounce d
bound
bout
***bow** bend / front of ship
bowel

brow
brown ed
***brows** more than one brow
***browse** d nibble / dip into books

* *

bouncing
boundary -ies
boundless
bounty -ies
bowel
bower

brownie
browsing

* * *

boundary -ies

* * * *

In these words you can hear the vowel sound ou as in owl

*

chow

cloud
clout
clown ed

couch es
couched
count
cow ed
cower ed

crouch es
crouched
crowd
crown ed

* *

cacao

chowder

cloudless
cloudy -ier, -iest

confound
*__council__ group for directing affairs
*__counsel__ advice
counselled
countdown
counted
counter
countess es
counting
countless
county -ies
*__coward__ person who lacks courage
cowboy
cower ed
*__cowered__ did cower
cowshed
cowslip

crowded

* * *

*__councillor__ member of a council
counselling
*__counsellor__ person who gives advice
countenance d
counteract
counterfeit
counterfoil
counterpart
counterpoint
countersink
cowardice

* * * * *

countenancing
counter-attack
counterexample

D

*

doubt
***dour** unsmiling
***douse / dowse** put into water / put out
doused / dowsed
dowel led
***dower** property of bride or widow
down ed
***dowse** use divining rod

drought
drown ed

**

denounce d
devour ed
devout

discount
dismount

doubtful ly
doubtless
***dousing / dowsing** putting into water / putting out
dowdy -ier, -iest
dowel led
dowelling
downcast
downfall
downhill
downland
download
downright
downstairs
downstream
downturn
downward
downwards
dowry -ies
dowser
***dowsing** using divining rod

drowsy -ier, -iest

***

denouncing

doubtfully
dowelling

****

E

*

**

empower ed

endow ed

***

empower ed

encounter ed

****

In these words you can hear the vowel sound ou as in owl

F

*

flounce d
***flour** ground grain
***flower** blossom
flowered

***foul** dirty
fouled
found
***fowl** bird

Frau [Frauen]
frown ed

for th . . .
see page 283

* *

flouncing
flounder ed
flowerpot

***fouler** dirtier
***founded** established
founder
***foundered** sank / collapsed
foundry -ies
fountain
***fowler** bird hunter

Frauen

* * *

flowerpot

foundation

* * * *

G

*

gouge d
gown

grouch es
grouched
ground
grouse d
growl ed

* *

glower ed

gouging

grouching
grouchy -ier, -iest
grounding
groundsel
groundwork
grousing

* * *

* * * *

H

*

hound
***hour** 60 minutes
house d
how
how'd
howl ed

*our belonging to us

* *

hourglass es
hourly
housefly -ies
household
houseplant
housewife [housewives]
housework
housing

* * *

householder
housekeeper
housekeeping
houseparent
however

* * * *

In these words you can hear the vowel sound ou as in owl

J

*	**	***	****
joust			
jowl			

for dr . . .
see page 278

L

*	**	***	****
***Laos** country	**louder**	**loudspeaker**	
	loudest		
loud	**loudly**		
lounge d	**lounging**		
***louse** insect	**lousy** -ier, -iest		
lout			

M

*	**	***	****
mound	**miaow / meow**	**mountaineer**	**mountaineering**
mount		**mountainous**	
mouse [mice]	**mountain**	**mountainside**	
mouth	**mounted**	**mountaintop**	
mouthed	**mousy** -ier, -iest		
	mouthful		
	mouthing		
	mouthpiece		

In these words you can hear the vowel sound ou as in owl

N

*

noun
now

* *

* * *

nowadays

* * * *

O

*

*hour 60 minutes

ounce
*__our__ belonging to us
ours
out

owl

* *

hourglass es

ourselves
outbid
[outbid]
outboard
outbox es
outbreak
outburst
outcome
outcrop
outcry -ies
outdo
[outdid]
[outdone]
outdoor
outdoors
outer
outfit
outflow
outgrow
[outgrew]
outing
outlaw ed
outlay
outlet
outline d
outlook
outpost
output
outrage d
outright
outrun
[outran]
outset
outshine
[outshone]
outside
outskirts
outstretch ed
outward
outwit ted
outwith

* * *

outbidding
outgoing
outlining
outlying
outnumber ed
outpatient
outrageous
outshining
outsider
outspoken
outstanding
outwardly
outwitted
outwitting

* * * *

for H . . .
see page 279

P

*

plough ed

pouch es
pouched
pounce d
pound
pout
power ed

proud
prow
prowl ed

* *

ploughman
[ploughmen]
ploughshare
pouncing
powder ed
power ed
powerful ly
powerless

profound
pronounce d
proudly
prowess

* * *

powerful ly
powerless

pronouncement
pronouncing

* * * *

powerfully

R

*

round
*__rouse__ d awaken / become more active
rout
row
*__rows__ quarrels

* *

rebound
recount
renown ed

rounded
rounders
rounding
roundup
rousing
router
rowdy -ier, -iest

* * *

roundabout

* * * *

S

*

scour ed
scout
scowl ed
scrounge d

shout
shower ed
shroud

slouch es
slouched

snout

sound
sour ed
south
sow

spouse
spout
sprout

stout

* *

Saudi
sauerkraut

scoundrel
scourer
scouring
scrounging

shouted
shouting
shower ed
showery

sounded
sounder
sounding
soundly
soundproof ed
soundtrack
sourdough
south-east
southward
south-west

surmount
surround

* * *

showery

south-eastern
southwester /
sou'wester
south-western

surrounded
surrounding
surroundings

* * * *

T

*

thou

tout
towel led
tower ed
town

trounce
trout
trowel led

* *

thousand
thousandth

tousle d
towel led
towelling
tower ed
towering
townhouse
township

trauma s [traumata]
trouncing
trousers
trowel led
trowelling

* * *

towelling
towering

traumata
traumatic
trowelling

* * * *

V

*	* *	* * *	* * * *
vouch es	**voucher**		
vouched	***vouchers** more than one voucher		
vow ed	***vouches** does vouch		
vowel	**vowel**		

W

*	* *	* * *	* * * *
wound			
wow			

Y

*	* *	* * *	* * * *
yowl ed	**yowling**		

In these words you can hear the vowel sound ou as in owl

Developing the ACE dictionary

The need for a new approach

There is justifiable concern about standards of reading and writing throughout the English-speaking world. Careful researchers such as Thorstad (1991), Upward (1992) and Spencer (2001, 2007) have repeatedly shown that the nature of English spelling is one of the reasons why children and young people in European countries with regular spelling systems perform much better than those in the United Kingdom. Both word recognition (especially for longer words) and spelling are affected. Moreover, Italian children can usually spell any word they can read, but British children can typically spell fewer than half of the words they can decode.

My own research (Moseley, 1996) has demonstrated that poor spellers will often use a restricted vocabulary in their writing, preferring short words that have one letter representing one sound, avoiding common words that are hard to spell and trying to play safe by repeating familiar words. Writing tasks are not enjoyed by many pupils and may become limited in quantity, range and frequency.

No amount of studying spelling patterns and learning spellings will do much to improve the situation if daily opportunities for meaningful writing are not provided across the curriculum. At the same time, there must be modelling, shared learning, encouragement and feedback regarding all aspects of writing, including spelling.

Beech (2004) found that 8-year-olds and 10-year-olds reported using a dictionary only once a week on average. He noted that such infrequent use would bring little benefit, but also showed that about a third of the children were slow and inaccurate. The younger children were much more likely to use a dictionary to check spellings than to find meanings and there was a strong relationship between speed of locating words, word recognition and spelling ability.

All this points to the need for a reference source that is quick and easy to access, structured to draw attention to spelling patterns, and rewarding to use whenever writing is undertaken. Shenton (2007) saw the ACE dictionary as addressing the user-unfriendly paradox that 'in order to access information within a source, the user must often apply knowledge that he or she does not yet possess'.

With a conventional dictionary children often do not possess the knowledge required to find the right page, let alone to find a specific word. The ACE Dictionary's Index was designed to direct the user to the right page, and finding the right word makes use of skills that even beginner readers possess. If the word is unfamiliar it is located by using both *analytic and synthetic phonics*, the reversible processes so strongly advocated in *Letters and Sounds* (DES, 2007).

For the field trials throughout the UK and in Ireland, a hundred copies of a pre-publication ACE dictionary were produced. It was important to demonstrate that all users could cope with the ACE page format and would not be put off by the number of words provided. Improvement suggestions were acted on for the first edition in 1985, including those concerning regional differences in pronunciation.

As a part of the field trials an A4 class set was provided to a Year 1 class in Whitley Bay as well as a half-size A5 version. The class coped very well with both versions and even sent a specially composed acrostic to the author. Timed trials showed that they were faster in finding words with the A5 version, indicating that small print presents no problems when scanning down columns.

How the words were chosen

Both British and American sources have been used in compiling the *ACE Spelling Dictionary*. Many words have been added in response to suggestions from users of the dictionary and this feedback process continues.

One major vocabulary source was the *American Heritage Word Frequency Book* (Carroll *et al*, 1971). This contains no fewer than 86,741 word types (words and word forms) from books used in schools by children in the age range 8 to 14. The complete range of school subjects was covered. Unless they were judged to be unfamiliar to British users, all words (but not all word forms) in the first 23,000 word types of the American heritage list were included in the *ACE Spelling Dictionary*.

In order to meet the needs of British students, lists supplied by subject teachers for all areas of the curriculum have been included, as has the subject-specific vocabulary from National Curriculum documents. Particular care has been taken to cover scientific, technical, mathematical and ICT vocabulary. The *Evans Technical Dictionary* (1982) and a list of mathematical terms published by the Scottish Qualifications Authority (2000) are among the sources used.

For the third edition, more than 3000 words were taken from the British National Corpus, from collections of children's writing at www.kidpub.com, from frequency counts of newspaper articles published on the internet and from various lists of new words added to well-known dictionaries.

A list of the major vocabulary sources is given at the end of the book.

Action research with ACE

A survey of research on ways of improving spelling (Moseley, 1994) suggests that those which combine a variety of powerful features are the most successful. It is also important to see spelling as an integral part of writing. Work by the author in which a weekly piece of creative writing was produced at home with the help of the *ACE Spelling Dictionary* showed that dyslexic learners could make very rapid progress in only five weeks when provided with individual targets and feedback. A similar approach was taken by Hancock (1992), working with a mixed-ability group of Year 6 children. The children used the ACE dictionary for checking their work and also chose six words to learn per week. Hancock reported an improvement in the overall quality of written work (as judged 'blind' by an independent evaluator), a 50 per cent reduction in spelling error rate and an improvement in written vocabulary. One boy with a spelling problem and a negative attitude towards spelling 'was extremely enthusiastic to succeed ... and ... his small and frequent achievements ... did much to boost his confidence and self-esteem'.

In an earlier classroom study (Moseley, 1989) it was those with weak spelling and reading who made the most progress. The pupils used the *ACE Spelling Dictionary* to proofread all written work, while the teacher was able to use one-to-one conferencing time for discussion of the content and structure of the writing. Spelling improved at an average rate of 1.7 months per month, while the seven poorest spellers progressed at more than twice this speed. These gains were accompanied by significant improvements in the quantity and quality of writing as well as rapid improvement in word recognition.

ACE Spelling Activities (Moseley and Singleton, 1993) grew out of earlier work with dyslexics in which learning activities were linked with the ACE Dictionary. Moseley (1994) reported that in classroom trials in which the learning strategies included at the end of the ACE dictionary were used, sixty-five pupils aged 8–11 improved in their spelling by nineteen months in only five months. The intervention was based on the daily learning at home of four to six words from the graded spelling lists provided. Both verbal and visual strategies proved effective, but two very important components were pronouncing the words in a different way, according to the spelling; and saying the letter names before writing each letter string.

One teacher and her pupils wrote to the author about her imaginative use of dictation passages, followed by an ACE checking activity limited to ten words. The pupils wrote with evident confidence and enjoyment, saying that 'over thirty children have bought their own dictionaries'. One reassured the author about the use of the 'smooth newt' sound clue by saying, 'My friend and I found a newt we brought it bake and built an aquarium for the newt, its a female. At the moment its hibernating.'

It is hoped that the *ACE Spelling Dictionary* will continue to encourage teachers and helpers to devise new ways of using it to suit all pupils, with individual strengths and weaknesses and with different approaches to learning.

How to look, listen and learn with ACE

Looking up words in order to spell them correctly is only one way of using the *ACE Spelling Dictionary*. Other ways of using it can be just as valuable and can help to increase your speed of word recognition as well as your knowledge about words. You can do this by timing yourself as you look for words of a certain type. You might like to work with someone and take turns in looking up words. The words can be chosen by topic, by use, by length, by stress pattern, by sound, by features of spelling or by grammatical function. It can also be fun to think of combinations of these – for example, to find as many long words as possible that can be used to express enjoyment of food, grouping them according to the stressed syllable.

Some of the activities at the end of this book demonstrate specific ways of using the dictionary. Many more ideas for actively exploring it will be thought of by those who use it. What is provided here is a detailed account of some of the rules that have been followed, especially those that relate to alphabetical order and to the inclusion of different forms of the same word. You do not need to understand all of these before you start to use the dictionary, but you may need to refer to them at times and they may suggest some useful activities.

Alphabetical grouping of words

Within each section words are grouped by initial letter, taken in alphabetical order. A letter is omitted if there are no words beginning with it in that particular section.

Within each column of words there are smaller sets, each beginning with the same two letters. This makes the columns easier to scan, and cuts down search time. It does not take long to learn that 'sc' is near the top of a set of words beginning with 'S', that 'sm' is about halfway through and that 'sw' is near the end.

Some words are entered in more than one place. This happens when the first sound in the word does not uniquely determine what the first letter is. For example, words beginning with a silent letter (like 'knife' and 'gnome') are entered under 'N' according to the initial sound as well as under the appropriate silent letter. Words like 'ceiling' and 'chassis' are entered under both 'S' and 'C'. Words like 'kangaroo' and 'karate' are entered under 'C' and under 'K'. Lighter print is used for double-entered words when they begin with a different letter from the rest of the words in a column.

In certain cases, cross-reference pointers are used instead of double or multiple entries. A cross-reference is always provided from 'K' to 'C' within the same section, instead of repeating a long list of 'C' words under 'K'. Dropped 'h's, confusion between initial 'e' and 'i' and between 'f' and 'th' as well as uncertainty about the spelling of words beginning with 'qu' are also taken care of by the use of cross-reference pointers.

Meanings

In cases where two words sound the same (or nearly the same) but have different meanings, you need to check that you have found the right word. All such words have an asterisk (*) against them and their meanings are given alongside. These words are called homonyms (words with the same sound but with different meanings). Some of them are also homographs (words with the same spelling but with different meanings).

If the meaning or meanings do not fit the word you are looking for, all you have to do is to try another similar-sounding word with an asterisk against it. That will be in the section you are looking at, but sometimes at the top or bottom of the list.

Plurals

If the plural form of a noun is not shown, it is safe to assume that you simply add an 's'. So, if you find 'journey', you will be able to spell 'journeys'.

All 'es' and '-ies' plurals are shown; for example 'box es' and 'baby -ies'. Where, as in 'baby -ies', there is a dash before the ending, part of the word has to be removed before the plural ending is added. The most common pattern is for a final 'y' to be removed before adding '-ies'. Plurals of Latin or Greek words and any unusual plurals such as 'calves' are printed in square brackets; for example, [criteria], [phenomena] and [calves].

Present participles

These are given for the more common words and in all cases where a final consonant is doubled before 'ing' is added (e.g. 'swim' and 'swimming').

When the present participle form (ending in 'ing') is not given, you can be sure that the spelling falls into one of two patterns:

a) for words not ending in 'e', add 'ing'
b) for words ending in 'e', remove the 'e' before adding 'ing'.

Past tenses

The past tense form is given for the more common words and whenever a final consonant is doubled before 'ed' is added (e.g. 'skid' and 'skidded').

In all words where the final 'ed' has the sound 't' (as in 'ticked') the past tense marker is given alongside: 'tick ed'. The past tense marker is also given for long vowel words ending in 'e': 'phone d'.

All irregular past tense forms are given in full. They are entered in the appropriate sections, but are also included, printed in square brackets, immediately below the corresponding present tense form. Two examples are the following:

bring	**buy**
[brought]	[bought]

Comparatives and superlatives

These are given in full for the more common words and whenever a final consonant is doubled (as in 'bigger' and 'biggest'). Where a final 'y' is changed to '-ier' or to '-iest' this is also always shown (e.g. 'saucy -ier, -iest'). If you cannot find a particular word with the ending 'er' or 'est', you can be sure that the spelling falls into one of the two following patterns:

a) for words not ending in 'e', add 'er' or 'est'
b) for words ending in 'e', remove the 'e' before adding 'er' or 'est'.

Dialects

The vowel sound sections are based on 'received' pronunciation (RP), but regional accents have been provided for. Trials were carried out throughout the British Isles, and wherever major shifts in the pronunciation of vowels required it, words were entered in more than one section. Wherever a dash appears in front of a word it means that for some speakers that word is pronounced with the same vowel sound as the other words in the section.

In the /a/ section words pronounced in RP with an /ar/ sound have a dash in front of them. These words are pronounced with an /a/ in Scotland, and in most cases in the north of England. In the /o/ section the words with a dash in front of them belong there only for Scottish speakers. In the short vowel /u/ and /oo/ section, two RP sounds have been put together, with a dash before the /oo/ sound words. In the north of England there may be no difference in pronunciation between the two groups. In the section containing words with the long /oo/ sound, the words with a dash before them belong there only for Scots. In parts of the Midlands and in Merseyside the sounds /air/ and /er/ are pronounced in the same way. The /air/ words are therefore entered in the /er/ section as well, a feature which also makes sense for some of the words as pronounced in Scotland.

A major feature of Scottish speech is the rolled **r** following a vowel. The RP /ar/, /air/, /er/ and /or/ sounds are therefore pronounced differently in Scotland. There are cross-reference pointers in the appropriate ACE sections, but these will not be needed if Scots always refer to the third part of the dictionary for words with vowels followed by an 'r'. This applies to all of the short vowels, and for the long vowels /ae/ and /oe/. It does not, however, apply to the long vowels /ee/, /ie/ and /ue/.

The following table is provided for the benefit of Scottish users:

Words with	**Section**	**Examples**
SHORT /a/ followed by 'r'	/ar/	shark, article
SHORT /e/ followed by 'r'	/er/	early, nervous
SHORT /i/ followed by 'r'	/er/	bird, firmly
SHORT /o/ followed by 'r'	/or/	horse, warning
SHORT /u/ followed by 'r'	/er/	hurt, worm
LONG /ae/ followed by 'r'	/air/	rare, airport
LONG /ee/ followed by 'r'	/ee/	clear, steer
LONG /ie/ followed by 'r'	/ie/	wire, tyre
LONG /oe/ followed by 'r'	/or/	hoarse, bored
LONG /ue//oo/ followed by 'r'	/ue//oo/	pure, poor

Strategies for improving spelling

Dealing with difficult and much-needed words

The following activities and strategies are suitable for use either by students working on their own – maybe with a helper – or in a classroom context. The techniques used in the activities can also be applied to other difficult words. Both content and techniques can be personalised.

We provide two spelling banks: 60 common tricky words and 660 other high frequency words used by young writers. The sixty common tricky words account for about 30 per cent of all misspellings made by children in Years 3–6 (Moseley, 1997). It is especially important that these are correctly written from the outset so that misspellings do not have to be unlearned. For this reason a reference card is recommended, to be used both while writing and when proofreading.

Three additional lists of frequently used words are provided for the regular study and learning of spellings. While the word list in *Letters and Sounds* (DES, 2007) is based on the vocabulary of reading schemes (Masterson *et al.*, 2003), these three lists are derived from combined samples of the words that children use. Taken together, the two ACE spelling banks account for between 40 per cent and 60 per cent of the words found in children's writing at ages 9–11.

Words you need to know

Some of the words you need to use a lot are not easy to spell. Once you can cope with those you will feel much more confident about spelling. To save you the trouble of looking up these words every time you need them, here is a *Master list of tricky words*. You will know some of these already, so the first thing to do is to shorten the list to the ones you really need.

Master list of tricky words

an	of	all	it's	off
saw	too	two	was	a lot
came	come	hour	into	kept
knew	know	said	then	they
want	went	were	when	again
could	heard	might	right	still
that's	their	there	tried	until
where	always	bought	caught	friend
houses	inside	myself	opened	people
played	police	school	turned	another
decided	outside	running	started	stopped
thought	through	because	suddenly	sometimes

What to do

1 Put a tick next to each word in the list that you know very well (or take a test, twenty at a time).

2 Get a piece of card that will fit into your *ACE Spelling Dictionary* or your jotter.

3 Copy out your own list of tricky words, in two columns. Leave a space or draw a box beside each word so you can write tally marks to show how many times you have recognised it. You can add some words of your own if you want to.

4 Ask a helper who is good at spelling to check your card when it is ready for use.

5 Get to know your tricky words. Take four words at a time and make up some sentences which include them. Write out your sentences. When you get to a tricky word, find it on your card so you spell it correctly. Take a good look and spell out the letters before and as you write. When you have finished, proofread all your sentences, using the Master list and the *ACE Spelling Dictionary*.

6 Get your card out every time you do some writing. Whenever a tricky word comes along, check it on your card before you write it down. Every time you do this, put a tally mark next to the word. You can cross off tricky words when you no longer need to check them on your card, but you should not do that until you have at least ten tally marks against a word.

7 Use your card to proofread work produced by you or by other writers.

8 Make a new card about every three months until you have narrowed down your list of tricky words to one or two. Eventually you will have no words at all on your list.

9 Try to learn your tricky words four at a time, always using letter names and at least one other method such as a memory aid (see pp. 295–296 for other effective methods).

Memory aids for tricky words

	LONG MEMORY AID	SHORT MEMORY AID
a lot	'A lot' is not one word.	two words (1) + (3)
again	Two wins: a gain and a gain **again**.	that pain **again**!
all	B**all**, c**all**, f**all**, h**all**, t**all**, w**all** – they **all** have 'all'.	We **all** f**all** down!
always	This is **always** one word with one 'l', all the time.	**al**(l) ...
an	An **e**gg, an **a**nything beginning with **A E I O U**.	an A- an E- an I- an O- an U-
another	**A N O**ther was dropped from the team.	one word (2 + 5 = 7)
because	**B**ig **e**lephants **c**an **a**lways **u**nderstand **s**mall **e**lephants.	be (2) + cause (5) = 7
bought	**B**eware **o**f **u**ntamed **g**reat **h**ungry **t**igers!	_ ough _
came	We c**ame** to have a g**ame** (magic E).	c**ame** (magic E)
caught	Her n**augh**ty d**augh**ter c**augh**t a cold.	c**augh**t: did catch
come	C**ome** h**ome** and have s**ome** tea.	C**ome** h**ome** for tea!
could	**Could/should/would O**ld **u**ncles **l**ove **d**ancing?	I **would** if I **could**.
decided	The CID de**cid**ed not to take sides.	decide on a de**cid**er
friend	**Fri**day and at the week**end** I'll see my friends.	fri-end
heard	Did hear, by **ear**.	_ ear _
hour	Our train leaves in an **hour** (60 minutes).	**H**ow long? An **h**our.
houses	How do you spell **houses**? There's no W and no Z!	a **h ou se** for sale
inside	You can hide **inside** or outside.	one word (2 + 4 = 6)
into	Run **into** the room and jump onto the chair.	one word (2 + 2 = 4)
it's	**It's** short for 'it is' and the ' stands for the letter **I**.	it is
kept	We **kept** on thinking about 11 **Sept**.	The keeper **kept** goal.
knew	(silent **K**) – understood?	k-n as in 'knobbly knee'
know	(silent **K**) – understand?	k-n as in 'knobbly knee'
might	I **might** get it right!	_igh_
myself	myself yourself himself herself	one word (2 + 4 = 6)
of	**'O-F'** is a one-off – one **of** a kind.	**Of** sounds like **ov**.
off	On and off, **off** is confused with **of**.	one F is not on
opened	The **ED** ending is needed in open**ed** and clos**ed**.	open (4) + ed (2) = 6
outside	You can hide inside or **outside**.	one word (3 + 4 = 7)
people	**P**eople **e**at **o**melettes: **p**eople **l**ove **e**ggs.	popular pe **o** ple
played	Yesterday I pl**ay**ed with words ending in **ED**.	pl **ay ed**
police	Be n**ice** and polite to the pol**ice**.	Pol**ice** not**ice**: **ICE**!
right	**I g**o **h**ome by going first left and then **right**.	I m**igh**t get it r **igh** t.
running	Doubled consonant before **ING** in words like ru**nn**ing.	run, running
said	**A-I** makes an /e/ sound in s**ai**d, ag**ai**n and ag**ai**nst.	A one-off (**AI**) again.

saw	I saw that **was** is **saw** spelt backwards.	See what I **saw** – a seesaw!
school	School is where you learn cool spellings.	sch (3) + ool (3) = 6
sometimes	**Sometimes** is one word for more than one time.	one word (4 + 5 = 9)
started	We start with **ST** and finish with **ED** (7 letters).	start (5) + ed (2) = 7
still	Many words end with **LL** after a short vowel.	Is **Bill still ill**?
stopped	Doubled consonant before **ED** in words like sto**pp**ed.	stop, stopped
suddenly	I suddenly forgot the middle part of sud **den** ly.	sudden (6) + ly (2) = 8
that's	**That's** short for 'that is' and the ' stands for the letter **i**.	That's short for 'that is'.
their	The dog we own is ours, not yours; **their** dog is theirs.	There is **their** heir!
then	But **th**en, **th**e walls of our d**en** are very thin!	**Then** and **th**en and th**en**.
there	There → to or in that place. There is/are/was/were/etc.	**There** is their heir!
they	The tricky bit may well be the **EY**.	Th**ey** did not ob**ey**.
thought	We th**ought** **o**f **u**ntamed **g**reat **h**ungry **t**igers!	**O U G**reat **H**ungry **T**iger!
through	It's a r**ough** path, but we **ough**t to get thr**ough**.	Thr**ough** a t**ough** exam.
too	**Too** many o's to put in a two-letter word.	My toe is **too** big **too**.
tried	Try to learn this pattern: no **Y**, but **I + ED** in **tried**.	I **try**, she tr**ies**, he tr**ied**.
turned	**U R** able to add **ED** to **turn**.	**turn** (4) + ed (2) = 6
until	One **l** as in **nil**: unlike fill, hill, kill, pill, till, will.	_ _ til
want	After a /w/ sound you often want **A** instead of **O**.	What do you want?
was	**W**asn't **A**nnie **s**tunning?	'Was' has an **A** and an **S**.
went	T**went**y of us **went** into the big tent.	WE NT: we **went** in.
were	Why is w**ere** spelt like wh**ere**?	**were**: in the past
when	**Wh**en do question words start with **WH-**?	**Wh**en they start with **W**.
where	**Where** were you when I took your place? Here.	**Where**? **Here**.

More much-needed words

Learn to spell these words so that you get them right when you write.

Lists 1, 2 and 3 (pp. 302–304), each containing 220 useful words, have been prepared from samples of children's speech and writing. Short regular words in which letter errors rarely occur are not included in the three lists. These spelling bank lists are graded, but do not include the sixty common words that are most often misspelt. Those are in the *Master list of tricky words* on page 293 and are best learned by using a reference card in the course of writing, as explained.

Using the lists at home

If you are using the lists to work on your spelling at home, the first thing to do is plan your own programme. Consult your T/H about this. You will need to have realistic targets that enable you to make steady progress without having too much to do. A lot will depend on how quickly you need to achieve results, and you should bear in mind any other activities you are committed to on a regular basis.

You will also need to find out which words you should concentrate on. It is not intended that you should always start with List 1. Use the test that follows to decide where to start.

Using the lists in school (for the T/H)

If these lists are used in school, one could be covered in one term, at the rate of twenty words a week. That allows for some repeated learning of words misspelt in weekly tests. Lists 1, 2 and 3 are suitable for NC Levels 2, 3 and 4–5 respectively, and for Scottish Levels A, B and C. Those who need an accelerated spelling programme can work on the lists for a whole year.

Note that it is not intended that the same list should be given to all members of a class. The following test can be used to decide which list should be used by which students.

Spelling test

Your T/H says each word, repeats it in a phrase or sentence, pauses briefly and then says the word again. You should not write it down until you hear it for the third time.

1 SHIP ... The passengers boarded the ship ... SHIP

2 FOOTBALL ... My football strip ... FOOTBALL

3 READING ... What are you reading? ... READING

4 TELL ... Tell me a story ... TELL

5 SEVEN ... Seven puppies in a basket ... SEVEN

6 SPOKE ... I spoke slowly to Gran on the phone ... SPOKE

7 SLOWLY ... We walked very slowly ... SLOWLY

8 NEAR ... We live near the park ... NEAR

9 PERSON ... Who is that person crossing the road? ... PERSON

10 ANYTHING ... Have you anything to report? ... ANYTHING

11 PRETTY ... The garden was looking very pretty ... PRETTY

12 BEFORE ... Tidy your room before you go out ... BEFORE

13 OWNER ... Who is the owner of this car? ... OWNER

14 MUSIC ... I listen to music on my MP3 player ... MUSIC

15 HAPPENED ... What happened in the playground? ... HAPPENED

16 FOLLOWED ... The stray dog followed me ... FOLLOWED

17 SUGAR ... Sugar in your tea ... SUGAR

18 MOUNTAIN ... The top of the mountain ... MOUNTAIN

19 USUAL ... I woke up at seven, as usual ... USUAL

20 INTERESTING ... An interesting story ... INTERESTING

When you have written down all the words, your T/H should check them. From your score, find out which list of words is right for you.

Score 0–4: Work with List 1: average word length 4 letters.
Score 5–14: Work with List 2: average word length 5 letters.
Score 15–20: Work with List 3: average word length 6 letters.

The 220 words in each list have been grouped into subsets of four words, on the basis of a topic or language pattern. There are five word sets across the page, which is normally enough for a week's work. Nouns, verbs, adjectives and adverbs have been grouped together, with some miscellaneous sets at the end. This has been done to help you to think of meaningful links between words and to use the words in sentences.

Note that words with an asterisk (*) against them may need special attention. These are ones for which it is hard or impossible to find a rhyming word with the same spelling pattern. You may be able to think of a non-rhyming word with the same letter string (e.g. watch/match) or find some other way of remembering the letters.

The word subsets are not arranged in order of difficulty.

Individual personalised lists

You can follow your own individual programme, so that you do not study words that you can already spell. You may like to begin with the shorter words in each list.

You will need to set your own target of how many words to learn over a certain period. Here are some suggestions for how a programme of learning could be drawn up. Adapt them to suit your situation. Remember to ask your T/H for advice about this.

Every fortnight choose 20, 40 or 60 words to learn from one of the lists, aiming to master at least 100, 200 or 300 words in a 12-week term. Underline the words and then write them down in sets of 4. If possible, there should be some meaningful link between the words in a set as this makes the words and their spellings easier to remember. You can choose words that will fit into the same sentence, that are linked by topic or that have the same spelling pattern. If you cannot find enough words you need to learn in the list, words may be taken from other sources.

With individually chosen lists, appropriate individual tests are needed. These are best organised by using a helper or helpers. In class, you and another student may test each other in turn.

Another kind of individual list, for use in correcting drafts (NC Level 3, Scottish level C and above) is described on pages 300–301.

How to learn

If you look at words in a list and get your T/H to test you, you may find you do not remember the spellings very well. A more active approach will lead to better results. You should Study – Copy – Check – Highlight and then Learn.

Study – spell the word aloud using helpful groups of letter strings
Copy – you are only allowed one glance per syllable
Check – letter by letter or in strings of up to four letters
Highlight – mark the tricky parts you need to remember
Learn – by one or more of the methods below.

Try the different methods of learning suggested below and decide which works best for you.

a) Pronounce the words in a different way, according to the spelling.

b) Trace over or write the word, saying the letter names before you write each letter string.

c) Shut your eyes and say or spell the word as you 'write' it in large letters with your finger.

d) With eyes shut see the word in your mind, count the letters in groups and then check.

e) Study the word so well that you can spell it backwards.

f) Study the word, say a tongue-twister or count to 10, then spell the word.

g) Think of a memory link or mnemonic for the whole word or just for the tricky part (e.g. On **Fri**day and at the week**end** I'll see my friends. **F**ind **r**eally **i**nteresting **fri**ends.).

h) IF there is a suffix, look for a common pattern such as an -es plural, an -ed tense ending, consonant doubling or y changing to -ies or -ied.

i) Use the *ACE Spelling Dictionary* to find a word that rhymes with the one you are learning and is spelt in the same way; think of a rhyme and then check the spelling, or simply look through the one- and two-syllable columns in a single vowel section. Remember that words in the lists that are marked * do not have suitable rhymes.

j) Find another word you already know that has the same spelling pattern (e.g. ton**gue**, ar**gue**).

k) Learn the tricky part (or parts) first, before trying the whole word.

Repeat – say, write and spell really rapidly, like a r-a-pp-e-r

Test – look, say, cover, write, check.

At the end of a learning session, write down a sentence containing the words you have studied. This should help you to spell those words correctly later on when you are writing.

Daily routine

Every day you will study two, four or six words from your list (or a different number, depending on your own programme). It is helpful if the words are related in some way. Enter the date and the words to be learned in a jotter.

Steps to success

1st word – learn (using chosen method)
self-test – look – say – cover – write – check

2nd word – learn
self-test – look – say – cover – write – check
double-check – look at both words – say – cover – write – check
Continue if both words are correct; otherwise practise and try again.

3rd word – learn
self-test – look – say – cover – write – check

4th word – learn
self-test – look – say – cover – write – check
double-check – look at both words – say – cover – write – check
Continue if both words are correct; otherwise practise and try again.

Final test – all four words should be written correctly when dictated in a random order

If you do not pass the final test, you should try to learn the words again, perhaps by a different method. On the other hand it may be better to reduce the number of words.

When you succeed in the final test, your T/H should initial the list in your jotter and record the learning method(s) you used (from the a) to k) list).

If you find it easy to learn the number of words you study each day, you might like to increase the number by one or two.

Note that if you are trying to learn six words you can double-check with groups of two or three words.

Weekly test

Once a week a test session should be held. In class this can be set up in pairs, so that each learner both gives and receives a test on the words chosen for that week. Words spelt correctly should be given a tick on their personal list. Those not spelt correctly should be studied again the following week. They should be spaced out over the week, not tackled on a single day along with the new words for that day.

Spelling correctly and correcting mistakes

If you use the STUDY – COPY – CHECK – HIGHLIGHT – LEARN approach, you will probably make fewer mistakes with words you have recently studied. You cannot expect that you will never again have to think about those words. Indeed, every time you realise that you have used a word that is on your list or seems to fit a familiar pattern, you score a success. All you have to do then is to check the spelling. If it is correct, that is excellent.

Good spellers are aware of common patterns between families of words. The more often you look up words in the *ACE Spelling Dictionary*, the more you will notice these patterns. Looking for word families based on Lists 1–3 will introduce you to thousands of words. Learning method i) (looking up rhyming words) is one of the best ways of 'getting to know' more word families. This method also encourages you to use a wider vocabulary when you write.

Most people miss spelling mistakes when they proofread a piece of work. You can improve in doing this if you make a personal alphabetical list of the words you want to learn from Lists 1, 2 and 3. It is sensible to include some interesting words from the same families and any hard-to-spell words you have previously attempted. If you arrange the list in syllable columns, as in the *ACE Spelling Dictionary*, it will be easier to scan. Read through the list before you check a draft; this will make it much more likely that you will recognise the words in the piece.

Your list might look like this:

*	**	*** (+)
aren't	against	ambulance
board	allow	arrival
break	answer	beautiful
brought	answered	disappeared
clothes	believe	February
course	buried	hospital
guard	curtain	idea
it's	harbour	investigate
knocked	haunted	parliament
let's	later	remembered
passed	people	suitable
past	present	unfortunately
piece	quickly	vegetables
race	really	
spare	swimming	
they're	themselves	
threw	without	
you're		

It is a good idea to check a draft at least three times, each time concentrating on a limited range of words. First, look for any words of three or more syllables that need to be checked. Then go through the passage again, looking for two-syllable words that might present problems. Finally, concentrate on one-syllable words, taking care not to skim over words such as 'its', 'they' and 'was'. These are so common that it is easy for your eye to pass over them without really noticing them.

The more often you identify and correct spelling mistakes, the better your spelling will become. You can give full attention to what you are writing if you know how to put things right.

List 1

father	*baby	dog	bus	money
dad	babies	hair	car	gold
mother	boy	way	road	bank
mum	girl	park	street	shop
look	ask	come	be	*are
looked	asked	*coming	been	will
find	call	came	*being	could
found	called	went	stay	couldn’t
one	some	bad	*front	*his
*two	left	good	ready	*her
three	all	better	nice	our
four	more	best	happy	your
garden	door	tea	book	king
farm	room	water	story	queen
wood	window	time	bed	lady
sea	fire	things	night	man
go	*was	woke	see	catch
goes	*wasn’t	help	saw	make
*going	would	told	*put	made
gone	wouldn’t	sleep	seen	eat
black	big	next	my	away
blue	little	last	*this	around
red	new	long	that	back
white	old	round	other	home
*children	*morning	*Christmas	*woman	*people
sister	*afternoon	tree	teacher	name
brother	week	day	school	hand
*aunt	year	dinner	work	*eyes
do	*has	give	dance	*watch
don’t	*have	gave	walk	*watching
did	*having	take	walking	start
didn’t	had	took	walked	started
when	how	first	no	by
just	so	*once	yes	for
now	down	out	*very	with
then	here	over	well	without
giant	he	him	*who	please
*castle	she	himself	*someone	me
ghost	we	you	which	*that’s
house	they	them	*something	much
play	named	like	upon	or
playing	think	married	about	but
played	say	live	*from	*because
fell	*said	*lived	after	while

List 2

*aeroplane
air
plane
*world

tell
spoke
shouted
hear

*these
those
any
many

wife
*husband
*person
*group

hope
hoped
hoping
getting

*young
*beautiful
*pretty
dear

*machine
wheel
hole
light

seemed
*imagine
guess
*understand

quickly
slowly
early
later

mountain
side
ice
winter

buy
wear
used
grown

*animals
bird
snake
*horse

listen
listened
*answer
*answered

high
*higher
smaller
short

*family
table
chair
*kitchen

pick
picked
pull
*pulled

whole
closed
past
seven

dragon
head
*heart
blood

die
died
jumped
killed

already
behind
ever
o'clock

piece
*picture
place
*village

before
why
whether
*whenever

present
balloon
*colour
*music

read
reading
mean
meant

*every
its
sure
true

*sugar
*breakfast
meat
*course

drop
dropped
break
*breaking

tired
*lonely
dark
*careful

ears
nose
mouth
*voice

sitting
waiting
*happen
*happened

*even
*also
*really
enough

*numbers
*nothing
*thousands
*difference

*I'd
*I'll
*I'm
*I've

*clothes
*body
*shoes
foot

point
write
writing
written

wide
*straight
near
real

boat
ship
shape
*owner

try
trying
cry
cried

dead
broken
dry
strange

*word
*idea
*notice
*language

meet
brought
passed
followed

nearly
*usually
*finally
together

few
half
*anyone
*anything

*you'd
*you'll
*you're
*you've

prince
princess
life
love

hold
*build
built
*covered

*usual
*different
*interesting
*coloured

*football
field
line
*corner

*finish
*finished
leave
fly

*nearby
*maybe
quite
alright

*radio
station
*minutes
*sentence

should
*does
*doesn't
done

onto
across
along
against

*no-one
*everyone
*everything
whose

*what
*what's
*let's
*themselves

List 3

mouse
mice
*puppy
*puppies

wash
washing
washed
dressed

*basket
*bowl
*board
brush

fishing
float
floated
drowned

shock
*ambulance
*hospital
*oxygen

*climb
tied
falling
slipped

pencil
*rubber
*ruler
*scissors

*dangerous
*terrible
massive
*enormous

*telephone
*message
rhyme
*tongue

*motor
racing
tight
*physical

*bicycle
bike
race
track

*squirrel
goat
*wolf
*elephant

*allow
*allowed
wished
*cannot

lawn
flowers
patch
*vegetables

believe
*wondering
*realised
*investigate

*uncle
*cousin
*grandfather
*neighbours

push
*pushed
knocked
smashed

*alphabet
*calendar
fractions
*graph

frightening
*poisonous
frightened
scared

*visitor
*Germany
*London
*countries

*excellent
*wonderful
*fantastic
*exciting

*hello
*everybody
*quietly
*sixth

creatures
*butterfly
*dinosaur
*monster

swim
swimming
rain
raining

shirt
skirt
sheet
*curtain

approach
*recognised
remember
*remembered

*February
*months
*holiday
*Saturday

hopped
hopping
pretended
hurt

*camera
*film
*submarine
*magazine

*favourite
*orange
*purple
*visible

*system
defence
*exhibition
*manager

*British
*Chinese
*Japanese
*Egyptian

he'd
he'll
*he's
*they're

fish
*rabbit
*potato
*potatoes

*arrived
*offered
received
grabbed

*drawer
shelf
shelves
stairs

lie
lying
lay
laid

*harbour
beach
*island
cave

*whisper
*whispered
*whistle
screamed

*parliament
*palace
*television
*programme

*curious
spare
*quiet
haunted

switch
*contact
*explosion
bridge

dining
*hungry
fried
*frozen

*aren't
we'd
we'll
*we're

*chocolate
coffee
flour
*apron

threw
throw
blew
blow

crash
surprise
fright
*skeleton

drag
dragged
*bury
*buried

pony
*ponies
saddle
stables

*burst
guard
*chase
*disappeared

noise
*policeman
*uniform
*court

lazy
dirty
*impossible
funny

flame
volcano
thunder
*lightning

*downstairs
*upstairs
*somewhere
*everywhere

*anyway
*somehow
*anybody
*somebody

Searching for patterns

The *ACE Spelling Dictionary* is an ideal resource for investigating aspects of language related to spelling and word recognition. Government strategy documents encourage the use of enquiry and investigation on the part of learners, recognising that we often remember what we have found out better than what we have been told.

A valuable analysis of spelling in GCSE English scripts is provided in *Improving Writing at Key Stages 3 and 4* (QCA, 1999). This draws attention to the persistence of homonym errors, phonetically plausible errors, omission of sounds and letters, problems with word endings and problems with word division. All of these areas can usefully be made the focus of an ACE investigation.

Here are some suggestions for investigating a range of spelling and other linguistic patterns, as well as exceptions to those patterns.

1 Spend five minutes looking for one-syllable words which have **es** added to the base word. Does this only happen after certain final consonant spellings?

2 Taking one vowel section at a time, count the vowel spellings in one or more columns and arrange them from the most to the least common.

3 **When you add ing to words ending with e, you knock off the e**. This does not apply if the ending is a double vowel (e.g. /ee/ as in 'see', /ie/ as in 'tie', /ue/ as in 'sue'). See how many words that fit this pattern you can find in ten minutes.

4 Find out what happens when you need the past tense form of long vowel words ending in **e**. The **e** is already there, so what is the consonant you add to the base word? This consonant can represent two different phonemes: what are they?

5 See how many three-syllable words you can find where a final **y** changes to **ie**. Group these under the endings: ies, ied and ier/iest. Spend ten minutes on this.

6 Take five minutes to find words of one and two syllables that have a plural ending (ves). **Let's say it's safe to use the ves spelling if you hear the sounds /v/ or /z/ at the end.**

7 **With words like 'wit'** (i.e. words having a single-letter short vowel and a single final consonant) **you double the final consonant when you add endings such as ed, ing, er, est, y, ier and iest.** That means you get: slow-witted, outwitting, witty, wittier, wittiest. See how many one-syllable words that fit this pattern you can find in ten minutes. Are there any exceptions?

8 **In a two-syllable word, double the final consonant only if the stress is on the last syllable, so 'begin' + ing is 'beginning' but 'open' + ing is 'opening').** Find ten words like 'beginning' with doubled consonants and ten like 'opening' where the stress is on the first syllable.

9 Find ten words like 'itch' (one syllable, with a single-letter short vowel and **tch** right after the vowel). Find ten more one-syllable words with a letter between the short vowel and the /ch/ sound, such as: belch, inch, lunch.
Find twenty words ending in **ch** from any of the long vowel sections.
What pattern do you notice? Are there any exceptions apart from 'rich', 'much' and 'such'?
Can you explain in a simple way when to use **tch**?
Carry out similar searches in order to establish when to use **dge** rather than **ge** and when to use **ck** rather than **k**.

10 Think about the spelling 'rule': **i** before **e** except after **c**. What is the ratio of hits to misses if this rule is applied to words in the long vowel /ee/ section? Can the rule be improved?

11 How many words of four or more syllables in which the last syllable contains a neutral vowel sound can you find in five minutes?

12 Make a list of homonym pairs from the /or/ section where spelling confusion is likely.

13 Full of ... ? truthful → truthfully helpful → helpfully grateful → gratefully.
Find five more words listed in the *ACE Spelling Dictionary* that fit the **ful** → **fully** pattern.

14 Look for word roots, prefixes, suffixes and spelling patterns; e.g. sign, signature, signal; form, deform, inform, formal, information. This extends vocabulary and provides support for spelling.

15 Find homonym pairs both of which can function as nouns, adjectives or adverbs. Then find some homonyms in which the words have different grammatical functions.

All of the investigations suggested above can be modified to suit the needs of the individuals or groups and it will often be found that a new investigation can be devised to address a particular query or problem.

Photocopiable activity sheets that reinforce and extend many of the pattern activities in this section can be found in *ACE Spelling Activities* (Moseley and Singleton, 1993).

Meeting National Curriculum objectives

An extensive range of activities and games for developing phonic skills and recognising and spelling words with 'tricky' parts is provided in *Letters and Sounds* (DES, 2007).

Where focused intervention is needed, it should be based on careful assessment. The detailed assessment statements for the six phases of *Letters and Sounds* provide a well-structured general framework. The present author has developed a complementary diagnostic assessment tool, the *Word Recognition and Phonic Skills Test* (Moseley, 2008). This yields objective measures of key aspects of word recognition normally acquired up to the age of 9. It provides a reliable profile of the stage reached in word recognition, of knowledge of higher frequency, lower frequency, regular and irregular words, of consonant and vowel spellings and of the tendency to omit elements. The manual also includes suggestions for teaching based on individual profiles of strengths and weaknesses. These are designed to provide a firm foundation for further word-level work in reading and writing. The diagnostic information can also be used to inform the choice of pattern investigation activities using, for example, *Letters and Sounds* and the *ACE Spelling Dictionary*.

Using the *ACE Spelling Dictionary* will help you to:

- show awareness of rhyme and alliteration
- recognise rhythm in spoken words
- apply the skills of segmenting words into their constituent phonemes
- learn variously from simultaneous visual, auditory and kinaesthetic activities which are designed to secure essential phonic knowledge and skills
- recognise and use alternative ways of spelling the graphemes already taught
- learn which words take which spellings
- spell common words correctly
- read and spell less common alternative graphemes including trigraphs
- identify the constituent parts of two- and three-syllable words to support the application of phonic knowledge and skills
- use knowledge of common inflections in spelling, such as plurals and -ly, -er
- read and spell phonically decodable two-syllable and three-syllable words
- read high and medium frequency words independently and automatically
- spell with increasing accuracy and confidence, drawing on word recognition and knowledge of word structure, and spelling patterns, including common inflections and use of double letters
- increase knowledge of word families, roots, derivations, morphology and regular spelling patterns
- use independent spelling strategies
- identify misspelt words in own writing; keep individual spelling logs; learn to spell them
- apply knowledge of spelling skills and strategies with increasing independence

- review and revise spelling strategies for dealing with words in familiar and unfamiliar contexts, or when imaginative and ambitious choices are made, or under time or other constraints
- spell most words correctly including some complex polysyllabic words and unfamiliar words
- spell correctly throughout a substantial text including ambitious or complex polysyllabic words
- apply skills in editing and proofreading in a range of different texts and contexts, reviewing and revising writing as it progresses
- identify some of the ways in which spoken English varies in different regions and settings
- investigate spoken English from a range of regions and settings and explain how it varies.

It's easier to get into good spelling habits early on than to correct poor spelling later.

References

Beech, J.R. (2004) Using a dictionary: its influence on children's reading, spelling, and phonology. *Reading Psychology*, 25, 19–36.

Department for Education and Skills (2007) *Letters and Sounds: Principles and Practice of High Quality Phonics*. London, Department for Education and Skills.

Hancock, R. (1992) *An appraisal of the Aurally Coded English Spelling Dictionary*. BEd. project, University of Sunderland.

Masterson, J., M. Stuart, M. Dixon, and S. Lovejoy (2003) *Children's Printed Word Database*. Economic and Social Research Council project (R00023406). At: http://www.essex.ac.uk/psychology/cpwd/

Moseley, D.V. (1989) Utilisation d'un dictionnaire à codage oral pour l'orthographe et la reconnaissance des mots: une étude en milieu scolaire. *Glossa*, 14, 14–19.

Moseley, D.V. (1994) From theory to practice: errors and trials. In G.D.A. Brown, and N.C. Ellis, (eds.) *Handbook of Spelling: Theory, Process and Intervention*. London, Wiley.

Moseley, D.V. (1996) How poor spelling affects children's written expression. *Topic*, 16, Item 8. Slough, NFER, 1–6.

Moseley, D.V. (1997) The assessment of spelling and related aspects of written expression. In J. Beech and C. Singleton (eds.) *Psychological Assessment of Reading and Spelling*. London, Routledge.

Moseley, D. (2008) *Word Recognition and Phonic Skills Test* (WraPS 3). London, Hodder Education.

Moseley, D. and G. Singleton (1993) *ACE Spelling Activities*. Cambridge, LDA.

Primary National Strategy (2007) *Letters and Sounds* (pack). London, Department for Education and Skills.

Qualifications and Curriculum Authority (1999) *Improving Writing at Key Stages 3 and 4*. London, QCA.

Shenton, A.K. (2007) The paradoxical world of young people's information behaviour. *School Libraries Worldwide*, 13 (2), 1–17.

Spencer, K.A. (2001) Differential effects of orthographic transparency on dyslexia: word reading difficulty for common English words. *Dyslexia*, 7, 217–228.

Spencer, K.A. (2007) Predicting children's word-spelling difficulty for common English words from measures of orthographic transparency, phonemic and graphemic length and word frequency. *British Journal of Psychology*, 98, 305–338.

Thorstad, G. (1991) The effect of orthography on the acquisition of literacy skills. *British Journal of Psychology*, 82, 527–537.

Upward, C. (1992) Is traditionl english spelng mor dificlt than jermn? *Journal of Research in Reading*, 15, 82–94.

Major vocabulary sources

[author(s) unknown] (1982) *Evans Technical Dictionary*. London, Evans.

Carroll, J.B., P. Davies and B. Richman (1971) *The American Heritage Word Frequency Book*. Boston, Houghton Mifflin.

Leech, G., P. Rayson and A. Wilson (2001) *Word Frequencies in Written and Spoken English: based on the British National Corpus*. London, Longman.

Scottish Qualifications Authority (2000) *Standard Grade Arrangements in Mathematics*. Glasgow, Scottish Qualifications Authority.